Romeo and Juliet

COLES NOTES TOTAL STUDY EDITION

Romeo and Juliet

Complete Text + Commentary + Glossary

John Wiley & Sons Canada, Ltd.

Coles Notes Total Study Edition Romeo and Juliet

Published by:

John Wiley & Sons Canada Ltd.

6045 Freemont Blvd.

Mississauga, Ontario

L5R 4J3

Copyright © 2012 John Wiley & Sons Canada, Ltd.

ISBN: 978-1-118-48677-1

Printed in the United States of America

1 2 3 4 5 DP 16 15 14 13 12

WILEY

COLES NOTES TOTAL STUDY EDITION

Romeo and Juliet

TABLE OF CONTENTS

ROMEO AND JULIET

INTRODUCTION TO WILLIAM SHAKESPEARE

William Shakespeare, or the "Bard" as people fondly call him, permeates almost all aspects of our society. He can be found in our classrooms, on our televisions, in our theatres, and in our cinemas. Speaking to us through his plays, Shakespeare comments on his life and culture, as well as our own. Actors still regularly perform his plays on the modern stage and screen. The 1990s, for example, saw the release of cinematic versions of *Romeo and Juliet, Hamlet, Othello, A Midsummer Night's Dream,* and many more of his works.

In addition to the popularity of Shakespeare's plays as he wrote them, other writers have modernized his works to attract new audiences. For example, *West Side Story* places *Romeo and Juliet* in New York City, and *A Thousand Acres* sets *King Lear* in Iowa corn country. Beyond adaptations and productions, his life and works have captured our cultural imagination. The twentieth century witnessed the production of a play and film about two minor characters from Shakespeare's *Hamlet* in *Rosencrantz and Guildenstern are Dead* and a fictional movie about Shakespeare's early life and poetic inspiration in *Shakespeare in Love.*

Despite his monumental presence in our culture, Shakespeare remains enigmatic. He does not tell us which plays he wrote alone, on which plays he collaborated with other playwrights, or which versions of his plays to read and perform. Furthermore, with only a handful of documents available about his life, he does not tell us much about Shakespeare the person, forcing critics and scholars to look to historical references to uncover the true-life great dramatist.

Anti-Stratfordians—modern scholars who question the authorship of Shakespeare's plays—have used this lack of information to argue that William Shakespeare either never existed or, if he did exist, did not write any of the plays we attribute to him. They believe that another historical figure, such as Francis Bacon or Queen Elizabeth I, used the name as a cover. Whether or not a man named William Shakespeare ever actually existed is ultimately secondary to the recognition that the group of plays bound together by that name does exist and continues to educate, enlighten, and entertain us.

An engraved portrait of Shakespeare by an unknown artist, ca. 1607. Culver Pictures, Inc./SuperStock

Family life

Though scholars are unsure of the exact date of Shakespeare's birth, records indicate that his parents—Mary and John Shakespeare—baptized him on April 26, 1564, in the small provincial town of Stratford-upon-Avon—so named because it sat on the banks of the Avon river. Because common practice was to baptize infants a few days after they were born, scholars generally recognize April 23, 1564 as Shakespeare's birthday. Coincidentally, April 23 is the day of St. George, the patron saint of England, as well as the day upon which Shakespeare would die 52 years later. William was the third of Mary and John's eight children and the first of four sons. The house in which scholars believe Shakespeare was born stands on Henley Street and, despite many modifications over the years, you can still visit it today.

Shakespeare's father

Prior to William Shakespeare's birth, John Shakespeare lived in Snitterfield, where he married Mary Arden, the daughter of his landlord. After moving to Stratford in 1552, he worked as a glover, a money-lender, and a dealer in agricultural products such as wool and grain. He also pursued public office and achieved a variety of posts including bailiff, Stratford's highest elected position—equivalent to a small town's mayor. At the height of his career, sometime near 1576, he petitioned the Herald's Office for a coat of arms and thus the right to be a gentleman. But the rise from the middle class to the gentry did not come right away, and the costly petition expired without being granted.

About this time, John Shakespeare mysteriously fell into financial difficulty. He became involved in serious litigation, was assessed heavy fines, and even lost his seat on the town council. Some scholars suggest that this decline could have resulted from religious discrimination. The Shakespeare family may have supported Catholicism, the practice of which was illegal in England. However, other scholars point out that not all religious dissenters (both Catholics and radical

Shakespeare's birthplace in Stratford-upon-Avon.
SuperStock

Puritans) lost their posts due to their religion. Whatever the cause of his decline, John did regain some prosperity toward the end of his life. In 1597, the Herald's Office granted the Shakespeare family a coat of arms at the petition of William, by now a successful playwright in London. And John, prior to his death in 1601, regained his seat on Stratford's town council.

Childhood and education

Our understanding of William Shakespeare's childhood in Stratford is primarily speculative because children do not often appear in the legal records from which many scholars attempt to reconstruct Shakespeare's life. Based on his father's local prominence, scholars speculate that Shakespeare most likely attended King's New School, a school that usually employed Oxford graduates and was generally well respected. Shakespeare would have started *petty school*—the rough equivalent to modern preschool—at the age of four or five. He would have learned to read on a *hornbook*, which was a sheet of parchment or paper on which the alphabet and the Lord's Prayer were written. This sheet was framed in wood and covered with a transparent piece of horn for durability. After two years in petty school, he would have transferred to grammar school, where his school day would have probably lasted from 6 or 7 o'clock in the morning (depending on the time of year) until 5 o'clock in the evening, with only a handful of holidays.

While in grammar school, Shakespeare would have studied primarily Latin, reciting and reading the works of classical Roman authors such as Plautus, Ovid, Seneca, and Horace. Traces of these authors' works can be seen in his dramatic texts. Toward his last years in grammar school, Shakespeare would have acquired some basic skills in Greek as well. Thus the remark made by Ben Jonson, Shakespeare's well-educated friend and contemporary playwright, that Shakespeare knew "small Latin and less Greek" is accurate. Jonson is not saying that when Shakespeare left grammar school he was only semi-literate; he merely indicates that Shakespeare did not attend University, where he would have gained more Latin and Greek instruction.

Wife and children

When Shakespeare became an adult, the historical records documenting his existence began to increase. In November 1582, at the age of 18, he married 26-year-old Anne Hathaway from the nearby village of Shottery. The disparity in their ages, coupled with the fact that they baptized their first daughter, Susanna, only six months later in May 1583, has caused a great deal of modern speculation about the nature of their relationship. However, sixteenth-century conceptions of marriage differed slightly from our modern notions. Though all marriages needed to be performed before a member of the clergy, many of Shakespeare's contemporaries believed that a couple could establish a relationship through a premarital contract by exchanging vows in front of witnesses. This contract removed the social stigma of pregnancy before marriage. (Shakespeare's plays contain instances of marriage prompted by pregnancy, and *Measure for Measure* includes this kind of premarital contract.) Two years later, in February 1585, Shakespeare baptized his twins Hamnet and Judith. Hamnet would die at the age of 11 when Shakespeare was primarily living away from his family in London.

For seven years after the twins' baptism, the records remain silent on Shakespeare. At some point, he travelled to London and became involved with the theatre, but he could have been anywhere between 21 and 28 years old when he did. Though some have suggested that he may have served as an assistant to a schoolmaster at a provincial school, it seems likely that he went to London to become an actor, gradually becoming a playwright and gaining attention.

The plays: On stage and in print

The next mention of Shakespeare comes in 1592 by a University wit named Robert Greene when Shakespeare apparently was already a rising actor and playwright for the London stage. Greene, no longer a successful playwright, tried to warn other University wits about Shakespeare. He wrote:

> For there is an upstart crow, beautified with our feathers, that with his "Tiger's heart wrapped in a player's hide" supposes he is as well able to bombast out a blank verse as the best of you, and, being an absolute Johannes Factotum, is in his own conceit the only Shake-scene in a country.

This statement comes at a point in time when men without a university education, like Shakespeare, were starting to compete as dramatists with the University wits. As many critics have pointed out, Greene's statement recalls a line from *3 Henry VI*, which reads, "O tiger's heart wrapped in a woman's hide!" (I.4.137). Greene's remark does not indicate that Shakespeare was generally disliked. On the contrary, another University wit, Thomas Nashe, wrote of the great theatrical success of *Henry VI*, and Henry Chettle, Greene's publisher, later printed a flattering apology to Shakespeare. What Greene's statement does show us is that Shakespeare's reputation for poetry had achieved enough prominence to provoke the envy of a failing competitor.

In the following year, 1593, the government closed London's theatres due to an outbreak of the bubonic plague. Publication history suggests that during this closure, Shakespeare may have written his two narrative poems, *Venus and Adonis*, published in 1593, and *The Rape of Lucrece*, published in 1594. These are the only two works that Shakespeare seems to have helped into print; each carries a dedication by Shakespeare to Henry Wriothesley, Earl of Southampton.

A ground plan of London after the fire of 1666, drawn by Marcus Willemsz Doornik. Guildhall Library, London/AKG, Berlin/SuperStock

Stage success

When the theatres reopened in 1594, Shakespeare joined the Lord Chamberlain's Men, an acting company. Though uncertain about the history of his early dramatic works, scholars believe that by this point he had written *The Two Gentlemen of Verona, The Taming of the Shrew,* the *Henry VI* trilogy, and *Titus Andronicus*. During his early years in the theatre, he primarily wrote history plays, with his romantic comedies emerging in the 1590s. Even at this early stage in his career, Shakespeare was a success. In 1597, he was able to purchase New Place, one of the two largest houses in Stratford, and secure a coat of arms for his family.

In 1597, the lease expired on the Lord Chamberlain's playhouse, called The Theatre. Because the owner of The Theatre refused to renew the lease, the acting company was forced to perform at various playhouses until the 1599 opening of the now famous Globe theatre, which was literally built with lumber from The Theatre. (The Globe, later destroyed by fire, recently has been reconstructed in London and can be visited today.)

Recent scholars suggest that Shakespeare's great tragedy, *Julius Caesar*, may have been the first of Shakespeare's plays performed in the original Globe theatre. When this open-air theatre on the Thames River opened, financial papers list Shakespeare's name as one of the principal investors. Already an actor and a playwright, Shakespeare was now becoming a "Company Man." This new status allowed him to share in the profits of the theatre rather than merely getting paid for his plays, some of which publishers were beginning to release in quarto format.

Publications

A *quarto* was a small, inexpensive book typically used for leisure books such as plays; the term itself indicates that the printer folded the paper four times. The modern day equivalent of a quarto would be a paperback. In contrast, the first collected works of Shakespeare were in folio format, which means that the printer folded each sheet only once. Scholars call the collected edition of Shakespeare's works the *First Folio*. A folio was a larger and more prestigious book than a quarto, and printers generally reserved the format for works such as the Bible.

No evidence exists that Shakespeare participated in the publication of any of his plays. Members of Shakespeare's acting company printed the First Folio seven years after Shakespeare's death. Generally, playwrights wrote their works to be performed on stage, and publishing them was an innovation at the time. Shakespeare probably would not have thought of them as books in the way we do. In fact, as a principal investor in the acting company (which purchased the play as well as the exclusive right to perform it), he may not have even thought of them as his own. He probably would have thought of his plays as belonging to the company.

For this reason, scholars generally have characterized most quartos printed before the Folio as "bad" by arguing that printers pirated the plays and published them illegally. How would a printer have received a pirated copy of a play? The theories range from someone stealing a copy to an actor (or actors) selling the play by relating it from memory to a printer. Many times, major differences exist between a quarto version of the play and a folio version, causing uncertainty about which is Shakespeare's true creation. *Hamlet*, for example, is almost twice as long in the Folio as in quarto versions. Recently, scholars have come to realize the value of the different versions. The *Norton Shakespeare*, for example, includes all three versions of *King Lear*—the quarto, the folio, and the *conflated* version (the combination of the quarto and folio).

Prolific productions

The first decade of the 1600s witnessed the publication of additional quartos as well as the production of most of Shakespeare's great tragedies, with *Julius Caesar* appearing in 1599 and *Hamlet* in 1600–1601. After the death of Queen Elizabeth in 1603, the Lord Chamberlain's Men became the King's Men under James I, Elizabeth's successor. Around the time of this transition in the English monarchy, the famous tragedy *Othello* (1603–1604) was most likely written and performed, followed closely by *King Lear* (1605–1606), *Antony and Cleopatra* (1606), and *Macbeth* (1606) in the next two years.

Shakespeare's name also appears as a major investor in the 1609 acquisition of an indoor theatre known as the Blackfriars. This last period of Shakespeare's career, which includes plays that considered the acting conditions both at the Blackfriars and the open-air Globe theatre, consists primarily of romances or tragicomedies such as *The Winter's Tale* and *The Tempest*. On June 29, 1613, during a performance of *All is True*, or *Henry VIII*, the thatching on top of The Globe caught fire and the playhouse burned to the ground. After this incident, the King's Men moved solely into the indoor Blackfriars theatre.

Final days

During the last years of his career, Shakespeare collaborated on a couple of plays with contemporary dramatist John Fletcher, even possibly coming out of retirement—which scholars believe began sometime in 1613—to work on *The Two Noble Kinsmen* (1613–1614). Three years later, Shakespeare died on April 23, 1616. Though the exact cause of death remains unknown, a vicar from Stratford in the mid-seventeenth-century wrote in his diary that Shakespeare, perhaps celebrating the marriage of his daughter, Judith, contracted a fever during a night of revelry with fellow literary figures Ben Jonson and Michael Drayton. Regardless, Shakespeare may have felt his death was imminent in March of that year because he altered his will. Interestingly, his will mentions no book or theatrical manuscripts, perhaps indicating the lack of value that he put on printed versions of his dramatic works and their status as company property.

Seven years after Shakespeare's death, John Heminge and Henry Condell, fellow members of the King's Men, published his collected works. In their preface, they claim that they are publishing the true versions of Shakespeare's plays partially as a response to the previous quarto printings of 18 of his plays, most of these with multiple printings. This Folio contains 36 plays to which scholars generally add *Pericles* and *The Two Noble Kinsmen*. This volume of Shakespeare's plays began the process of constructing Shakespeare not only as England's national poet but also as a monumental figure whose plays would continue to captivate imaginations at the end of the second millenium with no signs of stopping. Ben Jonson's prophetic line about Shakespeare in the First Folio—"He was not of an age, but for all time!"—certainly holds true.

Chronology of Shakespeare's plays

1590–1591	*The Two Gentlemen of Verona*
	The Taming of the Shrew
1591	*2 Henry VI*
	3 Henry VI
1592	*1 Henry VI*
	Titus Andronicus
1592–1593	*Richard III*
	Venus and Adonis
1593–1594	*The Rape of Lucrece*
1594	*The Comedy of Errors*
1594–1595	*Love's Labour's Lost*
1595	*Richard II*
	Romeo and Juliet
	A Midsummer Night's Dream
1595–1596	*Love's Labour's Won*
	(This manuscript was lost.)
1596	*King John*
1596–1597	*The Merchant of Venice*
	1 Henry IV
1597–1598	*The Merry Wives of Windsor*
	2 Henry IV
1598	*Much Ado About Nothing*
1598–1599	*Henry V*
1599	*Julius Caesar*

1599–1600	*As You Like It*
1600–1601	*Hamlet*
1601	*Twelfth Night, or What You Will*
1602	*Troilus and Cressida*
1593–1603	*Sonnets*
1603	*Measure for Measure*
1603–1604	*A Lover's Complaint*
	Othello
1604–1605	*All's Well That Ends Well*
1605	*Timon of Athens*
1605–1606	*King Lear*
1606	*Macbeth*
	Antony and Cleopatra
1607	*Pericles*
1608	*Coriolanus*
1609	*The Winter's Tale*
1610	*Cymbeline*
1611	*The Tempest*
1612–1613	*Cardenio (with John Fletcher; this manuscript was lost.)*
1613	*All is True (Henry VIII)*
1613–1614	*The Two Noble Kinsman (with John Fletcher)*

This chronology is derived from Stanley Wells' and Gary Taylor's *William Shakespeare: A Textual Companion,* which is listed in the "Works consulted" section later.

A note on Shakespeare's language

Readers encountering Shakespeare for the first time usually find Early Modern English difficult to understand. Yet, rather than serving as a barrier to Shakespeare, the richness of this language should form part of our appreciation of the Bard.

One of the first things readers usually notice about the language is the use of pronouns. Like the King James Version of the Bible, Shakespeare's pronouns are slightly different from our own and can cause confusion. Words like "thou" (you), "thee" and "ye" (objective cases of you), and "thy" and "thine" (your/yours) appear throughout Shakespeare's plays.

You may need a little time to get used to these changes. You can find the definitions for other words that commonly cause confusion in the glossary column on the right side of each page in this edition.

Iambic pentameter

Though Shakespeare sometimes wrote in prose, he wrote most of his plays in poetry, specifically blank verse. Blank verse consists of lines in unrhymed *iambic pentameter. Iambic* refers to the stress patterns of the line. An *iamb* is an element of sound that consists of two beats—the first unstressed (da) and the second stressed (DA). A good example of an iambic line is Hamlet's famous line "To be or not to be," in which you do not stress "to," "or," and "to," but you do stress "be," "not," and "be." *Pentameter* refers to the *meter* or number of stressed syllables in a line. *Penta*-meter has five stressed syllables. Thus, Romeo's line "But soft, what light through yonder window breaks?" (II.2.2) is a good example of an iambic pentameter line.

Wordplay

Shakespeare's language is also verbally rich as he, along with many dramatists of his period, had a fondness for wordplay. This wordplay often takes the forms of double meanings, called *puns*, where a word can mean more than one thing in a given context. Shakespeare often employs these puns as a way of illustrating the distance between what is on the surface—*apparent* meanings—and what meanings lie underneath. Though recognizing these puns may be difficult at first, the glosses (definitions) in the far right column point many of them out to you.

If you are encountering Shakespeare's plays for the first time, the following reading tips may help ease you into the plays. Shakespeare's lines were meant to be spoken; therefore, reading them aloud or speaking them should help with comprehension. Also, though most of the lines are poetic, do not forget to read complete sentences—move from period

to period as well as from line to line. Although Shakespeare's language can be difficult at first, the rewards of immersing yourself in the richness and fluidity of the lines are immeasurable.

Works consulted

For more information on Shakespeare's life and works, see the following:

Bevington, David, ed. *The Complete Works of Shakespeare.* New York: Longman, 1997.

Evans, G.Blakemore, ed. *The Riverside Shakespeare.* Boston: Houghton Mifflin Co., 1997.

Greenblatt, Stephen, ed. *The Norton Shakespeare.* New York: W.W. Norton and Co., 1997.

Kastan, David Scott, ed. *A Companion to Shakespeare.* Oxford: Blackwell, 1999.

McDonald, Russ. *The Bedford Companion to Shakespeare: An Introduction with Documents.* Boston: Bedford-St. Martin's Press, 1996.

Wells, Stanley and Gary Taylor. *William Shakespeare: A Textual Companion.* New York: W.W. Norton and Co., 1997.

INTRODUCTION TO EARLY MODERN ENGLAND

William Shakespeare (1564–1616) lived during a period in England's history that people have generally referred to as the English Renaissance. The term *renaissance*, meaning rebirth, was applied to this period of English history as a way of celebrating what was perceived as the rapid development of art, literature, science, and politics: in many ways, the rebirth of classical Rome.

Recently, scholars have challenged the name "English Renaissance" on two grounds. First, some scholars argue that the term should not be used because women did not share in the advancements of English culture during this time period; their legal status was still below that of men. Second, other scholars have challenged the basic notion that this period saw a sudden explosion of culture. A rebirth of civilization suggests that the previous period of time was not civilized. This second group of scholars sees a much more gradual transition between the Middle Ages and Shakespeare's time.

Some people use the terms *Elizabethan* and *Jacobean* when referring to periods of the sixteenth and seventeenth centuries, respectively. These terms correspond to the reigns of Elizabeth I (1558–1603) and James I (1603–1625). The problem with these terms is that they do not cover large spans of time; for example, Shakespeare's life and career spans both monarchies.

Scholars are now beginning to replace Renaissance with the term Early Modern when referring to this time period, but people still use both terms interchangeably. The term *Early Modern* recognizes that this period established many of the foundations of our modern culture. Though critics still disagree about the exact dates of the period, in general, the dates range from 1450 to 1750. Thus, Shakespeare's life clearly falls within the Early Modern period.

Shakespeare's plays live on in our culture, but we must remember that Shakespeare's culture differed greatly from our own. Though his understanding of human nature and relationships seems to apply to our modern lives, we must try to understand the world he lived in so we can better understand his plays. This introduction helps you do just that. It examines the intellectual, religious, political, and social contexts of Shakespeare's work before turning to the importance of the theatre and the printing press.

Intellectual context

In general, people in Early Modern England looked at the universe, the human body, and science very differently from the way we do. But while we do not share their same beliefs, we must not think of people during Shakespeare's time as lacking in intelligence or education. Discoveries made during the Early Modern period concerning the universe and the human body provide the basis of modern science.

Cosmology

One subject we view very differently than Early Modern thinkers is cosmology. Shakespeare's contemporaries believed in the astronomy of Ptolemy, an intellectual from Alexandria in the second century A.D. Ptolemy thought that the earth stood at the centre of the universe, surrounded by nine concentric rings. The celestial bodies circled the earth in the following order: the moon, Mercury, Venus, the sun, Mars, Jupiter, Saturn, and the stars. The entire system was controlled by the *primum mobile*, or Prime Mover, which initiated and maintained the movement of the celestial bodies. No one had yet discovered the last three planets in our solar system, Uranus, Neptune, and Pluto.

In 1543, Nicolaus Copernicus published his theory of a sun-based solar system, in which the sun stood at the centre and the planets revolved around it. Though this theory appeared prior to Shakespeare's birth, people didn't really start to change their minds until 1610, when Galileo used his telescope to confirm Copernicus's theory. David Bevington asserts in the general introduction to his edition of Shakespeare's works that during most of Shakespeare's writing career, the cosmology of the universe was in question, and this sense of uncertainty influences some of his plays.

Universal hierarchy

Closely related to Ptolemy's hierarchical view of the universe is a hierarchical conception of the Earth (sometimes referred to as the Chain of Being). During the Early Modern period, many people believed that all of creation was organized hierarchically. God existed at the top, followed by the angels, men, women, animals, plants, and rocks. (Because all women were thought to exist below all men on the chain, we can easily imagine the confusion that Elizabeth I caused when she became Queen of England. She was literally "out of order," an expression that still exists in our society.) Though the concept of this hierarchy is a useful one when beginning to study Shakespeare, keep in mind that distinctions in this hierarchical view were not always clear and that we should not reduce all Early Modern thinking to a simple chain.

Elements and humours

The belief in a hierarchical scheme of existence created a comforting sense of order and balance that carried over into science as well. Shakespeare's contemporaries generally accepted that four different elements composed everything in the universe: earth, air, water, and fire. People associated these four elements with four qualities of being. These qualities—hot, cold, moist, and dry—appeared in different combinations in the elements. For example, air was hot and moist; water was cold and moist; earth was cold and dry; and fire was hot and dry.

In addition, people believed that the human body contained all four elements in the form of *humours*—blood, phlegm, yellow bile, and black bile—each of which corresponded to an element. Blood corresponded to air (hot and moist), phlegm to water (cold and moist), yellow bile to fire (hot and dry), and black bile to earth (cold and dry). When someone was sick, physicians generally believed that the patient's humours were not in the proper balance. For example, if someone were diagnosed with an abundance of blood, the physician would bleed the patient (by using leeches or cutting the skin) in order to restore the balance.

Shakespeare's contemporaries also believed that the humours determined personality and temperament. If a person's dominant humour was blood, he was considered light-hearted. If dominated by yellow bile (or choler), that person was irritable. The

dominance of phlegm led a person to be dull and kind. And if black bile prevailed, he was melancholy or sad. Thus, people of Early Modern England often used the humours to explain behavior and emotional outbursts. Throughout Shakespeare's plays, he uses the concept of the humours to define and explain various characters.

Religious context

Shakespeare lived in an England full of religious uncertainty and dispute. From the Protestant Reformation to the translation of the Bible into English, the Early Modern era is punctuated with events that have greatly influenced modern religious beliefs.

The Reformation

Until the Protestant Reformation, the only Christian church in Western Europe was the Catholic, or "universal," church. Beginning in the early sixteenth century, religious thinkers such as Martin Luther and John Calvin, who claimed that the Roman Catholic Church had become corrupt and was no longer following the word of God, began what has become known as the Protestant Reformation. The Protestants ("protestors") believed in salvation by faith rather than works. They also believed in the primacy of the Bible and advocated giving all people access to reading the Bible.

Many English people initially resisted Protestant ideas. However, the Reformation in England began in 1527 during the reign of Henry VIII, prior to Shakespeare's birth. In that year, Henry VIII decided to divorce his wife, Catherine of Aragon, for her failure to produce a male heir. (Only one of their children, Mary, survived past infancy.) Rome denied Henry's petitions for a divorce, forcing him to divorce Catherine without the Church's approval, which he did in 1533.

A portrait of King Henry VIII, artist unknown, ca. 1542. National Portrait Gallery, London/SuperStock

The Act of Supremacy

The following year, the Pope excommunicated Henry VIII while Parliament confirmed his divorce and the legitimacy of his new marriage through the *Act of Succession*. Later in 1534, Parliament passed the *Act of Supremacy*, naming Henry the "Supreme Head of the Church in England." Henry persecuted both radical Protestant reformers and Catholics who remained loyal to Rome.

Henry VIII's death in 1547 brought Edward VI, his 10-year-old son by Jane Seymour (the king's third wife), to the throne. This succession gave Protestant reformers the chance to solidify their break with the Catholic Church. During Edward's reign, Archbishop Thomas Cranmer established the foundation for the Anglican Church through his 42 articles of religion. He also wrote the first *Book of Common Prayer*, adopted in 1549, which was the official text for worship services in England.

Bloody Mary

Catholics continued to be persecuted until 1553, when the sickly Edward VI died and was succeeded by Mary, his half-sister and the Catholic daughter of Catherine of Aragon. The reign of Mary witnessed the reversal of religion in England through the restoration of Catholic authority and obedience to Rome. Protestants were executed in large numbers, which earned the monarch the nickname *Bloody Mary*. Many Protestants fled to Europe to escape persecution.

Elizabeth, the daughter of Henry VIII and Anne Boleyn, outwardly complied with the mandated Catholicism during her half-sister Mary's reign, but she restored Protestantism when she took the throne in 1558 after Mary's death. Thus, in the space of a single decade, England's throne passed from Protestant to Catholic to Protestant, with each change carrying serious and deadly consequences.

Though Elizabeth reigned in relative peace from 1558 to her death in 1603, religion was still a serious concern for her subjects. During Shakespeare's life, a great deal of religious dissent existed in England. Many Catholics, who remained loyal to Rome and their church, were persecuted for their beliefs. At the other end of the spectrum, the Puritans were persecuted for their belief that the Reformation was not complete. (The English pejoratively applied the term *Puritan* to religious groups that wanted to continue purifying the English church by such measures as removing the *episcopacy,* or the structure of bishops.)

The Great Bible

One thing agreed upon by both the Anglicans and Puritans was the importance of a Bible written in English. Translated by William Tyndale in 1525, the first authorized Bible in English, published in 1539, was known as the Great Bible. This Bible was later revised during Elizabeth's reign into what was known as the Bishop's Bible. As Stephen Greenblatt points out in his introduction to the *Norton Shakespeare*, Shakespeare probably would have been familiar with both the Bishop's Bible, heard aloud in Mass, and the Geneva Bible, which was written by English exiles in Geneva. The last authorized Bible produced during Shakespeare's lifetime came within the last decade of his life when James I's commissioned edition, known as the King James Bible, appeared in 1611.

Political context

Politics and religion were closely related in Shakespeare's England. Both of the monarchs under whom Shakespeare lived had to deal with religious and political dissenters.

Elizabeth I

Despite being a Protestant, Elizabeth I tried to take a middle road on the question of religion. She allowed Catholics to practice their religion in private as long as they outwardly appeared Anglican and remained loyal to the throne.

Elizabeth's monarchy was one of absolute supremacy. Believing in the divine right of kings, she styled herself as being appointed by God to rule England. To oppose the Queen's will was the equivalent of opposing God's will. Known as *passive obedience*, this doctrine did not allow any opposition

A portrait of Elizabeth I by George Gower, ca. 1588. National Portrait Gallery, London/SuperStock

even to a tyrannical monarch because God had appointed the king or queen for reasons unknown to His subjects on earth. However, as Bevington notes, Elizabeth's power was not as absolute as her rhetoric suggested. Parliament, already well established in England, reserved some power, such as the authority to levy taxes, for itself.

Elizabeth I lived in a society that restricted women from possessing any political or personal autonomy and power. As queen, Elizabeth violated and called into question many of the prejudices and practices against women. In a way, her society forced her to "overcome" her sex in order to rule effectively. However, her position did nothing to increase the status of women in England.

One of the rhetorical strategies that Elizabeth adopted in order to rule effectively was to separate her position as monarch of England from her natural body—to separate her *body politic* from her *body natural*. In addition, throughout her reign, Elizabeth brilliantly negotiated between domestic and foreign factions—some of whom were anxious about a female monarch and wanted her to marry—appeasing both sides without ever committing to one.

She remained unmarried throughout her 45-year reign, partially by styling herself as the Virgin Queen whose purity represented England herself. Her refusal to marry and her habit of hinting and promising marriage with suitors—both foreign and domestic—helped Elizabeth maintain internal and external peace. Not marrying allowed her to retain her independence, but it left the succession of the English throne in question. In 1603, on her deathbed, she named James VI, King of Scotland and son of her cousin Mary, as her successor.

James I

When he assumed the English crown, James VI of Scotland became James I of England. (Some historians refer to him as James VI and I.) Like Elizabeth, James was a strong believer in the divine right of kings and their absolute authority.

Upon his arrival in London to claim the English throne, James made his plans to unite Scotland and England clear. However, a long-standing history of enmity existed between the two countries. Partially as a result of this history and the influx of Scottish courtiers into English society, anti-Scottish prejudice abounded in England. When James asked Parliament for the title of "King of Great Britain," he was denied.

As scholars such as Bevington have pointed out, James was less successful than Elizabeth was in negotiating between the different religious and political factions in England. Although he was a Protestant, he began to have problems with the Puritan sect of the House of Commons, which ultimately led to a rift between the court (which also started to have Catholic sympathies) and the Parliament. This rift between the monarchy and Parliament eventually escalated into the civil war that would erupt during the reign of James's son, Charles I.

In spite of its difficulties with Parliament, James's court was a site of wealth, luxury, and extravagance. James I commissioned elaborate feasts, masques, and pageants, and in doing so he more than doubled the royal debt. Stephen Greenblatt suggests that Shakespeare's *The Tempest* may reflect this extravagance through Prospero's magnificent banquet and accompanying masque. Reigning from 1603 to 1625, James I remained the King of England throughout the last years of Shakespeare's life.

Social context

Shakespeare's England divided itself roughly into two social classes: the aristocrats (or nobility) and everyone else. The primary distinctions between these two classes were ancestry, wealth, and power. Simply put, the aristocrats were the only ones who possessed all three.

Aristocrats were born with their wealth, but the growth of trade and the development of skilled professions began to provide wealth for those not born with it. Although the notion of a middle class did not begin to develop until after Shakespeare's death, the possibility of some social mobility did exist in Early Modern England. Shakespeare himself used the wealth gained from the theatre to move into the lower ranks of the aristocracy by securing a coat of arms for his family.

Shakespeare was not unique in this movement, but not all people received the opportunity to increase their social status. Members of the aristocracy feared this social movement and, as a result, promoted harsh laws of apprenticeship and fashion, restricting certain styles of dress and material. These laws dictated that only the aristocracy could wear certain articles of clothing, colours, and materials. Though enforcement was a difficult task, the Early Modern aristocracy considered dressing above one's station a moral and ethical violation.

The status of women

The legal status of women did not allow them much public or private autonomy. English society functioned on a system of patriarchy and hierarchy (see "Universal Hierarchy" earlier in this introduction), which means that men controlled society, beginning with the individual family. In fact, the family metaphorically corresponded to the state. For example, the husband was the king of his family. His authority to control his family was absolute and based on divine right, similar to that of the country's king. People also saw the family itself differently than today, considering apprentices and servants part of the whole family.

The practice of *primogeniture*—a system of inheritance that passed all of a family's wealth through the first male child—accompanied this system of patriarchy. Thus, women did not generally inherit their family's wealth and titles. In the absence of a male heir, some women, such as Queen Elizabeth, did. But after women married, they lost almost all of their already limited legal rights, such as the right to inherit, to own property, and to sign contracts. In all likelihood, Elizabeth I would have lost much of her power and authority if she married.

Furthermore, women did not generally receive an education and could not enter certain professions, including acting. Instead, society relegated women to the domestic sphere of the home.

Daily life

Daily life in Early Modern England began before sunup—exactly how early depended on one's station in life. A servant's responsibilities usually included preparing the house for the day. Families usually possessed limited living space; even among wealthy families, multiple family members tended to share a small number of rooms, suggesting that privacy may not have been important or practical.

Working through the morning, Elizabethans usually had lunch about noon. This midday meal was the primary meal of the day, much like dinner is for modern families. The workday usually ended around sundown or 5 p.m., depending on the season. Before an early bedtime, Elizabethans usually ate a light repast and then settled in for a couple of hours of reading (if the family members were literate and could bear the high cost of books) or socializing.

Mortality rates

Mortality rates in Early Modern England were high compared to our standards, especially among infants. Infection and disease ran rampant because physicians did not realize the need for antiseptics and sterile equipment. As a result, communicable diseases often spread very rapidly in cities, particularly London.

In addition, the bubonic plague frequently ravaged England, with two major outbreaks—from 1592–1594 and in 1603—occurring during Shakespeare's lifetime. People did not understand the plague and generally perceived it as God's punishment. (We now know that the plague was spread by fleas and could not be spread directly from human to human.) Without a cure or an understanding of what transmitted the disease, physicians could do nothing to stop the thousands of deaths that resulted from each outbreak. These outbreaks had a direct effect on Shakespeare's career, because the government often closed the theatres in an effort to impede the spread of the disease.

London life

In the sixteenth century, London, though small compared to modern cities, was the largest city of Europe, with a population of about 200,000 inhabitants in the city and surrounding suburbs. London was a crowded city without a sewer system, which facilitated epidemics such as the plague. In addition, crime rates were high in the city due to inefficient law enforcement and the lack of street lighting.

Despite these drawbacks, London was the cultural, political, and social heart of England. As the home of the monarch and most of England's trade, London was a bustling metropolis. Not surprisingly, a young Shakespeare moved to London to begin his professional career.

The theatre

Most theatres were not actually located within the city of London. Rather, theatre owners built them on the south bank of the Thames River (in Southwark) across from the city in order to avoid the strict regulations that applied within the city's walls. These restrictions stemmed from a mistrust of public performances as locations of plague and riotous behaviour. Furthermore, because theatre performances took place during the day, they took labourers away from their jobs. Opposition to the theatres also came from Puritans, who believed that they fostered immorality. Therefore, theatres moved out of the city, to areas near other sites of restricted activities, such as dog fighting, bear- and bull-baiting, and prostitution.

Despite the move, the theatre was not free from censorship or regulation. In fact, a branch of the government known as the Office of the Revels attempted to ensure that plays did not present politically or socially sensitive material. Prior to each performance, the Master of the Revels would read a complete text of each play, cutting out offending sections or, in some cases, not approving the play for public performance.

Performance spaces

Theatres in Early Modern England were quite different from our modern facilities. They were usually open-air, relying heavily on natural light and good weather. The rectangular stage extended out into an area that people called the *pit*—a circular, uncovered area about 21 metres in diameter. Audience members had two choices when purchasing admission to a theatre. Admission to the pit, where the lower classes (or *groundlings*) stood for the performances,

was the cheaper option. People of wealth could purchase a seat in one of the three covered tiers of seats that ringed the pit. At full capacity, a public theatre in Early Modern England could hold between 2,000 and 3,000 people.

The stage, which projected into the pit and was raised about 1.5 metres above it, had a covered portion called the *heavens*. The heavens enclosed theatrical equipment for lowering and raising actors to and from the stage. A trapdoor in the middle of stage provided theatrical graves for characters such as Ophelia and also allowed ghosts, such as Banquo in *Macbeth*, to rise from the earth. A wall separated the back of the stage from the actors' dressing room, known as the *tiring house*. At each end of the wall stood a door for major entrances and exits. Above the wall and doors stood a gallery directly above the stage, reserved for the wealthiest spectators. Actors occasionally used this area when a performance called for a difference in height—for example, to represent Juliet's balcony or the walls of a besieged city. A good example of this type of theatre was the original Globe Theatre in London in which Shakespeare's company, The Lord Chamberlain's Men (later the King's Men), staged its plays. However, indoor theatres, such as the Blackfriars, differed slightly because the pit was filled with chairs that faced a rectangular stage. Because only the wealthy could afford the cost of admission, the public generally considered these theatres private.

Actors and staging

Performances in Shakespeare's England do not appear to have employed scenery. However, theatre companies developed their costumes with great care and expense. In fact, a playing company's costumes were its most valuable items. These extravagant costumes were the object of much controversy because some aristocrats feared that the actors could use them to disguise their social status on the streets of London.

The recently reconstructed Globe theatre.
Chris Parker/PAL

Costumes also disguised a player's gender. All actors on the stage during Shakespeare's lifetime were men. Young boys whose voices had not reached maturity played female parts. This practice no doubt influenced Shakespeare's and his contemporary playwrights' thematic explorations of cross-dressing.

Though historians have managed to reconstruct the appearance of the early modern theatre, such as the recent construction of the Globe in London, much of the information regarding

A scene from Shakespeare in Love *shows how the interior of the Globe would have appeared.*
Everett Collection

how plays were performed during this era has been lost. Scholars of Early Modern theatre have turned to the scant external and internal stage directions in manuscripts in an effort to find these answers. While a hindrance for modern critics and scholars, the lack of detail about Early Modern performances has allowed modern directors and actors a great deal of flexibility and room to be creative.

The printing press

If not for the printing press, many Early Modern plays may not have survived until today. In Shakespeare's time, printers produced all books by *sheet*— a single, large piece of paper that the printer would fold in order to produce the desired book size. For example, a folio required folding the sheet once, a quarto four times, an octavo eight, and so on. Sheets would be printed one side at a time; thus, printers had to simultaneously print multiple nonconsecutive pages.

In order to estimate what section of the text would be on each page, the printer would *cast off* copy. After the printer made these estimates, *compositors* would set the type upside down, letter by letter. This process of setting type produced textual errors, some of which a proofreader would catch. When a proofreader found an error, the compositors would fix the piece or pieces of type. Printers called corrections made after printing began *stop-press* corrections because they literally had to stop the press to fix the error. Because of the high cost of paper, printers would still sell the sheets printed before they made the correction.

Printers placed frames of text in the bed of the printing press and used them to imprint the paper. They then folded and grouped the sheets of paper into gatherings, after which the pages were ready for sale. The buyer had the option of getting the new play bound.

The printing process was crucial to the preservation of Shakespeare's works, but the printing of drama in Early Modern England was not a standardized practice. Many of the first editions of Shakespeare's plays appear in quarto format and, until recently, scholars regarded them as "corrupt." In fact, scholars still debate how close a relationship exists between what appeared on the stage in the sixteenth and seventeenth centuries and what appears on the printed page. The inconsistent and scant appearance of stage directions, for example, makes it difficult to determine how close this relationship was.

We know that the practice of the theatre allowed the alteration of plays by a variety of hands other than the author's. This practice further complicated any efforts to extract what a playwright wrote and what was changed by either the players, the printers, or the government censors. Theatre was a collaborative environment. Rather than lament our inability to determine authorship and what exactly Shakespeare wrote, we should work to understand this collaborative nature and learn from it.

Shakespeare wrote his plays for the stage, and the existing published texts reflect the collaborative nature of the theatre as well as the unavoidable changes made during the printing process. A play's first written version would have been the author's *foul papers*, which invariably consisted of blotted lines and revised text. From there, a scribe would recopy the play and produce a *fair copy*. The theatre manager would then copy out and annotate this copy into a playbook (what people today call a *promptbook*).

At this point, scrolls of individual parts were copied out for actors to memorize. (Due to the high cost of paper, theatre companies could not afford to provide their actors with a complete copy of the play.) The government required the company to send the playbook to the Master of the Revels, the government official who would make any necessary changes or mark any passages considered unacceptable for performance.

Printers could have used any one of these copies to print a play. We cannot determine whether a printer used the author's version, the modified theatrical version, the censored version, or a combination when printing a given play. Refer to the "Publications" section of the "Introduction to William Shakespeare" for further discussion of the impact printing practices has on our understanding of Shakespeare's works.

Works cited

For more information regarding Early Modern England, consult the following works:

Bevington, David. "General Introduction." *The Complete Works of William Shakespeare*. Updated Fourth edition. New York: Longman, 1997.

Greenblatt, Stephen. "Shakespeare's World." *Norton Shakespeare*. New York: W.W. Norton and Co., 1997.

Kastan, David Scott, ed. *A Companion to Shakespeare*. Oxford: Blackwell, 1999.

McDonald, Russ. *The Bedford Companion to Shakespeare: An Introduction with Documents*. Boston: Bedford-St. Martin's Press, 1996.

INTRODUCTION TO *ROMEO AND JULIET*

In J.D. Salinger's *The Catcher in the Rye*, Holden Caulfield, the infamous spotter of phoniness, says that he likes *Romeo and Juliet* "a lot," but he has a few problems with the play. For example, Romeo and Juliet get "pretty annoying," and he doesn't like the fact that "smart, entertaining" Mercutio dies. Holden's comments remind us that *Romeo and Juliet* isn't just a play about love, nor is it a pure tragedy. Romeo may be romantic and meditative, but witty Mercutio is full of humour and vigour. The play is filled with contrasts like these: Tragedy mixes with comedy, love with hate, and death with life.

Although the names Romeo and Juliet will always be synonymous with deep and tragic love, Shakespeare's play is also about life itself. *Romeo and*

Leonardo DiCaprio in Baz Luhrmann's 1998 film version, Romeo + Juliet. *Everett Collection*

The story of Romeo and Juliet has a long history, but each author remade the tale in his own way. For example, although Brooke is faithful to his source, he also makes many additions that are influenced by Chaucer's *Troilus and Criseyde*. Following Chaucer, for example, Brooke's story emphasizes the powers of fate in shaping the tragedy.

Another direct source of Shakespeare's play is a novella written by William Painter, *The goodly History of the true and constant love betweene Romeo and Julietta,* published in 1567. Finally, in the preface to his poem, Brooke mentions a play version of the story that was performed in England. The play is lost, but many critics argue that Shakespeare may have referred to it when writing his drama.

Shakespeare chose to develop the story of Romeo and Juliet not only because of its popularity, but because he was interested in its themes, such as the idea of the star-crossed love. While the story of Romeo and Juliet did not originate with Shakespeare, he changed Brooke's version significantly enough to make the story his own.

Juliet is about the crazy, exciting, mixed-up world we live in, where we sometimes fight with our parents, we aren't always nice to our friends, we get bored and look for a fight, and we fall in love and it doesn't work out. The play also happens to be a well-crafted, poetically beautiful drama.

Sources of the story

Like most of Shakespeare's plays, the story in *Romeo and Juliet* doesn't originate with Shakespeare. Rather, the play is based on a folktale, which was developed into a series of novellas (short novels) in the fifteenth and sixteenth centuries.

In 1562, a famous version of the story was published in England: Arthur Brooke's *The Tragical History of Romeus and Juliet.* Brooke's work was Shakespeare's primary source for his play. Brooke's poem is a translation of a French version of the tale by Pierre Boaistuau (1559), whose version was an adaptation of Bandello (1554), based on Luigi da Porto's (1525) translation of a tale by Masuccio Salternitano (1476).

Shakespeare's variations

How did Shakespeare change Brooke's story? To begin, he cut the time frame of the story from nine months to five days. Romeo and Juliet meet on Sunday, marry on Monday, and die early on Friday morning. One reason for this change is that Shakespeare wanted to emphasize the quick passage of time, adding to the intensity of his drama. Shakespeare also decreases Juliet's age from 16 to 13 to emphasize her youth and to show that she is too young for marriage.

Shakespeare also changes the time of year from Christmas to July, but he occasionally forgets that he's made this change. The feast scenes, for example, seem to take place in winter, because Capulet tells his servants to "quench the fire, the room is grown too hot" (I.5.28). A warm fire probably wouldn't have been necessary in July in Italy.

Shakespeare enjoyed setting his plays in exotic locations, and he creates the spirited atmosphere and brilliant detail of an Italian city in this play, although critics argue that the domestic life represented in the play resembles the English merchant class more than Renaissance Italian nobility.

The birth of the play

Shakespeare probably wrote *Romeo and Juliet* between 1594 and 1596. Although the play has been popular from the time Shakespeare wrote it, the first recorded performance of the play was on March 1, 1662. Two primary versions, or *quartos,* of the play exist. The first was published in 1597, and the second in 1599.

As explained in the "Introduction to William Shakespeare," the first quartos of most of Shakespeare's dramas are considered corrupt, neither authorized nor written by Shakespeare. Often, actors or reporters constructed these first versions to make extra money. *Romeo and Juliet* is no exception. Critics believe that the first quarto of this play was published as a money-maker by arrangement with Shakespeare's company, when the play was still being shown on stage. The first version is significantly shorter than the second, probably because it was based on a staged version, perhaps one performed by a group of travelling players working in rural areas. (Travelling players would have wanted a short version to ensure that their audience didn't get bored.)

Structure

In addition to shortening the time frame of the play significantly, Shakespeare tightened Brooke's version of the story in many other ways. By increasing the roles of minor characters, creating tight structural parallels, and juxtaposing scenes of opposite emotion, Shakespeare put his personal stamp on this well-known story.

The roles of minor characters

Shakespeare increased the importance of minor characters to emphasize oppositions and similarities between various characters in the play. In doing so, he made his main characters' personalities more vivid.

Most significantly, Shakespeare developed the Nurse and Mercutio, who were only names in Brooke's poem. Mercutio contrasts with Romeo, and the Nurse contrasts with Juliet. While Mercutio is fiery, witty, belligerent, and humorous, his friend Romeo is dreamy, harmonious, meditative, and literary. Similarly, Juliet's Nurse is earthy and vulgar, while Juliet is spiritual, light, and poetic. Paris is another character that Shakespeare fleshes out; Paris becomes essentially Romeo's double. At the end of the play, the differences between Romeo and Paris show how completely Romeo has changed. Just as Romeo is stilted and literary at the beginning of the drama, Paris follows convention to the letter even when expressing grief for Juliet's death. In contrast, by the play's end, Romeo develops into an honest and authentic lover.

Structural parallels

Besides creating oppositions and similarities between characters, Shakespeare also creates structural parallels between scenes that make his drama cohesive. The scenes in which the Capulets prepare for the ball (I.5) and Juliet's marriage to Paris (IV.4), for example, are structurally similar. The lovers' three duets—their meeting at the masquerade, their interaction during the balcony scene, and their final conversation the morning after the consummation of their marriage—are also structurally similar. All three scenes end at dawn and all are interrupted by Juliet's Nurse.

Dawn is repeatedly used as a structuring device in the play. When we're first introduced to Romeo, he wanders through the woods at dawn dreaming of Rosaline. Romeo and Juliet spend most of their time together at dawn. In addition, the Nurse discovers Juliet's seemingly dead body at dawn on Thursday morning, and the lovers die at dawn on Friday. This emphasis on exact temporal moments gives the play a solid structure.

Shakespeare also carefully structures the Prince's appearances in the play. The Prince enters the action three times: at the opening, middle, and closing of the play. All of his appearances are in response to acts of violence, including the Montague-Capulet street brawl (I.1), Mercutio and Tybalt's deaths (III.1), and the deaths of Romeo, Juliet, and Paris (V.3). Likewise, all of the Prince's appearances involve the entire community, and all of his appearances result in his judgment on the community. The parallel structure of the Prince's actions in the play gives them a ritual or mythic tone. The Prince seems to be a voice of order, rendering judgment on Verona's chaotic society. His final speech has the effect of ritually purging Verona of its sins after the sacrificial deaths of Romeo and Juliet.

Dramatic tension

While the structurally parallel scenes of this drama create cohesion, the juxtaposition of scenes that have different emotional impact increases the play's intensity. Shakespeare weaves together tragic and comic moments throughout the play to increase dramatic tension. For example, Act IV, Scene 5 begins with the Capulets mourning Juliet's supposed death and ends with a comic conversation between the musicians who were scheduled to play at Juliet and Paris's wedding.

Glaring structural and thematic dichotomies abound in this play: society versus the lovers, age versus youth, hate versus love, death versus life, love poetry versus vulgar and bawdy language. For example, Romeo walks directly from his quiet marriage to Juliet into the street brawl in which Mercutio and Tybalt are killed. None of these oppositions are found in Shakespeare's source. He added them to increase the dramatic tension of the story, maintaining the audience's sympathies for the lovers and giving their deaths a ritual feeling. The juxtapositions emphasize

Leontina Vadura plays Juliet in a 1994 Royal Opera House production.
Clive Barda/PAL

one of Shakespeare's primary messages in the play: The collision between extreme oppositions results in violent and tragic explosion, which leads, ultimately, to a peaceful purging.

Language

Shakespeare's use of contrasts continues in the play's language. Varying from beautiful lyricism to colloquial and often vulgar speech, the play is filled with language games and punning on every level. Because puns show that words have multiple meanings, they prove that language is never transparent or singular. Following his secret wedding to Juliet, Romeo tells his former enemy and new cousin Tybalt, "[G]ood Capulet, which name I tender / As dearly as mine own, be satisfied" (III.1.70-71). Romeo implies that he now appreciates the name Capulet because of his marriage to Juliet, but Tybalt and Mercutio, who know nothing about the marriage, believe that that Romeo is simply being weak.

Romeo and Juliet is full of double entendres that prove the difficulty of interpreting another person's intentions, because language is capable of meaning many things at once. In the example in the previous paragraph, Romeo uses the word "tender," which means "value" but also infers "fondness," meaning that Romeo cares for his new kinsman. In suggesting that he no longer bears any enmity for the name "Capulet," Romeo also shows us how simultaneously arbitrary and significant names can be.

In the balcony scene, Juliet wonders what part of Romeo's body makes him her enemy. She tries to separate Romeo's name from his body, arguing "'Tis but thy name that is my enemy: / Thou art thyself, though not a Montague. What's Montague?" (II.2.38-39). What, indeed, is a Montague? Does a name or language truly define a person or an idea?

Continuing with her meditation on naming, Juliet asks, "What's in a name? That which we call a rose / By any other word would smell as sweet"

(II.2.43-44). Juliet believes that Romeo, like a rose, would be equally perfect by any other name. Thus, there is no relationship between his name and his true identity. On the other hand, Romeo's name has led to violence, because the feud between the Capulets and Montagues hinges almost completely on the families' names.

This questioning of the truth behind language continues throughout the play, and Shakespeare's almost excessive punning shows that word meanings aren't singular. Because of language's multiplicity, we always mean more than we say.

Shakespeare uses language in *Romeo and Juliet* not only to show that meaning is difficult to pinpoint, but also to show the relationship between language and emotions. Critics often see Romeo's early speeches to Rosaline as parodies of the conventions of traditional courtship, also known as *Petrarchanism*. Petrarch was a fourteenth-century Italian poet and scholar who, throughout his life, composed poems to praise his beloved, Laura. Petrarch's poems create an ideal lover who is melancholy, lovesick, emotionally extreme, and interested in paradox. Although Petrarch's work had a strong impact on world literature, Petrarch was viewed as old-fashioned in Shakespeare's day.

Early in *Romeo and Juliet*, Mercutio identifies Romeo as a student of Petrarch's poetry: He is "for the numbers that Petrarch flow'd in" (II.4.38-39). Mercutio intends his words as criticism, implying that Romeo's poems for Rosaline are intellectual and stilted, showing a lack of passion or honest emotion, as if Romeo wrote the poems for school instead of a lover. The artificiality of Romeo's words for Rosaline indicates that his feelings for her are equally false.

As the play progresses and Romeo falls in love with Juliet, his language becomes more natural and heartfelt, reflecting that his feelings for her are true. When Romeo and Juliet first meet, she complains that he kisses "by th'book." Their conversation in this scene is structured as a formal sonnet, and Juliet finds this form too literary and strict to express the excesses of her passion. During their wedding scene, Juliet again criticizes Romeo's language. Juliet wants Romeo to speak with a little more substance and a little less ornamentation (II.6.30-34). At this moment in the play, Juliet's feelings are so strong that they defy words; all language is too limiting to express her passion for her lover. By the end of the play, however, you see that Romeo's command of language has grown, especially when you compare his speech with Paris's. While Paris still speaks in formal, rhymed verses, Romeo uses blank verse (unrhymed iambic pentameter) to show his feelings for Juliet.

Imagery

One of Chaucer's primary influences on Shakespeare was his use of repeated patterns of images, or *motifs*, to create inner coherence. Recurring images related to the stars, seasons, blind cupid, and fate add unity and richness to *Romeo and Juliet*. In addition, Shakespeare associates certain images with particular characters. For example, Shakespeare associates both Romeo and Juliet with stars, light, dawn and, seafaring. Juliet frequently toys with images taken from falconry, and Friar Laurence repeats the idea of the earth being a womb and a tomb simultaneously. However, many of these symbols and motifs are ambiguous. For example, the young lovers "in their triumph die, like fire and powder / Which as they kiss consume" (II.6.10-11). Although fire generates warmth and energy, it also has the power to consume everything it touches, leaving only ash.

Light and darkness

One of the most often repeated image patterns in *Romeo and Juliet* involves the interplay of light and darkness. For example, Romeo compares Juliet to light throughout the play. Upon first sight of her, Romeo exclaims that she teaches "the torches to burn bright" (I.5.43). She's also "the sun" who can "kill the envious moon" (II.2.3). Later in the same scene,

he claims that her eyes are like "[t]wo of the fairest stars in all the heaven" (II.2.15). But Juliet's light shows best against the darkness; she "hangs upon the cheek of night / As a rich jewel in an Ethiop's ear" (I.5.44-45).

Juliet also associates Romeo with a light that illuminates the darkness. If Juliet dies, she wants Romeo cut "in little stars / And he will make the face of heaven so fine / That all the world will be in love with night, / And pay no worship to the garish sun" (III.2.22-25). This quotation reminds us that Romeo and Juliet's light shines most brightly in the dark—it is a muted glow associated primarily with stars, torches, and the dawn, rather than with sunlight, which is almost obscenely bright. Like the darkness, their love is associated with mystery, emotion, and imagination. In fact, the day works against them. At the end of their honeymoon night, Romeo says, "More light and light: more dark and dark our woes" (III.5.36). The lovers must part before the light arrives to ensure that Romeo isn't caught and killed.

Death

Images of death are also predominant in this play. Early in the drama, Shakespeare presents death as an essential aspect of life, simply a part of the cycle of nature. Following Tybalt's death, Lord Capulet says that "we were born to die" (III.4.4), echoing the Nurse's "death's the end of all" (III.3.91). Similarly, the Friar argues, "The earth that's nature's mother is her tomb: / What is her burying grave, that is her womb" (II.3.5-6). The Friar knows that life and death are simply different phases of earth's cyclical progression.

By the end of the play, death has become more ominous. Entering Juliet's tomb, Romeo imagines the "womb of death / Gorg'd with the dearest morsel of earth" (V.3.45-46). From a benign part of life, death becomes a gluttonous and rotting monster waiting to stuff itself with the bodies of the young lovers. Throughout the final scene, Romeo discusses death as Juliet's "paramour," which has sent his worms to be her "chambermaids" and to prepare her deathly wedding ceremony.

In Renaissance slang, the term *die* also suggests sexual consummation. Following the discovery of Juliet's seemingly dead body, Lord Capulet plays on the double meaning of this word, suggesting that death is a rapist who has "deflowered" Juliet (IV.5.37).

The death imagery is transformed again in the final passages of the play, when Romeo suggests that death grants him the beautiful power of transcendence that will lead him to eternal life with Juliet. For that reason, the poison Romeo buys from the apothecary is but a "cordial" that triumphantly leads him to Juliet.

Themes

Many of the themes in *Romeo and Juliet* involve the oppositions discussed earlier in this introduction. In particular, Shakespeare is interested in the contrasts between youth and old age, public and private, and love and hate. The play also explores the importance of fate or destiny in our lives. For example, how much control do humans actually have over their futures? Are we simply the pawns of a higher power, or can we determine our own destinies?

Love is another important thematic element in the play. *Romeo and Juliet* presents various types of love: the sensual, physical love that the Nurse enjoys; the proper or contractual love that Paris represents; and the passionate, romantic love of Romeo and Juliet. Shakespeare asks us to question

how these various types of love relate to one another. For example, is physical attraction a necessary component of romantic love? And how, if the meaning of language is so slippery, can we know if a lover speaks the truth about his feelings?

Another important theme is the dual nature of all creation. As the Friar reminds us, "Virtue itself turns vice being misapplied, / And vice sometime's by action dignified" (II. 3.17-18). Within a flower, for example, lies both poison and medicine. Similarly, the deaths of Romeo and Juliet are tragic but also bring new life to Verona. Even the Friar's role in the play contains this ambiguity. Although he tries to help the lovers, his actions lead to their suffering. Shakespeare's message is that nothing is purely good or evil; everything contains elements of both, and ambiguity rules.

A final theme that *Romeo and Juliet* considers is the meaning of gender. In particular, the play depicts a variety of versions of masculinity. One example is Mercutio, the showy male bird, who enjoys quarreling, fencing, and joking. Mercutio has definite ideas about what masculinity should look like. He criticizes Tybalt for being too interested in his clothes and for speaking with a fake accent. Similarly, Mercutio

Clare Danes and Leonardo DiCaprio in the 1998 film **Romeo + Juliet**. *Everett Collection*

suggests that Romeo's love-melancholy is effeminate, while his more sociable self is properly masculine. Mercutio is happiest when Romeo rejoins his witty, crazy group of male friends: "Now art thou sociable, now art thou Romeo; now art thou art, by art as well as by nature" (II.4.89-90).

Romeo's masculinity is constantly questioned. Following Mercutio's death, for example, Romeo fears that his love for Juliet has effeminized him: "Thy beauty hath made me effeminate / And in my temper soften'd valour's steel" (III.1.116-117). He worries that his reputation as a man is "stain'd"

(III.1.113). When Romeo is banished from Verona, the Friar accuses Romeo of being an "[u]nseemly woman in a seeming man" and says that his tears are "womanish" (III.3.109-111).

What is the proper role for a man? *Romeo and Juliet* seems to suggest that violence isn't it. Mediating between Mercutio's violent temper and Romeo's passivity, the Prince is possibly the best model of masculine behaviour in the play: Impartial and fair, he also opposes civil violence.

CHARACTERS IN THE PLAY

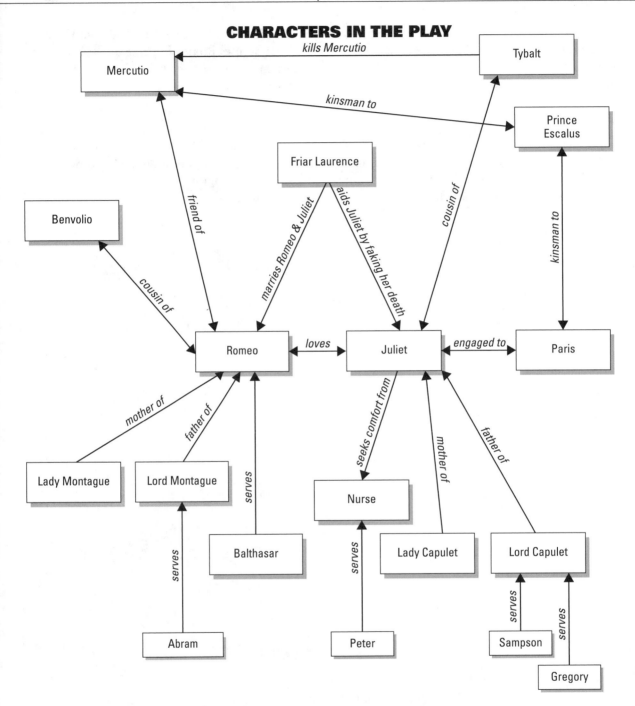

COLES NOTES TOTAL STUDY EDITION
ROMEO AND JULIET
ACT I

Romeo *If I profane with my unworthiest hand*
This holy shrine, the gentle sin is this;
My lips, two blushing pilgrims, ready stand
To smooth that rough touch with a tender kiss.

Juliet *Good pilgrim, you do wrong your hand too much,*
Which mannerly devotion shows in this;
For saints have hands that pilgrims' hands do touch,
And palm to palm is holy palmers' kiss.

Act I, Prologue

This introduction to the play emphasizes the power of fate over the lives of Romeo and Juliet, who are to some extent the victims of their parents' strife. Their love is described as being "death-marked." As in Greek tragedy, fate hovers over all.

ACT I, PROLOGUE

[Enter Chorus]

Chorus Two households, both alike in dignity,
  In fair Verona, where we lay our scene
  From ancient grudge break to new mutiny,
  Where civil blood makes civil hands unclean.
  From forth the fatal loins of these two foes   5
  A pair of star-crossed lovers take their life;
  Whose misadventured piteous overthrows
  Doth with their death bury their parents' strife.
  The fearful passage of their death-marked love,
  And the continuance of their parents' rage,   10
  Which, but their children's end, naught could remove,
  Is now the two hours' traffic of our stage;
  The which if you with patient ears attend,
  What here shall miss, our toil shall strive to mend.
[Exeunt]

NOTES

1.   *households:* the Capulets and the Montagues.
    alike: equal.
3.   *mutiny:* disorder, tumult—between anyone, not just in the armed forces.
4.   *civil blood makes civil hands unclean:* The blood of the citizens in civil war makes the hands of a civilized (well-mannered) people unclean.
5.   *fatal:* fated for misfortune.
6.   *star-crossed:* i.e., their fortunes were marred by the influence of the stars. That men's natures and fortunes were influenced by the star under which they were born was a widespread superstition of Elizabethan times.
7-8.   *Whose . . . strife:* the cessation of whose unfortunate pitiful struggles makes an end to their parents' strife; "overthrows" is used as a noun, not a verb.
9.   *death-marked:* destined (marked out) for death.
12.   *traffic:* business, concern.
14.   *miss:* fail, be missing, perhaps an implied metaphor, i.e., miss the mark.

COMMENTARY

Written in the form of a sonnet, the Prologue to Act I provides a clear summary of the play. From the beginning, we know that the story of Romeo and Juliet will end in tragedy. We also know that their tragic ends will result not from their own personality defects but from fate, which has marked them for sorrow. Emphasizing fate's control over their destinies, the Prologue tells us that the "star-crossed lovers'" relationship is "death-marked" (6,9).

The Prologue also sets up the juxtaposition of binary opposites that will be important throughout the play; for example, Romeo and Juliet's love contrasts the

WHEEL of FORTUNE

The Wheel of Fortune

"ancient grudge" between their parents (3). Likewise, the Prologue suggests that the play includes an important message about social violence. Because "civil blood makes civil hands unclean," the entire Verona community has been soiled from the fighting between the Montagues and Capulets (4). The lovers' deaths serve the ritual, sacrificial function of purging unclean Verona.

A rarity among Shakespeare's works, the Prologue is often considered superfluous and omitted from staged performances of the play. When included, the Prologue is usually spoken by the Prince (rather than a chorus as Shakespeare had intended).

Act I, Scene 1

Prompted by a fight between their servants, Benvolio (a Montague) and Tybalt (a Capulet) brawl in the public square of Verona. The Prince stops the fight and vows to execute any Capulet or Montague who disturbs the peace of Verona again. A melancholy Romeo tells Benvolio he is in love.

ACT I, SCENE 1
Verona, a public place.

[Enter SAMPSON and GREGORY, with swords and bucklers, of the house of Capulet]

Sampson Gregory, on my word, we'll not carry coals.

Gregory No, for then we should be colliers.

Sampson I mean, an we be in choler, we'll draw.

Gregory Ay, while you live, draw your neck out of collar.

Sampson I strike quickly, being moved.   5

Gregory But thou are not quickly moved to strike.

Sampson A dog of the house of Montague moves me.

Gregory To move is to stir, and to be valiant is to stand. Therefore, if thou art moved, thou runn'st away.

Sampson A dog of that house shall move me to stand. I   10 will take the wall of any man or maid of Montague's.

Gregory That shows thee a weak slave; for the weakest goes to the wall.

Sampson 'Tis true; and therefore women, being the weaker vessels, are ever thrust to the wall. Therefore I   15 will push Montague's men from the wall and thrust his maids to the wall.

Gregory The quarrel is between our masters, and us their men.

Sampson 'Tis all one. I will show myself a tyrant. When   20 I have fought with the men, I will be cruel with the maids—I will cut off their heads.

Gregory The heads of the maids?

Sampson Ay, the heads of the maids, or their maidenheads. Take it in what sense thou wilt.   25

NOTES

1.   *carry coals:* submit to insult, like servants.

2.   *colliers:* workmen who carry and trade in coal.

3.   *an we be in choler:* if we are angry, if our blood is up.

    draw: draw swords. (Note pun on carrying a collar equipped with buckets for drawing water from a well.)

6.   *moved:* roused to anger, stirred.

7.   *A dog:* i.e., any low-down fellow.

11.   *take the wall of:* prove superiority by fighting with back to the wall.

13.   *goes to the wall:* i.e., the other extreme, is pushed against the wall.

15.   *thrust to the wall:* a sexual joke.

20.   *'Tis all one:* i.e., 'tis all the same, it makes no difference to me.

Gregory They must take it in sense that feel it.

Sampson Me they shall feel while I am able to stand; and 'tis known I am a pretty piece of flesh.

Gregory 'Tis well thou art not fish; if thou hadst, thou hadst been poor-John. Draw thy tool! Here comes two of 30 the house of Montagues.

[Enter two other Servingmen, ABRAM and BALTHASAR]

Sampson My naked weapon is out. Quarrel! I will back thee.

Gregory How? turn thy back and run?

Sampson Fear me not.   35

Gregory No, marry. I fear thee!

Sampson Let us take the law of our sides; let them begin.

Gregory I will frown as I pass by, and let them take it as they list.

Sampson Nay, as they dare. I will bite my thumb at   40 them, which is disgrace to them if they bear it.

Abram Do you bite your thumb at us, sir?

Sampson I do bite my thumb, Sir.

Abram Do you bite your thumb at us, sir?

Sampson *[aside to GREGORY]* Is the law of our side if I say ay?   45

Gregory *[aside to SAMPSON]* No.

Sampson No, sir, I do not bite my thumb at you, sir; but I bite my thumb, sir.

Gregory Do you quarrel, sir?

Abram Quarrel, sir? No, sir.   50

Sampson But if you do, sir, I am for you. I serve as good a man as you.

Abram No better.

Sampson Well, sir.

[Enter BENVOLIO]

---

36. *marry:* an oath meaning "by the Virgin Mary," but in effect no stronger than "indeed."

37. *take the law of our sides:* make sure we have the law on our side.

39. *list:* choose, please.

40. *bite my thumb:* an insulting gesture in Shakespeare's time.

51. *I am for you:* I accept your challenge; I am ready to fight you.

54. *Well, sir:* Sampson cannot understand what Abram means by his noncommittal reply. He could mean that there was no better master than his own or that there was no better master than Sampson's.

Gregory *[aside to SAMPSON]* Say 'better.' Here comes 55
one of my master's kinsmen.

Sampson Yes, better, sir.

Abram You lie.

Sampson Draw, if you be men. Gregory remember thy
swashing blow.   60

[They fight]

Benvolio Part, fools!
Put up your swords. You know not what you do.

[Enter TYBALT]

Tybalt What, art thou drawn among these heartless hinds?
Turn thee, Benvolio! look upon thy death.

Benvolio I do but keep the peace. Put up thy sword,   65
Or manage it to part these men with me.

Tybalt What, drawn, and talk of peace? I hate the word,
As I hate hell, all Montagues, and thee.
Have at thee, coward!

[They fight]

*[Enter an Officer, and three or four Citizens with clubs or
     partisans]*

Officer Clubs, bills, and partisans! Strike! beat them down! 70

Citizens Down with the Capulets! Down with the
Montagues!

[Enter old CAPULET in his gown, and his Wife]

Capulet What noise is this? Give me my long sword, ho!

Wife A crutch, a crutch! Why call you for a sword?

Capulet My sword, I say! Old Montague is come   75
And flourishes his blade in spite of me.

[Enter old MONTAGUE and his Wife]

Montague Thou villain Capulet!—Hold me not, let me go.

Montague's Wife Thou shalt not stir one foot to seek a foe.

[Enter PRINCE ESCALUS, with his Train]

56.   *one of my master's kinsmen:* Tybalt; evidently he does not see Benvolio.

60.   *swashing blow:* knock-out blow, a blow that comes down with a swishing noise.

63.   *heartless hinds:* cowardly servants (pun on hinds [deer] without a male leader, or hart).

66.   *manage:* employ, use.

69.   *Have at thee:* on guard!

70.   *Clubs:* the cry of the London apprentices to call their fellows, sometimes to come with their clubs to keep the peace, as often as not to create a disturbance.

bills: long wooden staves with a blade or axe-head at one end.

partisans: long infantry spears.

73.   *long sword:* i.e., sword for action, not one to be worn merely for fashion's sake.

76.   *in spite of me:* to defy me.

Prince Rebellious subjects, enemies to peace,
Profaners of this neighbour-stained steel—   80
Will they not bear? What, ho! you men, you beasts,
That quench the fire of your pernicious rage
With purple fountains issuing from your veins!
On pain of torture, from those bloody hands
Throw your mistempered weapons to the ground   85
And hear the sentence of your moved prince.
Three civil brawls, bred of an airy word
By thee, old Capulet, and Montague,
Have thrice disturbed the quiet of our streets
And made Verona's ancient citizens   90
Cast by their grave beseeming ornaments
To wield old partisans, in hands as old,
Cank'red with peace, to part your cank'red hate.
If ever you disturb our streets again,
Your lives shall pay the forfeit of the peace.   95
For this time all the rest depart away.
You, Capulet, shall go along with me;
And, Montague, come you this afternoon,
To know our farther pleasure in this case,
To old Freetown, our common judgment place.   100
Once more, on pain of death, all men depart.

[Exeunt all but MONTAGUE, his Wife, and BENVOLIO]

Montague Who set this ancient quarrel new abroach?
Speak, nephew, were you by when it began?

Benvolio Here were the servants of your adversary
And yours, close fighting ere I did approach.   105
I drew to part them. In the instant came
The fiery Tybalt, with his sword prepared;
Which, as he breathed defiance to my ears,
He swung about his head and cut the winds,
Who, nothing hurt withal, hissed him in scorn.   110
While we were interchanging thrusts and blows,
Came more and more, and fought on part and part,
Till the Prince came, who parted either part.

Montague's Wife O, where is Romeo? Saw you him today?
Right glad I am he was not at this fray.   115

80.	*Profaners . . . steel:* i.e., you profane your weapons by staining them with the blood of your neighbours.
85.	*mistempered:* tempered for an evil end.
86.	*moved:* angry.
87.	*bred . . . word:* arising out of words lightly spoken.
91.	*beseeming ornaments:* weapons befitting them (i.e. walking sticks).
92.	*To:* in order to.
93.	*Cank'red . . . cankered:* rusty, malignant (a canker is a bud-destroying worm; hence cancer).
99.	*our farther pleasure:* what also we wish to do. The "our" is the royal plural, used throughout the speech.
100.	*Freetown:* the 'Villa Franca' of an old poem by Brooke, which in the poem was the name of Capulet's castle.
102.	*new abroach:* newly afoot (newly under way).
105.	*close:* i.e., in the thick of a fight.
110.	*Who:* antecedent "the winds."
	nothing hurt withal: not at all hurt thereby.
	hissed him in scorn: refers to the swish of his sword through the air.
112.	*on part:* on one side or the other.
113.	*parted either part:* separated both sides.

Benvolio Madam, an hour before the worshipped sun
  Peered forth the golden window of the East,
  A troubled mind drave me to walk abroad;
  Where, underneath the grove of sycamore
  That westward rooteth from this city side,   120
  So early walking did I see your son.
  Towards him I made, but he was ware of me
  And stole into the covert of the wood.
  I, measuring his affections by my own,
  Which then most sought where most might not be found,125
  Being one too many by my weary self,
  Pursued my humour, not pursuing his,
  And gladly shunned who gladly fled from me.

Montague Many a morning hath he there been seen,
  With tears augmenting the fresh morning's dew,   130
  Adding to clouds more clouds with his deep sighs;
  But all so soon as the all-cheering sun
  Should in the farthest East begin to draw
  The shady curtains from Aurora's bed,
  Away from light steals home my heavy son   135
  And private in his chamber pens himself,
  Shuts up his windows, locks fair daylight out,
  And makes himself an artificial night.
  Black and portentous must this humour prove
  Unless good counsel may the cause remove.   140

Benvolio My noble uncle, do you know the cause?

Montague I neither know it nor can learn of him.

Benvolio Have you importuned him by any means?

Montague Both by myself and many other friends;
  But he, his own affections' counsellor,   145
  Is to himself—I will not say how true—
  But to himself so secret and so close,
  So far from sounding and discovery,
  As is the bud bit with an envious worm
  Ere he can spread his sweet leaves to the air   150
  Or dedicate his beauty to the sun.

---

119. *sycamore:* traditionally associated with disappointed lovers.

120. *westward . . . side:* grows on the west side of the city.

127. *humour:* inclination of the title of Ben Jonson's play "Every Man in His Humour" (i.e., according to his mood, temperament, or disposition).

128. *shunned:* takes the object (understood) him.

134. *Aurora's:* goddess of dawn in classical mythology.

135. *heavy:* sad (note pun on "light").

139. *portentous:* boding evil, ominous, threatening.

143. *importuned:* persistently asked.

145. *his own . . . counsellor:* admitting to himself alone.

146. *true:* i.e.. true to himself.

148. *sounding:* being fathomed.

149. *bud . . . worm:* never opening to be overseen.

    envious: malignant.

Could we but learn from whence his sorrows grow,
We would as willingly give cure as know.

[Enter ROMEO]

Benvolio See, where he comes. So please you step aside,
I'll know his grievance, or be much denied.   155

Montague I would thou wert so happy by thy stay
To hear true shrift. Come, madam, let's away.

[Exeunt MONTAGUE, and Wife]

Benvolio Good morrow, cousin.

Romeo Is the day so young?

Benvolio But new struck nine.   160

Romeo Ay me! sad hours seem long.
Was that my father that went hence so fast?

Benvolio It was. What sadness lengthens Romeo's hours?

Romeo Not having that which having makes them short.

Benvolio In love?

Romeo   Out—

Benvolio   Of love?   165

Romeo Out of her favour where I am in love.

Benvolio Alas that love, so gentle in his view,
Should be so tyrannous and rough in proof!

Romeo Alas that love, whose view is muffled still,
Should without eyes see pathways to his will!   170
Where shall we dine? O me! What fray was here?
Yet tell me not, for I have heard it all.
Here's much to do with hate, but more with love.
Why then, O brawling love, O loving hate,
O anything, of nothing first create!   175
O heavy lightness, serious vanity,
Misshapen chaos of well-seeming forms,
Feather of lead, bright smoke, cold fire, sick health,
Still-waking sleep, that is not what it is!
This love feel I, that feel no love in this.   180
Dost thou not laugh?

Benvolio   No, coz, I rather weep.

---

153. *know:* i.e., know what the trouble is.

enter Romeo: Dramatically it is much more effective to "lead up" to Romeo like this, in the conversation of minor characters, than to bring him on the stage at the outset. This method has the advantage of creating suspense, and when the main character appears, he appears in response to a longing of the audience to see him. Our imagination has been worked upon by the talk of Benvolio, Montague, and his Lady so that when Romeo appears he already has our interest. From a practical point of view it also means that the first speeches of the main character are not disturbed by the entry of latecomers: by the time he speaks, the audience has settled down.

155. *be much denied:* force him to give me a strong refusal.

157. *shrift:* confession.

166. *where:* with whom.

167. *in his view:* in appearance ("his" effects the personification).

168. *in proof:* in experience or reality.

170. *his will:* i.e., make people fall in love. Cupid, the god of love, was represented as blind in classical mythology.

173. *to do:* trouble.

more with love: perhaps because Rosaline belonged to the Capulet family (as we see from the list of invited guests), or he may mean that there is more in his heart to do with love.

174. *loving hate:* This and the following pairings of opposites are examples of the figure of speech known as oxymoron.

179. *Still-waking:* keeping awake all the time.

180. *no love:* i.e., no really satisfying love.

181. *coz:* cousin (any relative or close friend).

Romeo Good heart, at what?

Benvolio   At thy good heart's oppression.

Romeo Why, such is love's transgression.
Griefs of mine own lie heavy in my breast,
Which thou wilt propagate, to have it prest   185
With more of thine. This love that thou hast shown
Doth add more grief to too much of mine own.
Love is a smoke raised with the fume of sighs;
Being purged, a fire sparkling in lovers' eyes;
Being vexed, a sea nourished with lovers' tears.   190
What is it else? A madness most discreet,
A choking gall, and a preserving sweet.
Farewell, my coz.

Benvolio   Soft! I will go along.
An if you leave me so, you do me wrong.

Romeo Tut! I have lost myself; I am not here;   195
This is not Romeo, he's some other where.

Benvolio Tell me in sadness, who is that you love?

Romeo What, shall I groan and tell thee?

Benvolio   Groan? Why, no;
But sadly tell me who.

Romeo Bid a sick man in sadness make his will.   200
Ah, word ill urged to one that is so ill!
In sadness, cousin, I do love a woman.

Benvolio I aimed so near when I supposed you loved.

Romeo A right good markman. And she's fair I love.

Benvolio A right fair mark, fair coz, is soonest hit.   205

Romeo Well, in that hit you miss. She'll not be hit
With Cupid's arrow. She hath Dian's wit,
And, in strong proof of chastity well armed,
From Love's weak childish bow she lives unharmed.

183. *transgression:* in making lovers suffer so.

185. *propagate:* increase.
      to have it prest: by having it oppressed.

186. *thine:* i.e., thy griefs.

192. *A choking . . . sweet:* a substance bitter enough to choke (anyone) and sweet enough to preserve (something).

193. *Soft:* a common exclamation of Shakespeare's time, equivalent to "Wait a minute!"

197. *in sadness:* seriously.

198. *groan:* Romeo purposely misunderstands "sadness," as if used in its modern sense, "Shall I groan in sadness?"

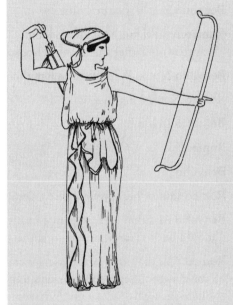

The Roman goddess Diana

201. *ill urged:* a suggestion made at an inopportune time.

203. *aimed so near:* guessed as much (Benvolio wants to know which woman Romeo loves).

205. *fair mark:* clear target. Benvolio plays on the word "fair" in a different sense, as Romeo does with Benvolio's "hit," using it in the sense as "guess." There are many metaphors from archery in Shakespeare and in Elizabethan literature in general.

207. *Dian's wit:* the good sense of Diana, huntress and Roman goddess of chastity.

She will not stay the siege of loving terms,   210
Nor bide th' encounter of assailing eyes,
Nor ope her lap to saint-seducing gold.
O, she is rich in beauty; only poor
That, when she dies, with beauty dies her store.

Benvolio Then she hath sworn that she will live chaste?   215

Romeo She hath, and in that sparing makes huge waste;
For beauty, starved with her severity,
Cuts beauty off from all posterity.
She is too fair, too wise, wisely too fair,
To merit bliss by making me despair.   220
She hath forsworn to love, and in that vow
Do I live dead that live to tell it now.

Benvolio Be ruled by me; forget to think of her.

Romeo O, teach me how I should forget to think!

Benvolio By giving liberty unto thine eyes.   225
Examine other beauties.

Romeo   'Tis the way
To call hers (exquisite) in question more.
These happy masks that kiss fair ladies' brows,
Being black puts us in mind they hide the fair.
He that is strucken blind cannot forget   230
The precious treasure of his eyesight lost.
Show me a mistress that is passing fair,
What doth her beauty serve but as a note
Where I may read who passed that passing fair?
Farewell. Thou canst not teach me to forget.   235

Benvolio I'll pay that doctrine, or else die in debt.

[Exeunt]

---

210. *stay the siege of loving terms:* allow herself to be besieged with expressions of love.

211. *assailing:* i.e., with looks of love.

214. *her store:* i.e., her store of wealth, which consists of her beauty. She will leave no beauty behind her in her offspring. This is a continual thought in Shakespeare's sonnets.

220. *merit bliss:* deserve the blessings of chastity.

221. *forsworn to:* sworn not to.

222. *live dead:* so do we talk of a "living death" (oxymoron).

223. *ruled:* advised.

224. *how . . . think:* i.e., he can think of nothing else.

231. *his eyesight:* what he saw once.

233. *note:* memorandum.

234. *passed:* surpassed

236. *I'll pay that doctrine:* i.e., I will pay you back in your own coin and show you that you cannot teach me to forget. Romeo says that Benvolio cannot teach him to forget, and in effect Benvolio says that he will have a good try.

COMMENTARY

The setting of the opening scene is the market place in Verona, Italy in July. The play begins with two of the Capulets' servants, Sampson and Gregory, complaining about the house of Montague. From their conversation, we learn that the two families are involved in a long and bitter feud.

Sampson and Gregory's conversation is full of puns referring to fighting and love, two of the play's predominant themes. For example, Sampson claims that he will "take the wall of any man or maid of Montague's" (11). Initially, this phrase means that the Capulet servants are superior to the Montague servants, but the comment quickly becomes bawdy. Sampson suggests that he'll "push Montague's men from the wall" while pushing the women toward it; in other words, he'll fight the Montague men and have sex with the Montague women (16). As is apparent from these opening remarks, despite the many tragic events it details, *Romeo and Juliet* is filled with wit, humour, and sexual innuendo, especially among the secondary characters.

Violence erupts in Verona

The comedy quickly turns to explosive violence when two Montague servants, Abram and Balthasar, enter the scene. *Romeo and Juliet* contains many such jarring juxtapositions of scenes that have opposite emotional tones. The fierce street fight following the entry of Abram and Balthasar shows that the feud between the Montagues and Capulets penetrates all levels of society, thus catching all of Verona in the violence. One of the play's goals is to purge this hatred so that a new, more peaceful society can emerge.

As the servants argue, Benvolio, a friend of Romeo's, enters the scene. Benvolio, whose name means "good-natured man," attempts to break up the fight, but the audience quickly learns how ineffective good intentions are in a world saturated with violence.

The violence becomes intense when Juliet's cousin (and Romeo's sworn enemy) Tybalt enters the fray. Tybalt misinterprets Benvolio's actions, assuming that Benvolio has drawn his sword on the servants. Tybalt wants to fight. Although Benvolio urges peace and asks Tybalt to put his sword away, the fiery Tybalt replies that he hates "the word [peace] / As I hate hell, all

Montagues, and thee" (67–68) This statement paints an insightful picture of Tybalt's hot temper and unreasonable nature. His words show the extent of his hatred for the Montague family (although he never gives a reason for his hatred). Likewise, his words prove that Benvolio has no power over Tybalt's fiery temper. We see throughout the play that good men have little authority within Verona. Time after time, Benvolio will urge peace, but his message will be ignored.

As the scene continues, a number of citizens enter the fray, vowing to beat down both the Montagues and the Capulets. The feud between families seems to be little more than an excuse for violence. Lord Capulet, Juliet's father, enters the street in his dressing gown, which demonstrates that the feud has disrupted domestic peace; in Verona, no time or place is free from the possibility of violence.

We get a good look at Capulet's personality in this moment. Like his kinsman Tybalt, he is quick to anger and immediately wants to join the violence. His wife makes fun of him, calling his sword "A crutch, a crutch!," which alerts us to Capulet's advanced age (74). Lady Capulet's

A scene from Franco Zeffirelli's 1968 film version of **Romeo and Juliet**. *Everett Collection*

statement highlights a division between youth and old age that continues throughout the play. The statement also makes us realize that as an old man, Capulet should break up the fight, retain order, and set a good example for the rest of the community. But Capulet, like the younger Tybalt, hasn't learned to control his temper. Ironically, as we see later, two youths will lose their lives because of the ancient feud fueled by old men like Capulet.

The prince orders peace

Prince Escalus—Verona's ruling authority—enters and calls the Montagues and Capulets "enemies to peace" and "beasts" (79, 81). According to the Prince, this is the third civil brawl "bred of an airy word" that has happened recently because of the feud between the two families (87).

The Prince's comment ritualizes the fights, because folk culture views three as a magical number. The number three has religious importance (for example, the holy trinity). But philosophers have also argued that the number three unites opposites, accepting both and leading to a new reality. For example, the famous German philosopher Hegel argued that one idea (a *thesis*) was always opposed by another equally valid idea (an *antithesis*), and the contradictions between these opposites were reconciled on a higher level of truth by a third idea (the *synthesis*).

By specifying that this brawl is the third, Prince Escalus implies that it will in some way lead to a balanced and functional society in Verona. By the end of the play, the arguments between the Montagues and Capulets *will* be resolved and a new society born.

The Prince begins this movement toward harmony by instituting a new rule: The next person caught disturbing the peace in Verona will be killed. In stating, "If ever you disturb our streets again / Your lives shall pay the forfeit of the peace," the Prince plays a prophetic role; his edict will result in several deaths by the play's end (94–95). As we will see, although neither Lord Montague nor Lord Capulet dies, each forfeits a child because of this ancient and meaningless feud.

The Prince's words in this scene are also important because they point out the contradictory impact of language on action. By suggesting that the fights between the Montagues and Capulets result from "airy" words, the Prince implies that the reasons for the feud are insubstantial; all of the violence is based on airy, light, trifling words. Yet words are also powerful, because they can lead to violent actions.

Romeo's seclusion

Following the Prince's pronouncement, Lady Montague wonders where her son Romeo has been. All talk of fighting now ends, and Benvolio employs images of the dawn (the "worshipped sun" and "the golden window of the East") and nature (the sycamore trees, which pun on the idea of "sick amour" or sick love)—two motifs associated with Romeo throughout the play (116–119). Benvolio reveals that Romeo has fled from him and the fighting in the city to the "covert of the wood," a natural world that's free from his family's feud (123).

Unlike his friends, who are generally eager to fight, Romeo seems to create his own secluded world. Romeo's is a natural world associated with the half-light of dawn rather than the full sunshine of the day. Montague expands the connection between Romeo and nature, arguing that Romeo's tears augment "the fresh morning's dew" and that his sighs add "to clouds more clouds" (130–131).

Romeo shuns sunlight. He prefers night and dawn—the realms of dreams, imagination, and fantasy—to day, the revealer of stark reality. Montague says that Romeo's beauty is not dedicated "to the sun" but is "secret" and "close" (151, 147). Romeo creates a private world that his inner visions can sustain. We learn in this scene that a strong opposition exists between the fiery, sun-loving Tybalt and the moody, moon-worshipping Romeo.

Petrarchan love

Along with imagination, Romeo is concerned with ideas of love—the many and often contradictory ways that a person can view love. Setting up this contrast,

Benvolio describes love as "gentle in his view" but also "tyrannous and rough in proof" (167–168). Based on his use of *oxymorons* (combinations of contradictory words) and his depiction of love as an infection or poison, Benvolio, like Romeo later in this scene, is presented as a Petrarchan lover.

The blind archer Cupid is a common Petrarchan image. In *Romeo and Juliet,* Shakespeare presents Cupid as an ambivalent figure—much like Fate—who symbolizes the fatal power of attraction that brings opposites together because of its blindness. For example, Cupid is to blame for Romeo's inability to distinguish Montague from Capulet when choosing a lover. (At this point in the play, Romeo is in love with Rosaline, the niece of Lord Capulet.) By upsetting traditional patterns of law and society, Cupid also has the power to bring new order and new life to a stale social system. Therefore, Cupid can work as a life-giving force that brings harmony to chaos. Blind to the importance of considering last names when choosing a lover, Romeo shows that he could be a catalyst for change in Verona.

Both the destructive and the creative impulses of love are recognized in this play. By loving Rosaline (who is as yet unnamed), for example, Romeo pursues a transgressive love that breaks all the barriers that society and his family create. By destroying boundaries, love can't be easily categorized because it quickly transforms itself. Romeo recognizes both the life-giving and death-dealing aspects of love in a series of oxymorons, describing love as both a "choking gall" and a "preserving sweet" (192). He also presents love as a battle: a "siege" that involves an "encounter" with "assailing eyes" (210–211). While love plays a serious role in the play, we might also wonder if Shakespeare is poking fun at Romeo here: Is Romeo's Petrarchanism excessive? Is he taking love too seriously?

Besides breaking social rules, love's battle also cracks the boundaries of the ego, making the lover lose his individual perception of the world. Romeo foreshadows the connection between love and death that will later define his relationship with Juliet by saying, "I have lost myself" (195).

Usually, this death of ego allows the lover to evolve toward a more communal view of life, but this doesn't happen to Romeo in his love for Rosaline because his love for her isn't true. Instead, Romeo's love for Rosaline is an intellectual exercise, based on the literary tradition of Petrarchan poetry. Romeo argues that chaos has grown out of "well-seeming forms" (177). In other words, the feud has flourished within the seemingly lawful, organized, and civil society of Verona, just as Romeo's unsatisfying love for Rosaline grows out of the seemingly organized forms created by the Petrarchan tradition of courtly love.

As a Petrarchan lover, Romeo is in love with the idea of love and enjoys the melancholy that his love produces. He revels in poetic language but has never felt real passion. It's significant, for example, that the chaste, aloof Rosaline never appears in the play but remains only an idea. As an idea, Rosaline (whose wit is as piercing as Cupid's arrow) is compared with Diana, the chaste goddess of hunting and the moon. This comparison suggests her inappropriateness as a lover. Moon imagery will be important later in the play; for example, Juliet critiques the "inconstancy" of the moon, which changes during its monthly orbit through the heavens. Keep an eye out for other references to the moon in the play to get a sense of whether it is used as a positive or negative image.

Romeo's language in this scene fits with the Petrarchan ideals that the introduction discusses. For example, Romeo speaks in couplets and uses oxymorons when defining love. Instead of presenting his love for Rosaline in a true or honest way, Romeo describes her in an overly intellectual fashion following the tradition of courtly love, which shows the shallowness of his feelings for her. Finding a new way of loving—one that literary tradition doesn't limit—will be one of Romeo's goals in the play. (As the play progresses, Romeo's language will become more natural and passionate, reflecting his deep love for Juliet.)

Themes introduced

This opening scene has many dramatic purposes that prepare the reader for the rest of the play. The introductory conversation between Sampson and Gregory shows the connections between love and violence, while also introducing a witty, comical, and bawdy language that interacts with the play's more serious discussions of love. As you read, consider the importance of the connection between language and feeling in the play. Note also what we learn about characters' personalities based on their manner of speech.

In his opening speeches, Romeo emphasizes the disconnection between appearance and reality. But Romeo's words lead us to question his love for Rosaline: Is the appearance of that relationship connected with its reality? Is the love itself based on appearances or something else? These questions lead to broader concerns about the nature of love. How can we distinguish true love from fake? Is real love based on physical appearance, spiritual bonding, or monetary possessions?

Shakespeare alerts us from the start that, at its best, life constantly transforms. In this scene, Verona is stale and violent. Because the Montague and Capulet feud has created a fragmented society, something needs to change to enable Verona's dismembered social body to reunite. While Shakespeare pokes fun at Romeo's fake love for Rosaline, the play later shows that true love (like Romeo's love for Juliet) can be powerful enough to mend the rifts in society: love, like death or violence, takes many forms in this play. From the beginning, Shakespeare breaks the distinctions between opposites such as love/hate and appearance/reality, leading to a synthesis on a higher level—one that will embrace these opposites in a new, more peaceful reality.

Act I, Scene 2

Paris, a young nobleman of Verona, asks Capulet for Juliet's hand in marriage. Capulet agrees (if Juliet will consent) and invites Paris to a feast. Romeo and Benvolio learn of the Capulet feast and decide to attend uninvited.

ACT I, SCENE 2
The same. A street.

[Enter CAPULET, COUNTY PARIS, and a Servant]

Capulet But Montague is bound as well as I,
In penalty alike; and 'tis not hard, I think,
For men so old as we to keep the peace.

Paris Of honourable reckoning are you both,
And pity 'tis you lived at odds so long.   5
But now, my lord, what say you to my suit?

Capulet But saying o'er what I have said before:
My child is yet a stranger in the world,
She hath not seen the change of fourteen years;
Let two more summers wither in their pride   10
Ere we may think her ripe to be a bride.

Paris Younger than she are happy mothers made.

Capulet And too soon marred are those so early made.
Earth hath swallowed all my hopes but she;
She is the hopeful lady of my earth.   15
But woo her, gentle Paris, get her heart;
My will to her consent is but a part.
An she agree, within her scope of choice
Lies my consent and fair according voice.
This night I hold an old accustomed feast,   20
Whereto I have invited many a guest,
Such as I love; and you among the store,
One more, most welcome, makes my number more.
At my poor house look to behold this night
Earth-treading stars that make dark heaven light.   25
Such comfort as do lusty young men feel
When well-apparelled April on the heel
Of limping Winter treads, even such delight
Among fresh fennel buds shall you this night

NOTES

1. *bound:* bound over to keep the peace.

4. *reckoning:* In view of Capulet's speech and the following line in Paris's speech, it would seem that Paris refers to the reckoning of their years, i.e., experience of life, not to their reputation in general.

5. *odds:* enmity.

9. *She hath not . . . years:* She is not fully fourteen.

10. *wither in their pride:* i.e., let their beautiful flowers wither.

13. *marred . . . made:* a thoroughly Shakespearean antithesis. This is a reference to the proverb, "Soon married, soon marred."

14. *earth . . . hopes:* i.e., all my other children are dead and buried.

15. *earth:* i.e., body, offspring. Capulet may mean that his daughter is the heiress of his land, but that interpretation does not seem likely because in this speech Capulet's mind is not on material things.

17. *My will . . . part:* My permission is but a part of her choice.

19. *fair according:* agreeing willingly.

25. *Earth-treading:* stars that make dark heaven light. Beauties are like stars come down to earth, sending rays of light upward.

27. *well-apparelled:* bringing foliage to clothe the trees.

28. *limping:* slowly retreating.

Inherit at my house. Hear all, all see,   30
And like her most whose merit most shall be;
Which, on more view of many, mine, being one,
May stand in number, though in reck'ning none.
Come, go with me.
[To Servant, giving him a paper]
                    Go, sirrah, trudge about
Through fair Verona; find those persons out   35
Whose names are written there, and to them say,
My house and welcome on their pleasure stay.

[Exit, with PARIS]

Servant Find them out whose names are written here?
It is written that the shoemaker should meddle with
his yard and the tailor with his last, the fisher with his   40
pencil and the painter with his nets; but I am sent to
find those persons whose names are here writ, and can
never find what names the writing person hath here
writ. I must to the learned. In good time!

[Enter BENVOLIO and ROMEO]

Benvolio Tut, man, one fire burns out another's burning;   45
One pain is less'ned by another's anguish;
Turn giddy, and be holp by backward turning;
One desperate grief cures with another's languish.
Take thou some new infection to thy eye,
And the rank poison of the old will die.   50

Romeo Your plantain leaf is excellent for that.

Benvolio For what, I pray thee?

Romeo   For your broken shin.

Benvolio Why, Romeo, art thou mad?

Romeo Not mad, but bound more than a madman is;
Shut up in prison, kept without my food,   55
Whipped and tormented and—God-den, good fellow.

Servant God gi' go-den. I pray, sir, can you read?

Romeo Ay, mine own fortune in my misery.

Servant Perhaps you have learned it without book.
But I pray, can you read anything you see?   60

32.–33. *Which . . . none:* This is differently punctuated in different editions, giving two different meanings. (1) When you have seen more of her whose merit is most (the antecedent of "which"), many—including my daughter—may be in the company, but none may be reckoned with her. (2) When you have seen many ladies, my daughter being one, she may be one of the company, but not one for whom you have any esteem. (1) has a comma at "of," and (2) at "many." The first seems more in character, in view of Capulet's words about what his daughter means to him, but if the second is accepted it could be said that he wants to save his daughter from an unhappy marriage, as well as to make sure that Paris's mind is made up and that his affection is not a passing fancy.

34. *sirrah:* a familiar (or contemptuous) form of "sir," generally used when speaking to inferiors.

39-41. The servant's confusion is deliberately contrived by Shakespeare: Shoemaker should be associated with last, tailor with yard, fisher with nets, and painter with pencil.

44. *I must to the learned:* I must go to someone who can read.

45. *one fire burns out another's burning:* i.e., a greater fire soon burns up the material of a lesser, or Benvolio may be referring to the superstition that the sun puts out a fire in a grate.

47. *holp:* archaic form of helped.

48. *cures with another's languish:* is cured when another grief appears.

51. *Your plantain leaf:* a dock-leaf. Romeo means that a dock-leaf is useful for minor ills—to stop bleeding from a scratch, for instance—but his ailment needs a more desperate remedy.

56. *God-den:* good evening, a contraction of the fuller "God give you a good even."

57. *gi':* give (you).

Romeo Ay, if I know the letters and the language.

Servant Ye say honestly. Rest you merry.

Romeo Stay, fellow; I can read.
[He reads the letter]
'Signior Martino and his wife and daughters;
County Anselmo and his beauteous sisters;   65
The lady widow of Vitruvio;
Signior Placentio and his lovely nieces;
Mercutio and his brother Valentine;
Mine uncle Capulet, his wife, and daughters;
My fair niece Rosaline and Livia;   70
Signior Valentio and his cousin Tybalt;
Lucio and the lively Helena.'
A fair assembly. Whither should they come?

Servant Up.

Romeo Whither? To supper?   75

Servant To our house.

Romeo Whose house?

Servant My master's.

Romeo Indeed I should have asked you that before.

Servant Now I'll tell you without asking. My master is   80
the great rich Capulet; and if you be not of the house
of Montagues, I pray come and crush a cup of wine.
Rest you merry.

[Exit]

Benvolio At this same ancient feast of Capulet's
Sups the fair Rosaline whom thou so loves;   85
With all the admired beauties of Verona.
Go thither, and with unattainted eye
Compare her face with some that I shall show,
And I will make thee think thy swan a crow.

Romeo When the devout religion of mine eye   90
Maintains such falsehood, then turn tears to fires;
And these, who, often drowned, could never die,
Transparent heretics, be burnt for liars!
One fairer than my love? The all-seeing sun
Ne'er saw her match since first the world begun.   95

---

62. *Rest you merry:* a colloquial term of farewell, comparable to our "All the best!"

65. *County:* another form of "count," often used by Shakespeare.

70. *Rosaline:* the first time Romeo's lady-love is named.

82. *crush a cup:* a common colloquial expression in Elizabethan English comparable to "crack a bottle."

84. *ancient:* one which has been held annually for a long time.

87. *unattainted:* impartial.

90. *devout religion:* implying that he worships Rosaline.

92. *these:* i.e., these eyes of mine "drowned" in tears.

Benvolio Tut! you saw her fair, none else being by,
   Herself poised with herself in either eye;
   But in that crystal scales let there be weighed
   Your lady's love against some other maid
   That I will show you shining at this feast,   100
   And she shall scant show well that now seems best.

Romeo I'll go along, no such sight to be shown,
   But to rejoice in splendor of my own. *[Exeunt]*

97.   *either eye:* i.e., in each of your eyes.

98.   *scales:* Romeo's eyes.

99.   *lady's love:* love for your lady. To interpret "the slight love of your lady for you" shifts the emphasis and is unlikely.

101.   *scant show well:* scarcely appear attractive.

103.   *splendor of mine own:* the splendid beauty of my own beloved.

COMMENTARY

In this scene, Lord Capulet speaks with Juliet's potential suitor, the County Paris, a young nobleman. Capulet tells Paris about the recent brawl and Prince Escalus's new decree. He claims, "'tis not hard, I think / For men so old as we to keep the peace" (2–3). But, as we saw in Act I, Scene 1, age hasn't improved the tempers of either Montague or Capulet; even in old age, they're always ready for a fight.

Juliet's suitor

Paris isn't interested in the feud, however; he has come to seek Juliet's hand in marriage. Capulet initially claims that Juliet is not ready for marriage, because she is only 13 years old and "yet a stranger in the world" (8). (Note that Shakespeare's sources for the play depict an older Juliet—she is 18 in Painter's version and 16 in Brooke's version. Shakespeare's alteration emphasizes Juliet's youth and sets up an even starker contrast with her father's age.) When Paris replies, "Younger than she are happy mothers made," Capulet counters that women who marry too young are often scarred (12). All of Capulet's other children have died, so he plans to take special care of Juliet, "the hopeful lady of my earth" (15). His emphasis on "earth" suggests not only that Juliet is the sole inheritor of his lands, but also that her children will carry on his bloodline. Despite these valid reasons to oppose the marriage, Capulet eventually tells Paris that he'll agree to the marriage if Paris convinces Juliet.

Capulet's inconstancy in this scene prepares you for his later reckless, sometimes violent, mood shifts. Even in matters that concern his only daughter, whom he supposedly loves and wants to protect, Capulet's moods and opinions can't be trusted. For this reason, we should not be surprised at his participation in the bitter and longstanding feud with the Montagues. Capulet's temperament makes him seem more youthful in some ways than the younger characters in the play, such as Paris, who presents his case for marriage so rationally in this scene.

Capulet invites Paris to a feast at his home that evening and says that the guest list includes many "[e]arth-treading stars"—women who "make dark heaven light" (25). The comparison of women (and love) with stars is a motif that repeats throughout the play, particularly concerning Juliet. In this scene, Capulet also refers to women as "fresh fennel buds," a traditional poetic invocation of youth and freshness (29). (Romeo is later called a "bud" and Paris a "flower.")

Capulet seems to suspect that Paris may prefer another woman at the party and forget about Juliet—a suggestion similar to one that Benvolio made earlier to Romeo concerning Rosaline. We see later that Paris stays true in his affections, while Romeo transfers his attentions from Rosaline to Juliet. Because Paris is more constant, he seems to be an appropriate lover for Juliet. The manner in which Paris pursues Juliet emphasizes his potential as an ideal son-in-law. Rather than follow Romeo's impetuous courtship of Juliet, Paris maintains proper protocol, discussing the marriage proposal with Lord Capulet and asking his permission to woo Juliet.

At this point in the play, Romeo and Paris both play the game of love "by the book." Romeo's love for Rosaline is ruled by Petrarchan protocol, while Paris's feelings for Juliet are guided by social conventions. But we will see later that Romeo leaves his books behind when he meets Juliet. By presenting a contrast between Paris and Romeo, the play asks us to consider the values of different types of love: Should Juliet choose a socially- and parentally-sanctioned (but reserved) lover like Paris? Or should she choose the passionate Romeo, whose secret and forbidden love for her transgresses the rules in feud-torn Verona? As you read, consider whether Shakespeare's depiction of Lord Capulet steers us in one direction or another on this question.

Preparing for the feast

Capulet's impetuous personality shines through again when he gives the guest list for that evening's feast to one of his servants, not realizing that the man can't read. The servant wittily remarks, "I am sent to / find those persons whose names are here writ, and can / never find what names the writing person hath here / writ" (41–44). The servant's playful manner of revealing that he can't read again emphasizes the importance *Romeo and Juliet* places on witticism and humour. To stress the different social status of characters in the play, Shakespeare has the servant speak entirely in prose while the upper-class characters speak in iambic pentameter (a form of rhythmic language explained in the "Introduction to William Shakespeare").

As the servant searches for someone who can read the guest list for him, Benvolio and Romeo enter the scene, still discussing Romeo's love problems. Benvolio argues that love is the cure for love—"one fire burns out another's burning" (45). Benvolio views love as an "infection," and he urges Romeo to accept a new infection so that the "rank poison of the old will die" (49–50). Romeo compares his love to madness and being shut up in prison, whipped, and tormented. Both Romeo and Benvolio continue to use Petrarchan devices in their discussion of love.

Fate intervenes

Completely by chance, Capulet's servant meets Romeo and Benvolio and asks if they know how to read. This accident emphasizes the importance of fate in the play. Shakespeare generally uses accidental meetings such as this more often in his comedies than in his tragedies. (Tragedy usually results from character flaws—such as Hamlet's inability to make a decision or Othello's blind faith in Iago—rather than from fate.) But the plot device works here because the play contains many other comic elements that interact with the tragedy, such as the bawdy language used by many of the secondary characters.

Romeo responds that it is his "fortune" to read— indeed, "fortune" or chance led Capulet's servant to him (58). This scene prepares us for the tragic inevitability of the events in the play. What eventually happens to Romeo and Juliet occurs not because of their own personal flaws but because fate works against them. Fate steps into this scene once more when the servant invites Romeo to Capulet's house to "crush a cup of wine" (82). (Ironically, the servant extends the invitation with the provision that Romeo can come as long as he isn't a Montague.) Only fate can manufacture this unlikely meeting with Capulet's illiterate servant, because only fate can devise a way for Romeo to trespass into the Capulet domain and meet Juliet.

Many questions emerge from the action in this scene. For example, why does Shakespeare accentuate Capulet's emotional volatility? What seem to be his true feelings for his daughter? Some of those questions again centre on the nature of true love: Does true love wrap itself in the protocol of proper courtship? Can true love only be described using poetic devices? And questions of fate emerge here as well; consider as you read if fate alone is responsible for what happens to Romeo and Juliet or if the personalities of the lovers contribute to their demise.

Act I, Scene 3

Capulet's wife informs Juliet that it is time for her to think about marriage, specifically with Paris. Juliet dutifully replies that she will be guided by her parents' choice. The Nurse reminisces about Juliet's childhood.

ACT I, SCENE 3
A room in Capulet's house.

[Enter CAPULET'S WIFE, and NURSE]

Wife Nurse, where's my daughter? Call her forth to me.

Nurse Now, by my maidenhead at twelve year old,
I bade her come. What, lamb! what, ladybird!
God forbid. where's this girl? What, Juliet!

[Enter JULIET]

Juliet How now? Who calls?

Nurse   Your mother.   5

Juliet Madam, I am here. What is your will?

Wife This is the matter—Nurse, give leave awhile,
We must talk in secret. Nurse, come back again;
I have rememb'red me, thou 's hear our counsel.
Thou knowest my daughter's of a pretty age.   10

Nurse Faith, I can tell her age unto an hour.

Wife She's not fourteen.

Nurse   I'll lay fourteen of my teeth—
And yet, to my teen be it spoken, I have but four—
She's not fourteen. How long is it now
To Lammastide?

Wife   A fortnight and odd days.   15

Nurse Even or odd, of all days in the year,
Come Lammas Eve at night shall she be fourteen.
Susan and she (God rest all Christian souls!)
Were of an age. Well, Susan is with God;
She was too good for me. But, as I said,   20
On Lammas Eve at night shall she be fourteen;
That shall she, marry; I remember it well.

NOTES

2.   *maidenhead:* virginity.

3.   *ladybird:* a term of endearment, similar to "lamb."

4.   *God forbid:* that Juliet should be harmed.

9.   *rememb'red me:* the "me" can be ignored. This is a reflexive use of the word "me," translating literally to "reminded myself."

     thou 's: thou shalt. The Elizabethan use of "thou" and "you" is clearly shown in this conversation. "Thou" was a sign of familiarity, "you" was a formal address used by servant to master. Compare also the conversation between Sampson and Gregory in the first scene and the conversation between Tybalt and Benvolio which follows (where Tybalt uses the second person contemptuously, as towards an inferior).

10. *pretty:* marriageable, ripe for marriage.

15. *Lammastide:* Lammas or Loaf Mass day (1 August) was a festival for the hallowing of bread.

22. *marry:* I swear (by Virgin Mary).

'Tis since the earthquake now eleven years;
And she was weaned (I never shall forget it),
Of all the days of the year, upon that day;   25
For I had then laid wormwood to my dug,
Sitting in the sun under the dovehouse wall.
My lord and you were then at Mantua.
Nay, I do bear a brain. But, as I said,
When it did taste the wormwood on the nipple   30
Of my dug and felt it bitter, pretty fool,
To see it tetchy and fall out with the dug!
Shake, quoth the dovehouse! 'Twas no need, I trow,
To bid me trudge.
And since that time it is eleven years,   35
For then she could stand high-lone; nay, by th' rood,
She could have run and waddled all about;
For even the day before, she broke her brow;
And then my husband (God be with his soul!
'A was a merry man) took up the child.   40
'Yea,' quoth he, 'dost thou fall upon thy face?
Thou wilt fall backward when thou hast more wit;
Wilt thou not, Jule?' and, by my holidam,
The pretty wretch left crying and said 'Ay.'
To see now how a jest shall come about!   45
I warrant, an I should live a thousand years,
I never should forget it. 'Wilt thou not, Jule?' quoth he,
And, pretty fool, it stinted and said 'Ay.'

Wife Enough of this. I pray thee hold thy peace.

Nurse Yes, madam. Yet I cannot choose but laugh   50
To think it should leave crying and say 'Ay.'
And yet, I warrant, it had upon it brow
A bump as big as a young cock'rel's stone;
A perilous knock; and it cried bitterly.
'Yea,' quoth my husband, 'fall'st upon thy face?   55
Thou wilt fall backward when thou comest to age;
Wilt thou not, Jule?' It stinted and said 'Ay.'

Juliet And stint thou too, I pray thee, nurse, say I.

Nurse Peace, I have done. God mark thee to his grace;
Thou wast the prettiest babe that e'er I nursed.   60
An I might live to see thee married once,
I have my wish.

---

23.   *since the earthquake:* There was an earthquake in England in 1580 and a bad one in Verona in 1570. Some have taken the reference to be to the 1580 earthquake and have deduced from there that the play was written in 1591.

26.   *wormwood:* a plant with a bitter juice to make the child stop drinking mother's milk.

29.   *do bear a brain:* have a retentive memory.

31.   *fool:* a term of endearment—darling or innocent.

32.   *tetchy:* fretful, peevish.

33.   *Shake, quoth the dovehouse:* The dovehouse began shaking.

34.   *trudge:* walk away.

36.   *high-lone:* quite alone.

      rood: cross (of Christ).

38.   *broke her brow:* cut her forehead.

43.   *Jule:* affectionate diminutive for Juliet.

      holidam: originally the holy relics upon which oaths were sworn; by the late sixteenth-century this word was used as a mild oath.

61.   *live . . . once:* only live to see you married.

Wife Marry, that 'marry' is the very theme
   I came to talk of. Tell me, daughter Juliet,
   How stands your disposition to be married? 65

Juliet It is an honour that I dream not of.

Nurse An honour? Were not I thine only nurse,
   I would say thou hadst sucked wisdom from thy teat.

Wife Well, think of marriage now. Younger than you,
   Here in Verona, ladies of esteem, 70
   Are made already mothers. By my count,
   I was your mother much upon these years
   That you are now a maid. Thus then in brief:
   The valiant Paris seeks you for his love.

Nurse A man, young lady! lady, such a man 75
   As all the world—why he's a man of wax.

Wife Verona's summer hath not such a flower.

Nurse Nay, he's a flower, in faith—a very flower.

Wife What say you? Can you love the gentleman?
   This night you shall behold him at our feast. 80
   Read o'er the volume of young Paris' face,
   And find delight writ there with beauty's pen,
   Examine every married lineament,
   And see how one another lends content;
   And what obscured in this fair volume lies 85
   Find written in the margent of his eyes.
   This precious book of love, this unbound lover,
   To beautify him only lacks a cover.
   The fish lives in the sea, and 'tis much pride
   For fair without the fair within to hide. 90
   That book in many's eyes doth share the glory,
   That in gold clasps locks in the golden story;
   So shall you share all that he doth possess,
   By having him making yourself no less.

Nurse No less? Nay, bigger! Women grow by men. 95

Wife Speak briefly, can you like of Paris' love?

---

63. *Marry, that 'marry':* The first is a corruption of the oath "by Mary," the second is the verb to wed.

67. *Were not I thine only nurse:* but since she is, to say so would be to praise herself.

68. *from thy teat:* from me (the Nurse had been Juliet's wet-nurse).

76. *of wax:* i.e., as handsome as if he had been modeled in wax, finer than men usually are.

83. *married:* harmonious, symmetrical, well balanced.

   lineament: part or feature of a face, with attention to outline.

84. *one another lends content:* one sets off another to advantage.

86. *margent:* margin; the general sense is that what you cannot find written in his face you will find out in his eyes.

87. *unbound:* unbounded, unmarried, free (pun on an unbound book).

88. *cover:* the binding (bonds) of marriage.

90. *fair without . . . hide:* i.e., for the beautiful sea to contain beautiful fish.

92. *That in . . . story:* i.e., is beautiful to look at on the outside as well as having a beautiful story within. The application is that Paris has a fair appearance "outside" and a good character "within."

94. *making yourself no less:* at the same time not lessening your own possessions.

Juliet I'll look to like, if looking liking move;
But no more deep will I endart mine eye
Than your consent gives strength to make it fly.

[Enter Servingman]

Servingman Madam, the guests are come, supper   100
served up, you called, my young lady asked for, the
nurse cursed in the pantry, and everything in extremity.
I must hence to wait. I beseech you follow straight.

Wife We follow thee. *[Exit Servingman]*
Juliet, the County stays.   105

Nurse Go, girl, seek happy nights to happy days.

[Exeunt]

97. *look to:* expect to.

looking liking move: what I see makes me like him. "Looking" is the subject of "move," "liking" the object.

98. *But no . . . fly:* i.e., I will go no farther than you approve.

102. *extremity:* a muddle.

103. *wait:* i.e., upon the guests.

COMMENTARY

As this scene begins, Lady Capulet searches for Juliet. The Nurse calls to Juliet using loving diminutives such as "ladybird" and "lamb" (3). (Some critics claim that "ladybird" also means "loose woman," which explains the Nurse's apology—"God forbid"—in the next line.) The Nurse says to Lady Capulet, "Now, by my maidenhead at twelve year old, / I bade her come," reminding us once again of Juliet's youthfulness and the possibility that she may be too young for marriage (2–3).

The Nurse's comment contains an explicit sexual reference (the term *maidenhead* refers to Juliet's virginity), which is significant. As in the conversation between Sampson and Gregory in Act I, Scene 1, sexual language becomes mixed with the language of true love and poses still further questions about the nature of love. For the Nurse, love and sex are necessarily intertwined. Consider, as you read, whether that holds true for Romeo and Juliet as well.

The Nurse's devotion

Although the Nurse is primarily a comic creation who balances the play's tragedy, her frank earthiness makes her one of Shakespeare's richest characters. Her love for and devotion to Juliet are apparent in this scene, particularly when she tells the story of Juliet falling on her head. But the scene also emphasizes the Nurse's role as servant when Lady Capulet capriciously sends her out of the room and then calls her back. Consider, as you read, how the Nurse balances her roles as servant and friend to Juliet throughout the play. Note whether one role predominates over the other at different points in the action.

The Nurse reveals that Juliet is almost 14 and that her birthday is on Lammas Eve or August 1. Lammas was a festival in England in which clergy blessed the bread made from the first corn harvest. Lammas is, therefore, a ritual that emphasizes abundance, wealth, and fertility. (We can speculate that the Nurse may believe the word "Lammas" comes from the words "lamb" and "mass," which explains her pet name for Juliet: lamb.)

In this scene, the Nurse remembers her own daughter, Susan, who shared a birthday with Juliet. The Nurse ominously states that Susan died because she was "too good for me" (20). Juliet will also prove "too good" before the play ends. The dialogue in this scene throws a shadow on the play, suggesting that life does indeed have a dark side and reminding us that the play's conclusion will be tragic.

While reminiscing about Juliet's childhood, the Nurse alludes to an earthquake: "'Tis since the earthquake now eleven years, / And she was weaned" (23–24). Numerous critics have tried to identify which earthquake the Nurse refers to. Some argue that the lines refer to the English earthquake of 1580, which means that the play is set in the year 1591. But several other earthquakes occurred in England and Italy around this time period, so pinpointing the earthquake that Shakespeare refers to or discovering the exact year in which the play was written is difficult. The reference to an earthquake would have added an element of reality for the original spectators of the play, who would have recognized the accuracy of the Nurse's claim.

The marriage proposal

While the Nurse reminisces about Juliet's childhood, Lady Capulet wants to discuss Paris's marriage proposal. Lady Capulet seems to favour Juliet's young marriage, saying, "Younger than you / Here in Verona, ladies of esteem, / Are made already mothers" (69–71). Lady Capulet says that she was a mother at Juliet's age, suggesting that she is a young woman (under 30) married to an older man. (When Capulet suggested in the previous scene that women who marry young end up spoiled, he may have been referring to his own wife.)

Juliet doesn't seem enthralled with the idea of marriage. She replies to her mother, "It is an honour that I dream not of" (66). By saying that she does not dream of marriage, Juliet rejects her mother's notion that Juliet is old enough for marriage. Juliet's forthright response to her mother seems surprising, because absolute obedience was expected of young women in Shakespeare's day. Her statement provides insight into her character; although she is a good daughter, she is not blindly obedient to her parents' wishes. As the play progresses, the fractures between Juliet and her parents will widen.

In discussing Paris, the women refer to him as a "flower, in faith—a very flower," creating a connection to Act I, Scene 2 in which the women at the party were called "buds" (78). Although these flower references emphasize Paris's youth and good looks, they also suggest the fragility of love. Like flowers, love blooms magnificently and then withers.

Lady Capulet champions Paris

The imagery of reading is also important in Lady Capulet's discussion of Paris. Juliet should read the "volume" of Paris's face, finding "delight writ there with beauty's pen" (81–82). What isn't apparent in the volume of Paris's face may appear in the page margins: his eyes. Paris is a "precious book of love" that is currently "unbound" (87). To be beautified, Paris needs only a "cover," which Juliet would provide (88). A woman as a cover, binding the man in marriage, makes him complete. The book of marriage is indeed a "golden story" that's clasped in gold locks (the wedding bands) (92).

As you read, consider how Lady Capulet's depiction of marriage in this scene differs from Shakespeare's representation of the Capulets' own marriage. Do Juliet's parents seem united in the positive way Lady Capulet describes? After seeing her parents' relationship, why might Juliet be suspicious of her mother? Why might she not want to follow too closely in her mother's marital footsteps?

In arguing that "[t]he fish lives in the sea, and 'tis much pride / For fair without the fair within to hide," Lady Capulet suggests that marriage is the proper element for Juliet, just as water is for fish (89–90). She suggests that by remaining unmarried and hiding the "fair within," Juliet is selfish or filled with pride. Marriage helps women, in Lady Capulet's opinion. She emphasizes that Juliet will "share" all that Paris possesses while "making [herself] no less"; Paris is Juliet's equal, so their marriage will be one of equality (93–94).

The Nurse humorously reinterprets Lady Capulet's words, arguing that women actually "grow by men" through pregnancy (95). The Nurse again emphasizes that love and sex are intertwined, and she obviously enjoys both. The Nurse finds Paris one of the most handsome men she knows and strongly favours the marriage. Although the Nurse's statements may be vulgar, she is refreshingly natural and honest in comparison to Lady Capulet who seems somewhat artificial.

Juliet's hesitance

Juliet, however, doesn't accept either view of love. Rather than giving her mother a straightforward yes or no answer about the proposed marriage to Paris, she cunningly promises to like Paris "if looking liking move" (97). Juliet undercuts even this ambiguous statement by claiming, "[N]o more deep will I endart mine eye / Than your consent gives strength to make it fly" (98–99). Implicitly, Juliet rejects her mother's advice and refuses to marry Paris. Although Paris may be a perfectly eligible man, she wants to marry a man of her own choosing. Juliet wants to create her own idea of love rather than accepting the views of others, including those of her parents and her Nurse. The conversation ends as a servant enters, calling the women to supper and claiming that everything is "in extremity" for the party (102).

Lady Capulet emphasizes the romantic aspects of marriage in this scene—the joining of two equal spirits in the golden book of love—but at the same time, she stresses that an equality of "possessions" in marriage is important. She is concerned not only with romance but with the material side of marriage, wanting her daughter to marry a man who is able to provide for her comfort. New questions arise: Does love depend on material wealth? Do we trust Lady Capulet? Does she seem genuinely concerned about her daughter's welfare?

The scene introduces us to the two most important women in this play: Juliet and her Nurse. Consider here what similarities and differences are apparent in their personalities. As the play progresses, note any changes in their characters. Do they grow and develop or do they remain static?

To understand how carefully Shakespeare crafted this drama, look back at this scene after reading Act IV, Scene 5. Echoing the opening of this scene, Act IV, Scene 5 will find Lady Capulet once again searching for Juliet and the Nurse once again calling her a "lamb," "lady," "love," and "sweetheart."

Act I, Scene 4

Romeo, Benvolio, Mercutio, and a group of other friends make their way to Capulet's house, where they plan to enter the masquerade unannounced and stay for a single dance. Romeo mourns his unrequited love, and Mercutio delivers an imaginative speech on Queen Mab, who brings strange dreams to mankind. As Romeo and his friends prepare to enter the Capulet's party, Romeo has a premonition of coming troubles.

ACT I, Scene 4
The same. A street.

*[Enter ROMEO, MERCUTIO, BENVOLIO, with five or six
    other Maskers; Torchbearers]*

Romeo What, shall this speech be spoke for our excuse?
　Or shall we on without apology?

Benvolio The date is out of such prolixity.
　We'll have no Cupid hoodwinked with a scarf,
　Bearing a Tartar's painted bow of lath,　　　　5
　Scaring the ladies like a crowkeeper;
　Nor no without-book prologue, faintly spoke
　After the prompter, for our entrance;
　But, let them measure us by what they will,
　We'll measure them a measure and be gone.　　10

Romeo Give me a torch. I am not for this ambling.
　Being but heavy, I will bear the light.

Mercutio Nay, gentle Romeo, we must have you dance.

Romeo Not I, believe me. You have dancing shoes
　With nimble soles; I have a soul of lead　　　15
　So stakes me to the ground I cannot move.

Mercutio You are a lover. Borrow Cupid's wings
　And soar with them above a common bound.

Romeo I am too sore enpierced with his shaft
　To soar with his light feathers; and so bound　　20
　I cannot bound a pitch above dull woe.
　Under love's heavy burden do I sink.

Mercutio And, to sink in it, should you burden love—
　Too great oppression for a tender thing.

Romeo Is love a tender thing? It is too rough,　　25
　Too rude, too boist'rous, and it pricks like thorn.

NOTES

s.d.　*Maskers:* men masked for a masquerade—a masked ball, not a masque (the elaborate entertainment which was coming into fashion among the nobility at the end of Shakespeare's career).

1.　*this speech:* i.e., speech of apology (for coming to the ball without a formal invitation) as the next line shows.

3.　*The date is out:* it is no longer the fashion.

　such prolixity: such long-winded verbosity.

4.　*Cupid:* a guest disguised as Cupid, as a spokesman to make their speech of apology.

　hoodwinked: blindfolded (like a hawk).

5.　*Tartar's painted bow of lath:* i.e., an imitation (painted and made of lath) of a Tartar bow such as Cupid is represented with.

6.　*crowkeeper:* boy acting as a scarecrow.

7.　*Nor no:* in Elizabethan English a double negative intensifies the idea instead of cancelling it.

　without-book: impromptu, or perhaps from memory.

10.　*measure them a measure:* dance a measure (a slow and stately dance).

11.　*Give me a torch:* i.e., I do not want to dance, so I will be one of the torch bearers.

　ambling: impolite term for rustic dancing.

12.　*heavy . . . light:* Romeo is rather fond of this punning antithesis. In Act I, Scene 1, he spoke of "heavy lightness," and Montague too said, "Away from light steals home my heavy son." ("Heavy" indicates heavy of heart.)

21.　*pitch:* a metaphor from falconry. The "pitch" was the technical word for the height to which a falcon soared before swooping on her prey.

23.　*to sink in it, should you burden love:* You would be too heavy a burden for love if you should sink in it.

Mercutio If love be rough with you, be rough with love,
Prick love for pricking, and you beat love down.
Give me a case to put my visage in.
A visor for a visor! What care I   30
What curious eye doth quote deformities?
Here are the beetle brows shall blush for me.

Benvolio Come, knock and enter; and no sooner in
But every man betake him to his legs.

Romeo A torch for me! Let wantons light of heart   35
Tickle the senseless rushes with their heels;
For I am proverbed with a grandsire phrase,
I'll be a candle-holder and look on;
The game was ne'er so fair, and I am done.

Mercutio Tut! dun's the mouse, the constable's own word! 40
If thou art Dun, we'll draw thee from the mire
Of this sir-reverence love, within thou stickest
Up to the ears. Come, we burn daylight, ho!

Romeo Nay, that's not so.

Mercutio   I mean, sir, in delay
We waste our lights in vain, like lamps by day.   45
Take our good meaning, for our judgment sits
Five times in that ere once in our five wits.

Romeo And we mean well in going to this masque,
But 'tis no wit to go.

Mercutio   Why may one ask?

Romeo I dreamt a dream to-night.

Mercutio   And so did I.   50

Romeo Well, what was yours?

Mercutio   That dreamers often lie.

Romeo In bed asleep, while they do dream things true.

Mercutio O, then I see Queen Mab hath been with you.
She is the fairies' midwife, and she comes
In shape no bigger than an agate stone   55
On the forefinger of an alderman,
Drawn with a team of little atomies
Over men's noses as they lie asleep;
Her wagon spokes made of long spinners' legs,

28.	*Prick love for pricking:* i.e., give love back as good (or as bad) as it gives you.
29.	*case:* mask or visor.
30.	*A visor for a visor!:* i.e., imagine putting a mask on my face, which is funny enough to be a mask by itself.
31.	*quote:* note carefully for future malicious use.
32.	*Here . . . me:* Mercutio means that he cares not what people think of him; if anyone blushes for him, it shall be himself.
34.	*betake him to his legs:* i.e., in dancing. He infers that they will then be lost in the crowd and less likely to be noticed.
37.	*proverbed with a grandsire phrase:* supported by an old man's proverb (that the candleholder, or looker-on, sees most of the game).
39.	*The game . . . done:* This is the best part of the proceedings, so I am giving up before worse comes. A proverb recommends that people give up while things are at their best, before the good impression is lost.
40.	*dun's the mouse:* a slang Elizabethan phrase meaning "keep quiet."
41.	*If . . . mire:* "Dun is in the mire" is an old country game. Dun was a log that represented a cart horse in the mire. Moving the log was a source of fun and games, such as pushing one another down and trying to make the log fall on one another's toes.
42.	*sir-reverence:* filth, dung (a special form of "mire"). "Sir-reverence" came to mean this because the word prefaced the mention of unpleasant things. The phrase is a corruption of "save your reverence" meaning "excuse my mentioning it."
43.	*we burn daylight:* i.e., we are wasting time (just as burning candles in the daylight is a waste).
47.	*in that:* i.e., in our "good meaning."
	five wits: i.e., being clever in playing with words.
49.	*to-night:* last night.
53.	*Queen Mab:* spoken of here as the Queen of the Fairies.
55.	*agate stone:* hard stone used for the engraved part of a seal ring.
57.	*atomies:* miniature beings.
59.	*spinners':* spiders'.

The cover, of the wings of grasshoppers;   60
Her traces, of the smallest spider web;
Her collars, of the moonshine's wat'ry beams;
Her whip, of cricket's bone; the lash, of film;
Her wagoner, a small grey-coated gnat,
Not half so big as a round little worm   65
Pricked from the lazy finger of a maid;
Her chariot is an empty hazelnut,
Made by the joiner squirrel or old grub,
Time out o' mind the fairies' coachmakers.
And in this state she gallops by night   70
Through lovers' brains, and then they dream of love;
O'er courtiers' knees, that dream on curtsies straight;
O'er lawyers' fingers, who straight dream on fees;
O'er ladies' lips, who straight on kisses dream,
Which oft the angry Mab with blisters plagues,   75
Because their breaths with sweetmeats tainted are
Sometimes she gallops o'er a courtier's nose,
And then dreams he of smelling out a suit;
And sometime comes she with a tithe-pig's tail
Tickling a parson's nose as 'a lies asleep,   80
Then dreams he of another benefice.
Sometimes she driveth o'er a soldier's neck,
And then dreams he of cutting foreign throats,
Of breaches, ambuscadoes, Spanish blades,
Of healths five fathom deep; and then anon   85
Drums in his ear, at which he starts and wakes,
And being thus frighted, swears a prayer or two
And sleeps again. This is that very Mab
That plats the manes of horses in the night
And bakes the elflocks in foul sluttish hairs,   90
Which once untangled much misfortune bodes.
This is the hag, when maids lie on their backs,
That presses them and learns them first to bear,
Making them women of good carriage.
This is she—

Romeo   Peace, peace, Mercutio, peace!   95
Thou talk'st of nothing.

Mercutio   True, I talk of dreams;
Which are the children of an idle brain,
Begot of nothing but vain fantasy;

---

60. *cover:* i.e., hood of the "wagon."

61. *traces:* straps joining the horses to the wagon.

62. *collars:* i.e., of the horses.

63. *film:* gossamer thread, like that spun by a spider.

64. *wagoner:* one who drives a wagon.

66. *lazy:* because laziness was thought to induce such growths.

68. *old grub:* The grub bores his way through nuts, as the squirrel cracks them.

joiner: carpenter (applied to the squirrel because of his chisel-sharp teeth).

76. *tainted:* presumably because their breaths are not naturally sweet and they use flavoured sweetmeats to smother the foulness.

79. *tithe-pig's:* a pig given as a tithe (tenth part) to a church; a payment of ecclesiastical tax.

84. *breaches:* gaps made (by the attackers) in fortifications.

ambuscadoes: ambushes.

85. *healths:* toasts.

anon: immediately, at once.

86. *Drums:* the signal for battle.

90. *elflocks:* When dirty hair became clotted together it was superstitiously attributed to elves. It happened only to filthy hair—"foul sluttish hairs."

91. *untangled:* entangled.

98. *fantasy:* fancy.

Which is as thin of substance as the air,
And more inconstant than the wind, who woos   100
Even now the frozen bosom of the North
And, being angered, puffs away from thence,
Turning his side to the dew-dropping South.

Benvolio This wind you talk of blows us from ourselves.
Supper is done, and we shall come too late.   105

Romeo I fear, too early; for my mind misgives
Some consequence, yet hanging in the stars,
Shall bitterly begin his fearful date
With this night's revels and expire the term
Of a despised life, closed in my breast,   110
By some vile forfeit of untimely death.
But he that hath the steerage of my course
Direct my sail! On, lusty gentlemen!

Benvolio Strike, drum.

---

100.   *woos . . . North:* i.e., blows warmly on the northern wastes.

104.   *This wind you talk of:* probably with the implication that Mercutio is a windbag.

        from ourselves: away from our purpose.

108.   *date:* season.

113.   *lusty gentlemen:* corresponding to "my fine fellows."

114.   *Strike, drum:* spoken to the drummer-boy, a sign that they shall march on.

COMMENTARY

The scene opens with Romeo and his friends dressed for the masquerade at the Capulet household, which they plan to attend uninvited. Suspense grows, because we know that something crucial will occur at the Capulets' party.

As Romeo and his friends get close to the Capulet mansion, they wonder if a speech is necessary before they enter the party. Traditionally, uninvited guests present a speech to their host to apologize for the intrusion, but Benvolio argues that such speeches are out of style and no longer necessary. Benvolio insists that their presence at the party will be brief, saying that the young men will "be gone" after one "measure," or dance (10).

Romeo's melancholy

Romeo continues his melancholy act in this scene, claiming that he'll not be able to dance because he is too "heavy" with his "soul of lead" (12, 15). Knowing that Rosaline will be there but probably won't dance with him, Romeo prefers to stand in the shadows watching, rather than dancing with another woman.

Just as we tire of Romeo's continued despondence, the jesting Mercutio lightens the mood. Mocking Romeo's Petrarchan excess, he suggests that his friend needs to borrow Cupid's wings and "soar with them above a common bound," above the boundaries that chain him to the ground (18). In contrast to the good "binding" that Lady Capulet thinks marriage will bring, for Romeo, love is a "heavy burden" under which he sinks (22). Mercutio jests that love is "a tender thing," but Romeo doesn't agree; for him, it is "too rough, / Too rude, too boist'rous" (24–26).

Mercutio responds to Romeo's complaint with vulgar humour, arguing that if love plays rough with Romeo, he should also "be rough with love" (27). But Romeo insists on nursing his mood, saying that he prefers to "be a candle-holder," watching the masquerade but not participating (38). Mercutio knows that because Romeo is stuck "[u]p to the ears" in the mire of love, he must be saved from melancholy by attending a party (43).

Mercutio's bawdy jesting links him with the Nurse. Both characters view love primarily in physical terms, though Mercutio takes love less seriously than the Nurse; for him, love is something of a joke. The teasing between Mercutio and Romeo highlights the difference in their moods and personalities. While the rest of the group is ready to enjoy the party, Romeo is stuck in an isolating depression.

As they prepare to enter the party, Romeo reveals that he "dreamt a dream to-night" (49). The details of his dream are never disclosed, but it seems to have been ominous, telling him that he shouldn't attend the party. Critics argue that Romeo's mention of a dream in this scene implicitly links him with Juliet, who in Act I, Scene 3 had said of marriage, "It is an honour that I dream not of." For both characters, dreams seem prophetic.

Queen Mab

Rather than pursuing the meaning of Romeo's dream, the text moves to Mercutio's richly textured speech about Queen Mab. Mercutio claims that Mab is the "fairies' midwife," a mischievous

A masquerador.

pixie who is responsible for bringing enticing dreams (54). As "fairy," Mab rules the airy world of dreams, fantasy, and love. As "midwife," she is more mundane, presiding over the realms of death and childbirth. Mercutio's depiction of Mab plays on these contradictions.

Although Mab brings pleasant dreams to some lovers, she plagues ladies' lips with blisters if they eat too many sweets, and she rides over soldiers' necks so they dream of "cutting foreign throats" (83). In fact, Mercutio spends more time discussing the effects that Mab has on soldiers than on lovers, which helps keep the violent, tragic, feud-ridden elements of the play in focus. This passage also shows that the jovial Mercutio has a more violent side, leading him to prefer war to love. His dream of Mab contains vulgar imagery, as do most of his

conversations: Mab is a nightmarish incubus who teaches women "to bear, / Making them women of good carriage," meaning good childbearers or good in bed (93–94).

The importance of dreams

Although Romeo believes that dreams bring true prophecies, Mercutio claims that dreams are "the children of an idle brain, / Begot of nothing but vain fantasy" (97–98). Mercutio neither understands nor sympathizes with Romeo's dreaming ways. In fact, he implies that Romeo is a narcissistic poseur who is emotionally immature and idle. For Mercutio, Romeo's visionary world is founded on the dangerous indulgence of whims and escapist scenarios instead of anything substantial.

Mercutio also suggests that fantasy, which includes love, is thin as "air" and "more inconstant than the wind" (99–100). Mercutio's emphasis on the "airy" nature of dreams here reminds us of the Prince's representation in Act I, Scene 1 of words as equally airy. But we will learn that just as airy words have powerful effects (leading to violence, even war), so do dreams. Throughout the play, dreams prove to be potently prophetic.

Romeo is caught up in his romantic daydreams, while Mercutio is pragmatic (though also imaginative, as his Queen Mab speech indicates). Benvolio's name suggests that he's a "good man," while Mercutio's links him to both the god and planet Mercury. Mercutio is *mercurial*, meaning that he's active, volatile, changeable, and erratic. In fact, his wit and humour make him a much more exciting character than the moody Romeo, and actors often prefer to play his part.

Despite Mercutio's argument that dreams are illusory, Romeo's premonitions seem ominous. As Romeo and his friends prepare to enter the Capulets' party, Romeo fears "[s]ome consequence, yet hanging in the stars" (107). He correctly intuits that he'll forfeit his life to an "untimely death" because of this party, yet he isn't afraid (111). His life is now moving in a direction that can't be changed.

Discussing his fate, Romeo uses the terminology of finance ("expire the term" and "forfeit") and seafaring ("steerage") (109, 111, 112). He also asks that whomever has control over his destiny direct his "sail" (113). Many of these images reoccur throughout the play. Notice how carefully Shakespeare uses imagery in order to emphasize the multiplicity of language; each image carries many connotations, adding more and more layers of meaning to the play.

At this point in the play, Romeo passively gives in to fate, allowing it to control his life. However, by the end of the play, Romeo takes greater control of his life and refuses to give "the inconsequential stars'" power over him. Romeo's final words in this scene provide a strong contrast with the seemingly festive intention of this occasion; he reminds us of the tragedy that undercuts all delight. In this play, love is never far from hate, happiness never distant from despair. Notice how quickly the moods of the play change from scene to scene, moment to moment.

Act I, Scene 5

At the masquerade, Romeo sees Juliet and, struck by her beauty, falls in love immediately. Tybalt recognizes Romeo's voice and wants to fight him, but Capulet steps in to prevent a brawl. Romeo and Juliet talk, and he kisses her. The Nurse informs each young lover of the other's family name.

ACT I, SCENE 5
The same. A hall in Capulet's house.

[They march about the stage, and Servingmen come forth with napkins]

1st Servingman Where's Potpan, that he helps not to take away? He shift a trencher? he scrape a trencher!

2nd Servingman When good manners shall lie all in one or two men's hands, and they unwashed too, 'tis a foul thing.   5

1st Servingman Away with the joint-stools, remove the court-cupboard, look to the plate. Good thou, save me a piece of marchpane and, as thou loves me, let the porter let in Susan Grindstone and Nell. *[Exit second Servingman]*
Anthony, and Potpan!   10

[Enter two more Servingmen]

3rd Servingman Ay, boy, ready.

1st Servingman You are looked for and called for, asked for and sought for, in the great chamber.

4th Servingman We cannot be here and there too. Cheerly, boys! Be brisk awhile, and the longer liver take all.   15

[Exit third and fourth Servingmen. Enter CAPULET, his WIFE, JULIET, TYBALT, NURSE, and all the Guests and Gentlewomen to the Maskers]

Capulet Welcome, gentlemen! Ladies that have their toes
Unplagued with corns will walk a bout with you.
Ah ha, my mistresses! which of you all
Will now deny to dance? She that makes dainty,
She I'll swear hath corns. Am I come near ye now?   20
Welcome, gentlemen! I have seen the day
That I have worn a visor and could tell

NOTES

2. *trencher:* wooden plate, literally one to cut food upon.

4. *When . . . hands:* i.e., when only one or two men do their duty.

6. *joint-stools:* folding stools (not all in one piece).

7. *court-cupboard:* movable sideboard, on which the food was placed.

    plate: silver plate.

8. *marchpane:* confectionery made of almond paste, sugar, and marzipan.

15. *the longer liver to take all:* a proverb meaning that he who lives longest will get the most.

17. *walk a bout:* dance a round.

19. *makes dainty:* comes shyly.

20. *come near ye:* touched you on the raw—where it hurts.

A whispering tale in a fair lady's ear,
Such as would please. 'Tis gone, 'tis gone, 'tis gone!
You are welcome, gentlemen! Come, musicians, play.   25
[Music plays, and they dance]
A hall, a hall! give room! and foot it, girls.
More light, you knaves! and turn the tables up,
And quench the fire, the room is grown too hot.
Ah, sirrah, this unlooked-for sport comes well.
Nay, sit, nay, sit, good cousin Capulet,   30
For you and I are past our dancing days.
How long is't now since last yourself and I
Were in a mask?

2nd Capulet   By'r Lady, thirty years.

Capulet What, man? 'Tis not so much, 'tis not so much;
'Tis since the nuptial of Lucentio,   35
Come Pentecost as quickly as it will,
Some five-and-twenty years, and then we masked.

2nd Capulet 'Tis more, 'tis more. His son is elder, sir;
His son is thirty.

Capulet   Will you tell me that?
His son was but a ward two years ago.   40

Romeo *[to a Servingman]* What lady's that, which doth enrich
    the hand
Of yonder knight?

Servingman I know not, sir.

Romeo O, she doth teach the torches to burn bright!
It seems she hangs upon the cheek of night   45
As a rich jewel in an Ethiop's ear—
Beauty too rich for use, for earth too dear!
So shows a snowy dove trooping with crows
As yonder lady o'er her fellows shows.
The measure done, I'll watch her place of stand   50
And, touching hers, make blessed my rude hand.
Did my heart love till now? Forswear it, sight!
For I ne'er saw true beauty till this night.

Tybalt This, by his voice, should be a Montague.
Fetch me my rapier, boy. What, dares the slave   55
Come hither, covered with an antic face,

---

27. *turn the tables up:* pack away the trestles and boards that constituted the tables.

28. *quench the fire:* Shakespeare here forgets that the play is supposed to take place in July (I.3.16).

33. *By'r Lady:* by our Lady, i.e., the Virgin Mary.

36. *Pentecost:* the feast of Whitsunday.

38. *His son is elder:* His (Lucentio's) son is older.

41. *enrich the hand:* i.e., by dancing with him, he holds her hand.

46. *Ethiop's:* Negro's, as used by Shakespeare (here and elsewhere), not Ethiopian in its narrower sense.

49. *fellows:* i.e., fellow-dancers.

50. *place of stand:* Between dances, dancers stood up, just as people did in church, at parish meetings and so on.

51. *rude:* common.

52. *sight:* He appeals to his sight to foreswear his previous love on account of what follows in the next line.

56. *antic:* grotesque mask.

To fleer and scorn at our solemnity?
Now, by the stock and honour of my kin,
To strike him dead I hold it not a sin.

Capulet Why, how now, kinsman? Wherefore storm you so? 60

Tybalt Uncle, this is a Montague, our foe;
A villain, that is thither come in spite
To scorn at our solemnity this night.

Capulet Young Romeo is it?

Tybalt   'Tis he, that villain Romeo.

Capulet Content thee, gentle coz, let him alone.   65
'A bears him like a portly gentleman,
And, to say truth, Verona brags of him
To be a virtuous and well-governed youth.
I would not for the wealth of all this town
Here in my house do him disparagement.   70
Therefore be patient, take no note of him.
It is my will, the which if thou respect,
Show a fair presence and put off these frowns.
An ill-beseeming semblance for a feast.

Tybalt It fits when such a villain is a guest.   75
I'll not endure him.

Capulet   He shall be endured.
What, goodman boy! I say he shall. Go to!
Am I the master here, or you? Go to!
You'll not endure him, God shall mend my soul!
You'll make a mutiny among my guests!   80
You will set cock-a-hoop, you'll be the man!

Tybalt Why, uncle, 'tis a shame.

Capulet   Go to, go to!
You are a saucy boy. Is't so, indeed?
This trick may chance to scathe you, I know what.
You must contrary me! Marry, 'tis time—   85
Well said, my hearts!—You are a princox—go!
Be quiet, or—More light, more light!—For shame!
I'll make you quiet; what!—Cheerly, my hearts!

---

57. *fleer:* jeer.

solemnity: ceremonial festival.

66. *bears him:* carries himself.

portly: dignified, honourable, of good carriage or bearing.

70. *disparagement:* discourtesy.

71. *patient:* calm. Capulet does not mean, "Wait patiently for another opportunity."

77. *goodman boy:* my fine fellow, with the implication in "boy" that he is only an underling after all.

78. *Go to:* stop it, behave yourself.

79. *God . . . soul:* an oath meaning "God spare me if I will permit this!"

81. *set cock-a-hoop:* to drink without stint, make good cheer recklessly, cast off all restraint, give the rein to disorder.

84. *This trick may chance to scathe you:* I'll use this as an opportunity to injure you.

what: Capulet is obviously hinting that if Tybalt's behaviour does not improve it will affect his income, or his legacy in Capulet's will.

85. *contrary me:* go against my will.

86. *hearts:* good fellows. The rest of this speech is interspersed with remarks to the guests.

*princox: prin*ce of *cox*combs; a saucy boy or upstart.

Tybalt Patience perforce with willful choler meeting
Makes my flesh tremble in their different greeting.   90
I will withdraw; but this intrusion shall,
Now seeming sweet, convert to bitt'rest gall.
[Exit]

Romeo If I profane with my unworthiest hand
This holy shrine, the gentle sin is this;
My lips, two blushing pilgrims, ready stand   95
To smooth that rough touch with a tender kiss.

Juliet Good pilgrim, you do wrong your hand too much,
Which mannerly devotion shows in this;
For saints have hands that pilgrims' hands do touch,
And palm to palm is holy palmers' kiss.   100

Romeo Have not saints lips, and holy palmers too?

Juliet Ay, pilgrim, lips that they must use in prayer.

Romeo O, then, dear saint, let lips do what hands do!
They pray; grant thou, lest faith turn to despair.

Juliet Saints do not move, though grant for prayers' sake.   105

Romeo Then move not while my prayer's effect I take.
Thus from my lips, by thine my sin is purged.

[Kisses her]

Juliet Then have my lips the sin that they have took.

Romeo Sin from my lips? O trespass sweetly urged!
Give me my sin again *[Kisses her]*   110

Juliet You kiss by th' book.

Nurse Madam, your mother craves a word with you.

Romeo What is her mother?

Nurse   Marry, bachelor,
Her mother is the lady of the house,
And a good lady, and a wise and virtuous.   115
I nursed her daughter that you talked withal.
I tell you, he that can lay hold of her
Shall have the chinks.

Romeo   Is she a Capulet?
O dear account! my life is my foe's debt.

---

89.   *Patience perforce:* compulsory (enforced) patience.

choler: anger.

90.   *their different greeting:* meeting of opposites.

91.   *intrusion:* i.e., of Romeo.

93.   *hand:* Romeo takes her hand as he says this. The next few speeches are in the form of a Shakespearean sonnet. It is significant that the first words between Romeo and Juliet are in sonnet form, as the sonnet was the accepted form for the language of love.

94.   *This holy shrine:* Juliet's body.

105.   *move:* alter, stir from what they know to be right.

though grant: though they answer prayers.

106.   *my prayer's effect:* what is granted in answer to my prayer.

109.   *trespass:* i.e., accusation of sin.

111.   *kiss by th' book:* kiss according to the rules and techniques described by the erotic books, which reduce the art to a science.

113.   *What:* i.e., what position does she hold, what is her family and title.

Marry: an exclamation based on the oath "by Mary."

118.   *chinks:* cash (from the clatter of the coins).

119.   *dear account:* sad reckoning. In Elizabethan English, the word "dear" intensified the meaning—you could have a "dear friend" and a "dear enemy."

my foe's debt: at the mercy of my foe (because he loves his foe).

Benvolio Away, be gone; the sport is at the best.   120

Romeo Ay, so I fear; the more is my unrest.

Capulet Nay, gentlemen, prepare not to be gone;
We have a trifling foolish banquet towards.
Is it e'en so? Why then, I thank you all.
I thank you, honest gentlemen. Good night.   125
More torches here! Come on then, let's to bed.
Ah, sirrah, by my fay, it waxes late;
I'll to my rest.

[Exeunt all but JULIET and NURSE]

Juliet Come hither, Nurse. What is yond gentleman?

Nurse The son and heir of old Tiberio.   130

Juliet What's he that now is going out of door?

Nurse Marry, that, I think, be young Petruchio.

Juliet What's he that follows there, that would not dance?

Nurse I know not.

Juliet Go ask his name.—If he be married,   135
My grave is like to be my wedding bed.

Nurse His name is Romeo, and a Montague,
The only son of your great enemy.

Juliet My only love, sprung from my only hate!
Too early seen unknown, and known too late!   140
Prodigious birth of love it is to me
That I must love a loathed enemy.

Nurse What's this? what's this?

Juliet   A rhyme I learnt even now
Of one I danced withal. *[One calls within, 'Juliet']*

Nurse   Anon, anon!
Come, let's away; the strangers all are gone.   145

[Exeunt]

---

120. *the sport is at the best:* We have had the best of the fun.

121. *the more is my unrest:* Realizing what dangers there are in this sudden love for Juliet, Romeo applies Benvolio's comment to his own affairs.

123. *towards:* coming, at hand.

124. *Is it e'en so:* corresponding to the modern "Must you really go?"

127. *fay:* faith.

waxes: grows.

136. *My grave . . . bed:* i.e., I am not likely to marry anyone else.

140. *too late:* i.e., to make any difference—I cannot help loving him.

141.-142. *Prodigious . . . enemy:* (the fate) that I must love a loathed enemy is the portentous birth that love has given to me.

COMMENTARY

Romeo and his friends have finally arrived at the Capulet mansion for the masquerade. This scene begins with Capulet's witty servants clearing away the dinner dishes. Playing the happy host, Capulet welcomes the masked Romeo to the party and the dancing begins. The emphasis on the contrast between youth and age reappears in this scene as Capulet and his cousin quibble about how long it's been since they last masqueraded. Although Capulet claims to be too old for dancing now, he was quite a ladies' man when he was younger. Watching the dancing, Capulet seems content, and we see a new, calmer side of his personality.

Capulet's emphasis on the quick passage of time at the opening of the scene—"'Tis gone, 'tis gone, 'tis gone"—is a motif that occurs throughout the play (24). Although his sources spread the action of the play over nine months, Shakespeare compresses it into less than five days. As the play progresses, time appears to move more and more quickly.

Juliet's beauty

As Capulet reminisces, the most important event in the play has happened: Romeo has spotted Juliet. The imagery that Romeo uses to describe her provides important insights into their relationship. He says that she teaches the torches to burn bright and "hangs upon the cheek of night / As a rich jewel in an Ethiop's ear" (45–46). She is also "for earth too dear" (47). The association of Juliet and light is repeated throughout the play, but hers is not sunlit beauty; instead, it appears best when viewed against a dark background, because she is a jewel in the night's ear. Similarly, their blazing love, born at a candlelit party, is carried on primarily at night and rarely sees the light of day. Throughout the play, Juliet's bright happiness with her love for Romeo is shadowed by darkness; she always seems aware of the tragic direction they're heading in. Romeo's statement that her beauty is "for earth too dear" is sadly prophetic.

Although Romeo's enraptured description of Juliet seems sincere, the scene is almost comical after we have read four scenes full of Romeo's protestations of undying love for Rosaline. The speed with which he alters the object of his affections suggests the immaturity and superficiality of his love. Should we trust Romeo? How do we know that his love for Juliet is real? Based on the fickleness of his character, Shakespeare makes us wonder whether Romeo will be a true and faithful lover for the innocent, young Juliet. But he adds to Romeo's credibility later in the scene by showing Capulet's respect for him as an admired member of Verona's society.

Tybalt's fury

Overhearing Romeo's statements about Juliet's beauty, Tybalt recognizes a Montague voice. Love and violence collide as fiery Tybalt calls for his *rapier* (double-edged sword). Despite the families' feud, Capulet asks Tybalt to leave Romeo alone because "Verona brags of him / To be a virtuous and well-governed youth" (67–68). As the master of the house and host of the party, Capulet refuses to allow Tybalt to fight with Romeo. Capulet has again changed his tune; rather than the hotheaded man we see earlier in the play, he's now willing to forget temporarily about the feud, primarily because he doesn't want his party to be ruined. The festival spirit has levelled some of the familial differences; however, Tybalt wants the feud to take priority in all situations.

Rather than respecting Capulet's "will," Tybalt insists that he can't endure Romeo's presence. Faced with Tybalt's lack of respect for his authority, Capulet becomes hotheaded. He responds to Tybalt's insolence by calling him "goodman boy" and "saucy boy," belittling his kinsman and affirming his own status as the "master" of the house (77, 83). Capulet becomes so angry with Tybalt's insolence that he vows to "make [Tybalt] quiet," ironically showing that his personality is just as explosive as Tybalt's (88).

The religion of love

Following this angry exchange between two Capulets, Shakespeare abruptly shifts the mood of the scene, presenting Romeo and Juliet's first meeting. The quick change in mood reminds us that this play is about extremes: love versus hate, age versus youth, light versus dark, and ultimately, life versus death. Juxtaposed with the angry exchange between Tybalt and Capulet, the interaction between Romeo and Juliet seems calm and private, outside of the boundaries of the crowded ballroom.

The lovers' first conversation uses the intense language of lyrical poetry and is structured in the form of a sonnet in which Romeo and Juliet speak alternately. The conversation ends with a kiss. The sonnet is heavy with religious imagery including references to palmers, pilgrims, saints, and shrines. Juliet's body is transformed into a "holy shrine," and Romeo's lips are "two blushing pilgrims" waiting to offer a "tender kiss" (94–96). (Critics suggest that by using the pilgrim image,

Clare Danes and Leonardo DiCaprio in the 1998 film version of Romeo and Juliet. *Everett Collection*

combines spiritual and physical pleasures. Although the lovers' first conversation is structured in the stylized form of a sonnet, their later conversations use blank verse, expressing the growth of their passion past the limits of literary form.

The importance of names

Sonnet-making is so intriguing to the lovers that they forget to ask one another's names before they are interrupted by the Nurse. Romeo discovers from the Nurse that Juliet is a Capulet. The Nurse assures him that Juliet's future husband will "have the chinks," meaning he will have a lot of money (118). But this statement figuratively plunges Romeo into debt. Continuing with the Nurse's monetary imagery, he says, "[M]y life is my foe's debt" (119). Romeo owes his new interest in life to his family's rivals.

Shakespeare may be playing upon the Italian meaning of Romeo's name, which is "roamer" or "wanderer.") Juliet is the "saint" who uses her lips for praying rather than kissing (103). The motif of the religious quest emphasizes Romeo's pilgrimage to find true love. Romeo wants their lips to "do what hands do"—pray (103). By kissing Juliet in prayer, Romeo claims that his sins are purged. As pilgrim and saint, Romeo and Juliet create a vision of the world that vies with the church in its power. In fact, romantic love appears to be its own religion.

The sonnet interchange emphasizes Juliet's modesty—she will allow Romeo to kiss her but will not return the kiss. In claiming that Romeo kisses "by th' book," Juliet suggests that he follows the traditional rules of love, and she urges him to create something new (111). The bodily focus of their interchange—the palming and kissing—shows that this is an erotically charged moment.

The imagery that Shakespeare used shows that their love has a spiritual component, which distinguishes it from the purely earthy pleasures advocated by the Nurse and the material pleasures that Lady Capulet recommends. Earlier in the play, Romeo was isolated in a Petrarchan world of melancholy and failed love; now he and Juliet create their own world of love, one that

Juliet asks the Nurse to find out Romeo's name and prophetically claims, "If he be married, / My grave is like to be my wedding bed" (135–136). Although Romeo is not married, Juliet's statement will prove true. Upon discovering that Romeo is a Montague, she cries, "My only love, sprung from my only hate!" (139). Again, love and hate mesh; they can't be separated in this play.

Act I, Scene 5 is important to the play because it clearly depicts the fiery natures of Capulet and Tybalt. However, the scene also shows an interesting juxtaposition of moods that heightens the dramatic tension. The scene begins comically with the servants and the conversation between Capulet and his cousin, and then moves to the fight between Tybalt and Capulet, which foreshadows danger for Romeo. How do these juxtapositions of moods within and between scenes influence our interpretation of Romeo and Juliet's love? Does their conversation seem more sincere when contrasted with Tybalt's irrational anger?

This scene creates a strong link between love and religion. Keep an eye out for this connection throughout the play. The scene raises further questions about love as well. Is the relationship between Romeo and Juliet simply an adolescent crush, or does it seem deeper? Is the play suggesting that love at first sight is the only true love? In Act I, Scene 3, Juliet said that she would love Paris if "looking liking move"; how much does her love for Romeo seem based on "looking" (physical attraction)? Is Romeo's love for Juliet motivated purely by her physical beauty?

Note that the lovers' meeting is interrupted by the Nurse; this will happen again later in the play, contributing to its structural unity.

Notes

Notes

COLES NOTES TOTAL STUDY EDITION

ROMEO AND JULIET
ACT II

Juliet *'Tis but thy name that is my enemy.*
Thou art thyself, though not a Montague.
What's Montague? It is nor hand, nor foot,
Nor arm, nor face, nor any other part
Belonging to a man. O, be some other name!
What's in a name? That which we call a rose
By any other word would smell as sweet.

Act II, Prologue

The Prologue summarizes the events of Act I, reminding us that Romeo has now switched his affections from Rosaline to Juliet. Juliet returns Romeo's sentiment, but the lovers will be unable to meet freely because of their feuding families. The Prologue ends on a hopeful note, telling us that passion gives the lovers power so that they will find a way to meet.

ACT II, PROLOGUE

[Enter Chorus]

Chorus Now old desire doth in his deathbed lie,
And young affection gapes to be his heir;
That fair for which love groaned for and would die,
With tender Juliet matched, is now not fair.
Now Romeo is beloved and loves again,   5
Alike bewitched by the charm of looks;
But to his foe supposed he must complain,
And she steal love's sweet bait from fearful hooks.
Being held a foe, he may not have access
To breathe such vows as lovers use to swear,   10
And she as much in love, her means much less
To meet her new beloved anywhere;
But passion lends them power, time means, to meet,
Temp'ring extremities with extreme sweet. *[Exeunt]*

NOTES

1. *old desire:* Romeo's previous love, for Rosaline.
2. *young affection:* Romeo's fresh love, for Juliet.
   gapes: is keen.
3. *That fair (one):* Rosaline.
6. *Alike bewitched:* Each of them is equally enchanted.
7. *foe supposed:* Juliet, who as a member of the rival house, would normally be regarded as an enemy.
10. *use:* are in the habit of.
13. *time:* (lend them the) means.
14. *Temp'ring extremities:* making their difficult positions easier by the sweetness of their meeting.

COMMENTARY

The Prologue to Act II, like the Prologue to Act I, functions like a Greek chorus. In modern productions of *Romeo and Juliet*, the prologues are usually spoken by a single narrator—often Prince Escalus. The Prologue to Act II summarizes the events of Act I, reminding us that Romeo has now switched his affections from Rosaline to Juliet, the daughter of his enemy, Lord Capulet. Juliet returns Romeo's sentiment, but the lovers will be unable to meet freely because of their feuding families. The Prologue ends on a hopeful note, telling us that passion gives the lovers power, and they will, therefore, find a way to meet. The dangers—"[t]emp'ring extremities"—of their meetings will make their meetings extremely sweet.

Critics always question the function of this Prologue. Does it add anything useful to the play, or is it simply providing a useless summary? For example, the famous eighteenth-century literary critic Dr. Samuel Johnson wrote about the Prologue, "The use of this chorus is not easily discovered. It conduces nothing to the progress of the play, but relates what is already known, or what the next scenes will shew; and relates it without adding the improvement of any moral sentiment." As Johnson suggests, the Prologue neither adds to the action of the play nor enhances our understanding of the play's meaning.

Act II, Scene 1

Romeo's isolation from his friends grows as he leaps into the Capulet's garden, hoping for one more look at Juliet. As Benvolio and Mercutio search for him, they discuss their views of love.

ACT II, SCENE 1
Verona. A lane by the wall of Capulet's orchard.

[Enter ROMEO alone]

Romeo Can I go forward when my heart is here?
  Turn back, dull earth, and find thy centre out.

[Enter BENVOLIO with MERCUTIO. ROMEO retires]

Benvolio Romeo! My cousin Romeo! Romeo!

Mercutio   He is wise,
  And, on my life, hath stol'n him home to bed.

Benvolio He ran this way and leapt this orchard wall.   5
  Call, good Mercutio.

Mercutio   Nay, I'll conjure too.
  Romeo! humours! madman! passion! lover!
  Appear thou in the likeness of a sigh!
  Speak but one rhyme, and I am satisfied!
  Cry but 'Ay me!' pronounce but 'love' and 'dove';   10
  Speak to my gossip Venus one fair word,
  One nickname for her purblind son and heir
  Young Abraham Cupid, he that shot so true
  When King Cophetua loved the beggar maid!
  He heareth not, he stirreth not, he moveth not;   15
  The ape is dead, and I must conjure him.
  I conjure thee by Rosaline's bright eyes,
  By her high forehead and her scarlet lip,
  By her fine foot, straight leg, and quivering thigh,
  And the demesnes that there adjacent lie,   20
  That in thy likeness thou appear to us!

Benvolio An if he hear thee, thou wilt anger him.

Mercutio This cannot anger him, 'Twould anger him
  To raise a spirit in his mistress' circle
  Of some strange nature, letting it there stand   25

NOTES

2.   *earth:* body.

7.   *humours:* evil moods.

11.   *gossip:* friend.

     Venus: goddess of love.

12.   *purblind:* quite blind or merely dimsighted.

13.   *Abraham Cupid:* This expression has not been satisfactorily explained by any commentator, but may be an allusion to a famous archer of the day.

14.   *King Cophetua:* The story was a favourite ballad topic. Cupid shot "so trim" to bring about so unlikely an occurrence.

16.   *ape:* poor fellow.

17.   *conjure:* solemnly appeal to.

20.   *demesnes:* domains (of pleasure).

Till she had laid it and conjured it down.
That were some spite; my invocation
Is fair and honest: in his mistress' name,
I conjure only but to raise up him.

Benvolio Come, he hath hid himself among these trees   30
To be consorted with the humorous night.
Blind is his love and best befits the dark.

Mercutio If love be blind, love cannot hit the mark.
Now will he sit under a medlar tree
And wish his mistress were that kind of fruit   35
As maids call medlars when they laugh alone.
O, Romeo, that she were, O that she were
An open et cetera and thou a pop'rin pear!
Romeo, good night. I'll to my truckle-bed;
This field-bed is too cold for me to sleep.   40
Come shall we go?

Benvolio   Go then, for 'tis in vain
To seek him here that means not to be found.

[Exit with MERCUTIO]

31. *humorous:* damp (climate and physiology).

34. *medlar:* a fruit like a small brown apple. The name lent itself to puns, because it sounds like "meddler."

38. *An open et cetera:* a nice phrase for an unpleasant one.

39. *truckle- bed:* small bed on wheels (cf. "truck") which was pushed under a larger bed when not in use. Mercutio means that even a truckle-bed would be better than "this field-bed."

COMMENTARY

This scene takes place near a wall in Capulet's orchard. Romeo stands alone, contemplating his life without Juliet. She has instantly become the centre of his universe, and without her, he feels dull. When Benvolio and Mercutio try to find him, Romeo leaps over the orchard wall.

Mercutio's banter

Love leaves Romeo so isolated and separate that he can't communicate with his friends. As in Act I, Scene 5, Mercutio shows little sympathy for Romeo's Petrarchan lovesickness, associating it with madness. Calling to Romeo, Mercutio mockingly pretends to conjure a spirit: "Romeo! humours! madman! passion! lover!" (7).

Neither Mercutio nor Romeo's other friends know that Romeo has found new love in Juliet. Mercutio's use of the term *humours* refers to the medieval conception of physiology in which the body consists of four primary

fluids that determine a person's physical and psychological disposition. (See the Introduction to Early Modern England for further discussion of this subject.)

Mercutio's playful speech asking Romeo to speak with "Venus" or the "[y]oung Abraham Cupid" makes fun of Romeo's courtly mannerisms (11, 13). Mercutio's references to Rosaline are bawdy—commenting on her "scarlet lip" and "quivering thigh" and the delights "there adjacent" (18–20). His irreverence reminds us of the physical aspects of love that he and the Nurse advocate in the play. Neither Mercutio nor the Nurse believes in the glory of chastity.

Benvolio's concern

Sympathetic toward Romeo's melancholy, Benvolio worries that Mercutio's playfulness will anger Romeo. Defending himself, Mercutio claims that his comments are "fair and honest" because he uses Rosaline's name merely to conjure Romeo from the woods (28). Benvolio suggests that Romeo plays in the trees to consort with "humorous night," again emphasizing Romeo's association with night, fantasy, and illusion (31).

Benvolio also argues that Romeo's love is blind (another reference to blind Cupid, who randomly shoots his arrows at ill-starred lovers) and, therefore, "best befits the dark" (32). Both Benvolio and Mercutio recognize that Romeo bases his ideas of love on a courtly ideal rather than on a true understanding of his lover's personality—this is Romeo's blindness. But neither of Romeo's friends knows about Romeo's new affection for Juliet.

Romeo's love can only flourish if it lives in the fantastical land of night, dreams, and illusions. Like the Queen Mab speech in which he focuses on soldiers' dreams, Mercutio presents love as war in this scene. Mercutio says, for example, that the "field-bed is too cold" (meaning that the war zone of Romeo's courtship is too cold or chaste for him), so he decides to go home and sleep (40).

Act II, Scene 1 provides further insights into the personality differences between Mercutio, Benvolio, and Romeo. Romeo's friends think he's still trapped by his melancholy love for the aloof Rosaline. Mercutio presents a view of love that emphasizes its physical aspects and links love with war. Mercutio's vulgar references to Rosaline make Romeo and Juliet's love seem even more pure and spiritual by comparison.

This scene also dramatizes Romeo's growing isolation. By jumping over the wall into the Capulets' garden, Romeo further separates himself from his friends. Consider whether Romeo could learn something from Mercutio's more humorous view of love. Are both Mercutio and Romeo excessive in their ideas about love? Perhaps Shakespeare is guiding us toward a definition of love that synthesizes Romeo's seriousness and Mercutio's playfulness.

Act II, Scene 2

Unaware that Romeo is in the Capulet orchard listening to her confession, Juliet expresses her longing and love for Romeo. Romeo steps from the shadows and declares his love for her. They agree to marry, and they part as dawn breaks.

ACT II, SCENE 2
The same. Capulet's orchard.

Romeo [*coming forward*]

   He jests at scars that never felt a wound.

   [*Enter JULIET above at a window*]

   But soft! What light through yonder window breaks?

   It is the East, and Juliet is the sun!

   Arise, fair sun, and kill the envious moon,

   Who is already sick and pale with grief   5

   That thou her maid art far more fair than she.

   Be not her maid, since she is envious.

   Her vestal livery is but sick and green,

   And none but fools do wear it. Cast it off.

   It is my lady; O, it is my love!   10

   O that she knew she were!

   She speaks, yet she says nothing. What of that?

   Her eye discourses; I will answer it.

   I am too bold; 'tis not to me she speaks.

   Two of the fairest stars in all the heaven,   15

   Having some business, do entreat her eyes

   To twinkle in their spheres till they return.

   What if her eyes were there, they in her head?

   The brightness of her cheek would shame those stars

   As daylight doth a lamp; her eyes in heaven   20

   Would through the airy region stream so bright

   That birds would sing and think it were not night.

   See how she leans her cheek upon her hand!

   O that I were a glove upon that hand,

   That I might touch that cheek!

Juliet   Ay me!

Romeo   She speaks.   25

   O speak again, bright angel! for thou art

   As glorious to this night, being o'er my head,

NOTES

1. *He . . . wound:* Romeo is no doubt thinking of the scars made by Cupid's arrows, which Mercutio has never felt. This line creates a couplet with the previous one, before the change to the scene which Romeo and Juliet have to themselves. The scene division is obviously wrong.

7. *Be not her maid:* in other words, love and marry me.

8. *sick and green:* Shakespeare is probably thinking of the "greensickness," an anemic disease causing a lingering death in young women.

vestal livery: virgin uniform.

13. *discourses:* the language of love.

18. *they in:* the stars in.

26. *thou:* Romeo and Juliet address one another ("thou" and "thee") as close friends. Bear in mind, however, that the address is imaginary to begin with—they do not actually speak to one another.

As is a winged messenger of heaven
Unto the white-upturned wond'ring eyes
Of mortals that fall back to gaze on him   30
When he bestrides the lazy-pacing clouds
And sails upon the bosom of the air.

Juliet O Romeo, Romeo! wherefore art thou Romeo?
Deny thy father and refuse thy name;
Or, if thou wilt not, be but sworn my love,   35
And I'll no longer be a Capulet.

Romeo *[aside]* Shall I hear more, or shall I speak at this?

Juliet 'Tis but thy name that is my enemy.
Thou art thyself, though not a Montague.
What's Montague? It is nor hand, nor foot,   40
Nor arm, nor face, nor any other part
Belonging to a man. O, be some other name!
What's in a name? That which we call a rose
By any other word would smell as sweet.
So Romeo would, were he not Romeo called,   45
Retain that dear perfection which he owes
Without that title. Romeo, doff thy name;
And for thy name, which is no part of thee,
Take all myself.

Romeo   I take thee at thy word.
Call me but love, and I'll be new baptized;   50
Henceforth I never will be Romeo.

Juliet What man art thou that, thus bescreened in night,
So stumblest on my counsel?

Romeo   By a name
I know not how to tell thee who I am.
My name, dear saint, is hateful to myself,   55
Because it is an enemy to thee.
Had I it written, I would tear the word.

Juliet My ears have yet not drunk a hundred words
Of thy tongue's uttering, yet I know the sound.
Art thou not Romeo, and a Montague?   60

Romeo Neither, fair maid, if either thee dislike.

---

29.   *white-upturned:* the whites of the eyes turned upwards.

37.   *this:* this point, before she goes any farther.

46.   *owes:* possesses.

47.   *doff:* relinquish.

48.   *for:* in exchange for.

50.   *new baptized:* freshly renamed.

53.   *stumblest on my counsel:* overhears by accident my secret thoughts.

Juliet How camest thou hither, tell me, and wherefore?
The orchard walls are high and hard to climb,
And the place death, considering who thou art,
If any of my kinsmen find thee here.   65

Romeo With love's light wings did I o'erperch these walls;
For stony limits cannot hold love out,
And what love can do, that dares love attempt.
Therefore thy kinsmen are no stop to me.

Juliet If they do see thee, they will murder thee.   70

Romeo Alack, there lies more peril in thine eye
Than twenty of their swords! Look thou but sweet,
And I am proof against their enmity.

Juliet I would not for the world they saw thee here.

Romeo I have night's cloak to hide me from their eyes;   75
And but thou love me, let them find me here.
My life were better ended by their hate
Than death prorogued, wanting of thy love.

Juliet By whose direction found'st thou out this place?

Romeo By love, that first did prompt me to inquire.   80
He lent me counsel, and I lent him eyes.
I am no pilot; yet, wert thou as far
As that vast shore washed with the farthest sea,
I should adventure for such merchandise.

Juliet Thou knowest the mask of night is on my face;   85
Else would a maiden blush bepaint my cheek
For that which thou hast heard me speak tonight.
Fain would I dwell on form—fain, fain deny
What I have spoke; but farewell compliment!
Dost thou love me? I know thou wilt say 'Ay';   90
And I will take thy word. Yet, if thou swear'st,
Thou mayst prove false. At lovers' perjuries,
They say Jove laughs. O gentle Romeo,
If thou dost love, pronounce it faithfully.
Or if thou thinkest I am too quickly won,   95
I'll frown, and be perverse, and say thee nay,
So thou wilt woo; but else, not for the world.
In truth, fair Montague, I am too fond,

Blind Cupid with his arrow.

66.   *o'erperch:* fly over, a metaphor from a bird hopping
from perch to perch.

67.   *stony limits:* boundaries of stone.

76.   *but:* except.

          them: the Capulets (enemies to Romeo, who is a
Montague).

78.   *prorogued:* adjourned (postponed).

81.   *I lent him eyes:* Cupid is blind.

84.   *adventure for:* speculate in—the regular word for
overseas trading in Shakespeare's day.

          merchandise: Juliet (note the sustained mercantile
metaphor).

88.   *fain:* gladly, willingly.

          dwell on form: do the proper thing (in the formal,
conventional way).

89.   *farewell compliment!:* goodbye, polite conventions!

93.   *Jove:* King of the Roman gods.

97.   *else:* otherwise, i.e., I will not do this ("frown and
be perverse and say thee nay") unless you think that
I am too quickly won.

98.   *fond:* foolish.

And therefore thou mayst think my 'haviour light:
But trust me, gentleman, I'll prove more true   100
Than those that have more cunning to be strange.
I should have been more strange, I must confess,
But that thou overheard'st, ere I was ware,
My true-love passion. Therefore pardon me,
And not impute this yielding to light love,   105
Which the dark night hath so discovered.

Romeo Lady, by yonder blessed moon I vow,
That tips with silver all these fruit-tree tops—

Juliet O, swear not by the moon, th' inconstant moon,
That monthly changes in her circled orb,   110
Lest that thy love prove likewise variable.

Romeo What shall I swear by?

Juliet   Do not swear at all;
Or if thou wilt, swear by thy gracious self,
Which is the god of my idolatry,
And I'll believe thee.

Romeo   If my heart's dear love—   115

Juliet Well, do not swear. Although I joy in thee,
I have no joy of this contract to-night.
It is too rash, too unadvised, too sudden;
Too like the lightning, which doth cease to be
Ere one can say 'It lightens.' Sweet, good night!   120
This bud of love, by summer's ripening breath,
May prove a beauteous flow'r when next we meet.
Good night, good night! As sweet repose and rest
Come to thy heart as that within my breast!

Romeo O, wilt thou leave me so unsatisfied?   125

Juliet What satisfaction canst thou have to-night?

Romeo Th' exchange of thy love's faithful vow for mine.

Juliet I gave thee mine before thou didst request it;
And yet I would it were to give again.

Romeo Wouldst thou withdraw it? For what purpose, love? 130

Juliet But to be frank and give it thee again.
And yet I wish but for the thing I have.
My bounty is as boundless as the sea,

99.   *'haviour:* behaviour (shortened because of the metrical necessity).

101.   *strange:* reserved, off-putting.

109.   *inconstant:* changeable or unfaithful.

110.   *changes in her circled orb:* referring to the moon's changes within the full circle; or, possibly, to the changes of the moon as it goes through its path in the heavens.

114.   *Which . . . idolatry:* which I worship (as if you were an idol).

The inconstant moon.

129.   *I would . . . again:* so that I might have the pleasure all over again.

131.   *frank:* generous, bountiful.

132.   *the thing I have:* my love.

My love as deep; the more I give to thee,
The more I have, for both are infinite.   135
I hear some noise within. Dear love, adieu!
[Nurse calls within]
Anon, good nurse! Sweet Montague, be true.
Stay but a little, I will come again. *[Exit]*

Romeo O blessed, blessed night! I am afeard,
Being in night, all this is but a dream,   140
Too flattering-sweet to be substantial.

[Enter JULIET above]

Juliet Three words, dear Romeo, and good night indeed.
If that thy bent of love be honourable,
Thy purpose marriage, send me word to-morrow,
By one that I'll procure to come to thee,   145
Where and what time thou wilt perform the rite;
And all my fortunes at thy foot I'll lay
And follow thee my lord throughout the world.

Nurse *[within]* Madam!

Juliet I come, anon.—But if thou meanest not well,   150
I do beseech thee—

Nurse *[within]*   Madam!

Juliet By and by I come.—
To cease thy suit and leave me to my grief.
To-morrow will I send.

Romeo   So thrive my soul—

Juliet A thousand times good night! *[Exit]*   155

Romeo A thousand times the worse, to want thy light!
Love goes toward love as schoolboys from their books;
But love from love, toward school with heavy looks.

[Enter JULIET, above, again]

Juliet Hist! Romeo, hist! O for a falc'ner's voice
To lure this tassel-gentle back again!   160
Bondage is hoarse and may not speak aloud,
Else would I tear the cave where Echo lies

---

141.   *substantial:* real.

145.   *procure:* cause, arrange.

150.   *anon:* in a short time (not immediately).

152.   *By and by:* at once (not in a short time).

156.   *worse:* worse night.

            to want thy light: being deprived of the light (cast by Juliet's presence).

159.   *hist!:* silence! or listen!

            falc'ner's voice: special tone employed to attract a falcon back to the owner's wrist.

160.   *tassel-gentle:* male falcon of the peregrine variety.

161.   *Bondage is hoarse:* my bondage in (a secret) love makes me speak in a whisper.

162.   *Echo:* a mountain-nymph in Roman mythology (hence "the cave").

And make her airy tongue more hoarse than mine
With repetition of 'My Romeo!'

Romeo It is my soul that calls upon my name.   165
How silver-sweet sound lovers' tongues by night,
Like softest music to attending ears!

Juliet Romeo!

Romeo   My sweet?

Juliet   At what o'clock to-morrow
Shall I send to thee?

Romeo   By the hour of nine.

Juliet I will not fail. 'Tis twenty years till then.   170
I have forgot why I did call thee back.

Romeo Let me stand here till thou remember it.

Juliet I shall forget, to have thee still stand there,
Rememb'ring how I love thy company.

Romeo And I'll still stay, to have thee still forget,   175
Forgetting any other home but this.

Juliet 'Tis almost morning. I would have thee gone—
And yet no farther than a wanton's bird,
That lets it hop a little from her hand,
Like a poor prisoner in his twisted gyves,   180
And with a silken thread plucks it back again,
So loving-jealous of his liberty.

Romeo I would I were thy bird.

Juliet   Sweet, so would I.
Yet I should kill thee with much cherishing.
Good night, good night! Parting is such sweet sorrow   185
That I shall say good night till it be morrow. *[Exit]*

Romeo Sleep dwell upon thine eyes, peace in thy breast!
Would I were sleep and peace, so sweet to rest!
Hence will I to my ghostly father's cell,
His help to crave and my dear hap to tell. *[Exit]*   190

163. *airy tongue:* The words Echo utters are so insubstantial that her tongue seems made merely of air.

166. *silver-sweet:* as sweet as silver bells.

178. *wanton's bird:* pet bird of an irresponsible girl, who (as is shown by what follows) teases her pets.

180. *gyves:* chains (used to shackle prisoners).

182. *So loving-jealous of his liberty:* so fond of the bird that she is jealous of its regaining its liberty.

189. *ghostly:* pertaining to the Holy Ghost, spiritual father—a priest who hears confession and gives absolution.

190. *dear hap:* good luck, good fortune.

COMMENTARY

Romeo walks alone through the Capulet garden as this scene begins. He's upset at Mercutio's lack of sympathy and believes that Mercutio can easily tease him because he has "never felt a wound," meaning that Mercutio has never been in love (1). The statement ironically foreshadows Mercutio's fate later in the play.

The light from the balcony

Suddenly, Romeo notices a light at Juliet's bedroom window. Upon seeing it, Romeo claims that Juliet is the sun, lighting up his fantastical nighttime world. This image of the sun echoes Romeo's first description of Juliet teaching "the torches to burn bright" (I.5.46). Throughout the play, Romeo describes Juliet with imagery that depicts her as "light" and "bright." As in Act I, Scene 5, Juliet's light shows best against darkness. According to Romeo,

John Trevealen and Valerie Masterson in an English National Opera production in 1983. Clive Barda/PAL

Juliet's eyes, for example, are two of the brightest stars in heaven. In fact, her eyes are so bright that she creates an artificial daylight that would confuse even the birds.

Romeo's use of light imagery in his descriptions of Juliet contrasts with the moon imagery he uses to describe Rosaline. Remember that Romeo compared Rosaline to Diana, the goddess of the moon, earlier in the play, suggesting that Rosaline's love was chaste, cold, and dark. By indicating that Juliet should rise like the sun and "kill the envious moon," Romeo implicitly wants to replace Rosaline with Juliet (4).

Waxing and waning, the moon is fickle, and Romeo prefers the sun's more constant light. Unlike Rosaline's love, which was icy as a "field-bed," Juliet's affections are warm and revitalizing (II.1.40). Even though it's night, Juliet's warmth makes the time of day feel like mid-afternoon. She is a "bright angel," an image that combines in Juliet a heavenly light and the holy imagery from the lovers' first conversation at the masquerade (26).

From her bedroom balcony, Juliet longingly speaks Romeo's name. She doesn't realize that he's listening from the shadows below. In a heartfelt soliloquy, Juliet reveals her love for Romeo and asks him to "[d]eny [his] father and refuse [his] name" (34). In turn, she says, she'll "no longer be a Capulet" (36).

The duality of names

In Act I, Prince Escalus made us aware of the duality of language, calling it airy even as it threatened to disrupt the entire city. Names have a similar duality for Juliet. Although Romeo isn't her enemy, his name is. She asks what part of him is Montague, and then suggests that it's not his "hand, nor foot, / Nor arm, nor face, nor any other part" (40–41). Juliet argues that a name can't define a person, although their feuding families seem to feel otherwise. This scene is also the source of the play's most famous lines, "What's in a name? That which we call a rose / By any other word would smell as sweet" (43–44). In parallel fashion, Juliet says that Romeo would maintain his "dear perfection" even if his name weren't Romeo (46). Naming, therefore, has a dual nature—while arbitrary, it can be socially powerful. A name cannot change a person, but it can dramatically impact his relationships with others.

At one level, *Romeo and Juliet* is fundamentally about language, puns, and witticisms that expand the possibilities of meaning. The play is about correct reading and interpretation of messages. Therefore, Juliet's investigation of language in this scene seems appropriate. By questioning names and identity— "What's Montague?"—Juliet suggests that the source of the feuding is probably not substantial (40). She wonders if the families simply quibble over names or if a more significant reason for their argument exists. Juliet believes that names do not define a person, so she asks Romeo to get rid of his name and to take her instead.

Romeo's vow

Romeo comes out of hiding and responds to what he has heard. He vows to take Juliet at her "word," asking that she rename him "love" and saying that from now on he "never will be Romeo" (49–51). When Juliet asks who is speaking to her, Romeo can't answer: "By a name / I know not how to tell thee who I am" (53–54). Because he shed the name Romeo, he no longer knows how to identify himself. Besides reminding us of the danger that these lovers face as members of feuding families, Romeo's play with names also shows the loss of ego that results from true love. All love involves a type of death, because all lovers must give up part of themselves as they move into a deep relationship with someone.

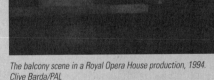

The balcony scene in a Royal Opera House production, 1994.
Clive Barda/PAL

Juliet is concerned for Romeo's safety and wonders how he managed to jump the high walls that surround the Capulet property. Romeo claims that his feelings for her have given him "love's light wings" (another reference to winged Cupid) and enabled him to fly over the orchard walls (66). This description presents another contrast with his love for Rosaline, which left him so "heavy" that he couldn't dance at the Capulet's party (I.4.12).

Describing his voyage to Juliet, Romeo uses seafaring imagery. He says that he isn't a pilot, but he would venture for her even "as far / As that vast shore washed with the farthest sea" (82–83). Remember that in Act I, Scene 4, Romeo used seafaring imagery to indicate his understanding that fate controlled his destiny. Consider whether the imagery has a different meaning here. For example, Romeo seems active in this scene—he's an adventurer, guiding his ship on a quest for true love. In Act I, Scene 4, he conceded that fate was steering his course. Romeo's seafaring imagery is ominously repeated in the play's final scene. As you read, think about why Shakespeare may use this watery imagery so often in the play.

Juliet's response

Juliet is initially embarrassed by what she unintentionally said to Romeo while he hid below her balcony, but she decides to forget about "compliment" (the conventional rules of polite speech) when speaking with him (89). Juliet creates a world and language of love that transcends courtly tradition. Act I questioned the usefulness of poetic devises for expressing true love—through Shakespeare's critique of Romeo's formal language and Juliet's claim that Romeo kissed by the book, for example. It is significant that Juliet takes additional steps away from convention here. She seems to believe that true love can't express itself within parentally and socially sanctioned boundaries.

Savvy for a 13-year-old, Juliet is trying to discover the meaning of true love; however, she isn't sure that she should trust Romeo. She knows that his words may lie and that he can claim to love her even if he doesn't. If Romeo really loves Juliet, she wants him to "pronounce it faithfully" (94). Although Lady Capulet suggested earlier in the play that Juliet read Paris like a book, in this scene, Juliet tries to interpret the truth behind Romeo's words.

Just as language may lie, so may actions. Some who appear honest may prove dishonest. Therefore, Juliet must prove that her words and her actions are true. She wants to know the difference between reality and appearance: How can you distinguish truth and falsity in either language or looks? Although some people who pretend to love only fake it, Juliet vows to "prove more true / Than those that have more cunning to be strange" (100–101). In other words, Romeo shouldn't think that her love for him is "light" because he discovered it secretly and at night (99).

In her replies to Romeo, Juliet uses the imagery of lightness and darkness—images that repeat throughout the play. Romeo attempts to make a traditional vow of love to Juliet, swearing to the "blessed moon" that he'll be faithful (107). However, Juliet asks him not to follow this traditional form of declaring his love. In choosing the inconstant moon as the focus of his vow, Romeo again invokes his ex-love Rosaline, and it seems appropriate that he should find some other icon to describe his love. At first, Juliet says that he should instead swear by his own "gracious self," but later she decides

that she doesn't want Romeo to swear at all (113). Juliet wants Romeo to declare his love for her authentically, rather than following a literary style.

Defining love

In this scene, both lovers wonder if their love is, indeed, "true-love passion" (104). In describing her ideal love, Juliet uses many of the images that occurred previously in the play. Thinking realistically about their situation, she first wonders if their love is "too rash, too unadvised, too sudden; / Too like the lightning" (118–119). Once again, we are asked to reflect on the nature of true love. What differentiates Romeo and Juliet's love from a typical adolescent crush?

Rather than a "light" love, Juliet prefers a more lasting relationship—one that grows from a "bud of love" into a "beauteous flow'r" (121–122). Flower images traditionally represent youth, but they also represent fragility. Juliet hopes that Romeo's love is as lasting as a flower rather than fleeting as lightning, yet flowers are also delicate and soon wilt.

Juliet modifies her description of love yet again at the end of the scene, saying that her love for Romeo is deep, infinite, and "boundless as the sea," and therefore isn't the binding, restricted love that her mother advocated in her discussion of Paris's marriage proposal (133). Juliet echoes Romeo's use of sea imagery earlier in the scene but adds a new shade of meaning to that image. Romeo worries that Mercutio may be right and that their love may be "[t]oo flattering-sweet to be substantial"—it may be just a dream (141).

Despite all of these worries, the lovers exchange vows and promise to be faithful. Before Romeo leaves, Juliet insists that only the act of getting married will adequately show their true intentions. She tells Romeo that she'll send a messenger to him by nine o'clock that morning to discover his plans. As Romeo leaves, Juliet declares, "Parting is such sweet sorrow" (185), echoing the Act II Prologue, which foretold that the lovers' "extremities" would make their time together more "sweet." Like Juliet, Romeo is eager to marry. After leaving her, he goes directly to Friar Laurence's cell to ask the holy man for guidance and to arrange a time for the wedding ceremony.

To increase the coherence of the play, Shakespeare creates many parallels between this scene and the lovers' first conversation at the masquerade. For example, the Nurse calls Juliet to bed to interrupt both conversations. Likewise, both scenes end with the dawn, heightening the connection between these lovers and night or early morning. Romeo and Juliet have a nighttime romance, and their conversations must end with the arrival of the "grey-eyed morn" (II.3.1).

In addition, this scene shows that Romeo and Juliet's love has flourished since their last meeting. By insisting that Romeo not swear on the moon and not use traditional literary modes to express his love, Juliet urges him toward a deeper, more authentic language of love. Like their encounter at the masquerade, in this scene, the lovers seem sheltered from the outside world, moving more deeply into an intimate world of their own creation.

This scene also continues to question the function of language, suggesting that both words and actions are used to deceive, making the discovery of a "true-love passion" difficult. The beauty of the lyrical language in this scene reflects Romeo and Juliet's deepening affection. Romeo says, "How silver-sweet sound lovers' tongues by night, / Like softest music to attending ears!"—a poetically complex representation of the lovers' growing emotional bond (166–167). Romeo's suggestion that music has a "silver-sweet" sound will be echoed by the Nurse's servant Peter in Act IV, Scene 5 in his conversation with the musicians.

Act II, Scene 3

After leaving Juliet, Romeo rushes to see Friar Laurence, who is philosophizing about human nature and medicine as he tends his herb garden. Romeo begs Friar Laurence to marry the two young lovers, and the Friar agrees in hopes that Romeo and Juliet's marriage will end the feud between the Capulets and Montagues.

ACT II, SCENE 3
The same. Friar Laurence's cell.

NOTES

[Enter FRIAR LAURENCE alone, with a basket]

Friar The grey-eyed morn smiles on the frowning night,
  Check'ring the Eastern clouds with streaks of light;
  And flecked darkness like a drunkard reels
  From forth day's path and Titan's fiery wheels.
  Now, ere the sun advance his burning eye   5
  The day to cheer and night's dank dew to dry,
  I must up-fill this osier cage of ours
  With baleful weeds and precious-juiced flowers.
  The earth that's nature's mother is her tomb.
  What is her burying grave, that is her womb;   10
  And from her womb children of divers kind
  We sucking on her natural bosom find,
  Many for many virtues excellent,
  None but for some, and yet all different.
  O, mickle is the powerful grace that lies   15
  In plants, herbs, stones, and their true qualities;
  For naught so vile that on the earth doth live
  But to the earth some special good doth give;
  Nor aught so good but, strained from that fair use,
  Revolts from true birth, stumbling on abuse.   20
  Virtue itself turns vice, being misapplied,
  And vice sometime 's by action dignified.
[Enter ROMEO]
  Within the infant rind of this weak flower
  Poison hath residence, and medicine power;
  For this, being smelt, with that part cheers each part;   25
  Being tasted, slays all senses with the heart.
  Two such opposed kings encamp them still
  In man as well as herbs—grace and rude will;
  And where the worser is predominant,

4.   *From forth:* out of the way of.

  Titan's fiery wheels: chariot belonging to the flaming god of the sun.

7.   *osier cage:* willow basket.

  ours: the monastery to which he belonged.

8.   *baleful:* harmful, poisonous.

  previous-juiced: containing wonderful properties in their juices.

9.   *The earth . . . tomb:* All life springs from the earth and when dead goes back to it. The next line contains the same thought, with the two parts in the reverse order.

14.   *but for some:* There are none which are not useful for something.

15.   *mickle:* great (refers to the Scots proverb "mony a muckle maks a mickle.")

19.   *strained:* twisted away.

  that fair use: the use for which it was intended.

22.   *by action dignified:* by the way it is used (presumably in a good cause) becomes dignified.

23.   *infant rind:* seedling stalk.

25.   *that part:* its scent.

26.   *with the heart:* by stopping ("slaying") the heart.

28.   *grace and rude will:* good and ill.

Full soon the canker death eats up that plant.   30

Romeo Good morrow, father.

Friar   Benedicite!
What early tongue so sweet saluteth me?
Young son, it argues a distempered head
So soon to bid good morrow to thy bed.
Care keeps his watch in every old man's eye,   35
And where care lodges, sleep will never lie;
But where unbruised youth with unstuffed brain
Doth couch his limbs, there golden sleep doth reign.
Therefore thy earliness doth me assure
Thou art uproused with some distemp'rature;   40
Or if not so, then here I hit it right—
Our Romeo hath not been in bed to-night.

Romeo That last is true—the sweeter rest was mine.

Friar God pardon sin! Wast thou with Rosaline?

Romeo With Rosaline, my ghostly father? No.   45
I have forgot that name and that name's woe.

Friar That's my good son! But where hast thou been then?

Romeo I'll tell thee ere thou ask it me again.
I have been feasting with mine enemy,
Where on a sudden one hath wounded me   50
That's by me wounded. Both our remedies
Within thy help and holy physic lies.
I bear no hatred, blessed man, for lo,
My intercession likewise steads my foe.

Friar Be plain, good son, and homely in thy drift.   55
Riddling confession finds but riddling shrift.

Romeo Then plainly know my heart's dear love is set
On the fair daughter of rich Capulet;
As mine on hers, so hers is set on mine,
And all combined, save what thou must combine   60
By holy marriage. When, and where, and how
We met, we wooed, and made exchange of vow,
I'll tell thee as we pass; but this I pray,
That thou consent to marry us to-day.

Friar Holy Saint Francis! What a change is here!   65

---

30.   *canker:* canker-worm.

31.   *Benedicite!:* an ecclesiastical greeting—"Bless (you)" or "Blessed be (God)!"

33.   *argues:* proves.

       distempered: disturbed, upset, uneasy.

35.   *his watch:* awake.

37.   *unbruised:* unspoiled.

       unstuffed: by care (anxiety).

38.   *golden:* priceless, invaluable.

40.   *distemp'rature:* disturbance of mind (probably accompanied by physical disturbance).

46.   *that name's woe:* the woe Rosaline brought me (by rejecting my suit).

49.   *mine enemy:* the Capulets.

50.   *one:* refers to Juliet.

       wounded: by love.

54.   *steads:* benefits.

56.   *Riddling:* puzzling, doubtful.

       shrift: forgiveness and pardon.

60.   *combined:* agreed.

       combine: unite. The word is used in two senses in the line.

Is Rosaline, that thou didst love so dear,
So soon forsaken? Young men's love then lies
Not truly in their hearts, but in their eyes.
Jesu Maria! What a deal of brine
Hath washed thy sallow cheeks for Rosaline!   70
How much salt water thrown away in waste
To season love, that of it doth not taste!
The sun not yet thy sighs from heaven clears,
Thy old groans ring yet in mine ancient ears.
Lo, here upon thy cheek the stain doth sit   75
Of an old tear that is not washed off yet.
If e'er thou wast thyself, and these woes thine,
Thou and these woes were all for Rosaline.
And art thou changed? Pronounce this sentence then:
Women may fall when there's no strength in men.   80

Romeo Thou chid'st me oft for loving Rosaline.

Friar For doting, not for loving, pupil mine.

Romeo And bad'st me bury love.

Friar   Not in a grave
To lay one in, another out to have.

Romeo I pray thee chide not. She whom I love now   85
Doth grace for grace and love for love allow.
The other did not so.

Friar   O, she knew well
Thy love did read by rote, that could not spell.
But come, young waverer, come go with me.
In one respect I'll thy assistant be;   90
For this alliance may so happy prove
To turn your households' rancour to pure love.

Romeo O, let us hence! I stand on sudden haste.

Friar Wisely and slow. They stumble that run fast.

[Exeunt]

---

69.   *Maria:* Son of Mary.

          brine: salt water (tears).

72.   *season:* preserve (by salt water, the same word as in "seasoning.") Salting and drying were the two chief methods of preserving in Shakespeare's days.

          it: true love.

73.   *sighs:* Romeo's sighs for Rosaline are thought of as clouds rising into the air. (Note what Romeo says in I.1, "Love is a smoke raised with the fume of sighs.")

77.   *thyself:* true to thyself.

          thine: genuine.

80.   *Women may:* no wonder women do.

          fall: fall from grace (be unfaithful).

81.   *chid'st:* rebuked.

82.   *doting:* unreasoning infatuation.

84.   *to lay one . . . have:* as if you are on with the new love almost before you are off with the old.

86.   *grace for grace:* favour in return for favour.

88.   *did read . . . spell:* had learnt it by heart and could not read, i.e., you repeated the words of love without understanding what love meant.

90.   *In one respect:* on account of one thing.

92.   *households' rancour:* bitterness between the two families.

COMMENTARY

This scene takes place in Friar Laurence's cell on the same morning as the balcony scene. Romeo rushes from Juliet's house to the Friar's cell to make arrangements for their wedding later that day. When he arrives, Friar Laurence is in his garden, gathering healing herbs. Later in the play, the Friar will make use of his herbs when preparing a potion for Juliet.

The Friar's garden

While clipping plants, the Friar philosophizes about medicine and human nature. The Friar says the earth is nature's womb as well as her tomb—nature is cyclical, so whatever dies becomes the fuel for new life.

Linking birth and death, the Friar echoes the play's earlier presentations of love's duality. Like nature, love is both creative and destructive, something that becomes more apparent as the play progresses. His words parallel Juliet's argument in the balcony scene that truth and falsity often look and sound alike.

The Friar develops these conflicting ideas further when he says, "Virtue itself turns vice being misapplied, / And vice sometime 's by action dignified" (21–22). Nothing in life is ever purely good or purely evil; you can use the good for evil purposes, just as you can use the good for evil. This statement foreshadows the Friar's paradoxical role in the play. Although he's a holy man who supposedly tries to bring spiritual healing to his community, his actions lead to disaster.

The Friar's logic points out the difficulty in making immutable value judgments. You can't clearly define good and bad, because such values depend upon the situation. For example, the deaths of Romeo and Juliet later in the play will be tragic, but they'll also provide a larger good for the community by ending the feud between the Capulets and Montagues.

The Friar's discussion about the ambiguous nature of flowers attaches an ominous image to Juliet's wish that her love for Romeo grow into a "beauteous flower" (II.2.122). According to the Friar, flowers and people can contain both medicine and poison: "Two such opposed kings encamp them still / In man as well as herbs" (27–28). When evil presides, "canker death eats up that plant" (30). Similarly, the canker can destroy the beauty of youth or the beautiful flower of love, providing a dismal image of the fate of Romeo and Juliet's flowerlike love. By the end of the play, the canker of hate that the feud between the Montagues and the Capulets caused will blight the "bud of love" that Romeo and Juliet create.

Romeo's announcement

Romeo arrives at Friar Laurence's cell in the middle of his speech about good and evil. The Friar is disturbed because Romeo is up so early in the morning. In the Friar's opinion, Romeo's early arrival means trouble— young people should be caught in "golden sleep" at that time of day (38). The Friar immediately assumes that Romeo was with Rosaline, once again reminding us how quickly Romeo's affections shifted from one woman to another.

Playing on Friar Laurence's facility as a healer, Romeo tells the Friar that he has come to him for a remedy that lies within his confessor's "holy physic" (52). The Friar asks Romeo to speak plainly, because a "[r]iddling confession" results only in a riddling cure (56). Romeo tells the Friar that he wants to marry Juliet that very day. The sudden shift in Romeo's affections shocks the Friar because Romeo appeared lovesick for Rosaline the day before.

The Friar's garden.

The Friar naturally assumes that Romeo's love lies not in his "heart" but in his "eyes," meaning that Romeo is enamoured with Juliet's beauty rather than her spirit (68). Like Juliet, Friar Laurence wonders how a person can differentiate true love and infatuation, because they look the same, producing the same tears, sighs, and groans. The Friar says that Romeo's "love did read by rote, that could not spell," suggesting that Romeo simply mimics other lovers rather than truly feeling love (88). Romeo disagrees, arguing that his love for Juliet is real because it is mutual; while Rosaline didn't return his love, Juliet responds to him "love for love" (86). A cynical reader may wonder if Romeo loves Juliet simply because she loves him. Does the reciprocity of their love mean that it is necessarily true?

The Friar's consent

Despite all of his worries about the depth of Romeo's affections for Juliet, the Friar agrees to marry them because their wedding could lead to reconciliation between the Montagues and Capulets. Echoing Juliet, the Friar says that Romeo should move slowly because those who travel fast often fall. (It seems, though, that the Friar shifts his opinion as quickly as Romeo shifts his passions. If he didn't make his decision to marry Romeo and Juliet so quickly, perhaps the lovers would have avoided tragedy.)

Critics have often viewed the Friar as a pompous character, and Baz Luhrman, in his film version of the play titled *William Shakespeare's Romeo + Juliet*, presents the Friar as downright evil. Consider how someone could arrive at this characterization as you read further. Note evidence that the Friar's character may combine good and evil, just as herbs provide both medicine and poison. Think about whether his decision to support the lovers is a good one, and consider how his decision determines the outcome of the play.

Act II, Scene 4

Romeo reunites with his friends, Mercutio and Benvolio, in Verona's square, and Romeo appears to have been cured of his lovesickness. Romeo plots with Juliet's nurse to facilitate their nuptials and consummation of the marriage.

ACT II, SCENE 4
The same. A street.

[Enter BENVOLIO and MERCUTIO]

Mercutio Where the devil should this Romeo be?
Came he not home to-night?

Benvolio Not to his father's. I spoke with his man.

Mercutio Why, that same pale hard-hearted wench, that
Rosaline,
Torments him so that he will sure run mad.   5

Benvolio Tybalt, the kinsman to old Capulet,
Hath sent a letter to his father's house.

Mercutio A challenge, on my life.

Benvolio Romeo will answer it.

Mercutio Any man that can write may answer a letter.   10

Benvolio Nay, he will answer the letter's master, how
he dares, being dared.

Mercutio Alas, poor Romeo, he is already dead!
stabbed with a white wench's black eye; run through
the ear with a love song; the very pin of his heart cleft   15
with the blind bow-boy's butt-shaft; and is he a
man to encounter Tybalt?

Benvolio Why, what is Tybalt?

Mercutio More than Prince of Cats, I can tell you. O, he's the
courageous captain of compliments. He fights as you   20
sing pricksong—keeps time, distance, and proportion;
he rests his minim rests, one, two, and the third in

NOTES

2.   *to-night:* last night.

15.   *pin:* centre-pin. In archery competitions the white target was fastened to a post by a wooden pin: it was thus a sign of extremely good marksmanship to hit the pin in the very centre.

16.   *butt-shaft:* arrow used in archery practice at the butts (mounds of earth behind the targets, as used in rifle practice today).

17.   *man:* fit and proper person.

19.   *Prince of Cats:* In the old story of Reynard the Fox, the cat is called "Tibert" or "Tybert, " a variant of the name Tybalt (Theobald), and it was a name often given to cats.

21.   *pricksong:* music noted down exactly.

22.   *minim:* short note in music.

your bosom! The very butcher of a silk button, a
duellist, a duellist! a gentleman of the very first
house, of the first and second cause. Ah, the   25
immortal passado! The punto reverso! The hay!

Benvolio The what?

Mercutio The pox of such antic, lisping, affecting
fantasticoes—these new tuners of accent! 'By Jesu, a
very good blade! a very tall man! a very good whore!'   30
Why, is not this a lamentable thing, grandsir,
that we should be thus afflicted with these strange
flies, these fashion-mongers, these pardon-me's, who
stand so much on the new form that they cannot sit
at ease on the old bench? O, their bones, their bones!   35

[Enter ROMEO]

Benvolio Here comes Romeo! here comes Romeo!

Mercutio Without his roe, like a dried herring. O
flesh, flesh, how art thou fishified! Now is he for the
numbers that Petrarch flowed in. Laura, to his lady,
was a kitchen wench (marry, she had a better love to   40
berhyme her), Dido a dowdy, Cleopatra a gypsy,
Helen and Hero hildings and harlots, Thisbe a grey
eye or so, but not to the purpose. Signior Romeo,
bonjour! There's a French salutation to your French slop.
You gave us the counterfeit fairly last night.   45

Romeo Good morrow to you both. What counterfeit
did I give you?

Mercutio The slip, sir, the slip. Can you not conceive?

Romeo Pardon, good Mercutio. My business was great,
and in such a case as mine a man may strain   50
courtesy.

Mercutio That's as much as to say, such a case as yours
constrains a man to bow in the hams.

Romeo Meaning, to curtsy.

Mercutio Thou hast most kindly hit it.   55

Romeo A most courteous exposition.

Mercutio Nay, I am the very pink of courtesy.

23-24. *butcher of a silk button:* the mark of a good duellist, the sort of thing young men used to boast about in those days.

24-25. *a gentleman . . . cause:* expert at duelling.

25. *house:* rank (of duellists).

29. *fantasticoes:* absurd, irrational persons.

new tuners of accents: speakers in the latest fashion, who affect all the new idioms and mannerisms of speech.

30. *blade:* fighter (metonymy).

tall: spirited, bold.

31. *grandsir:* said humorously to Benvolio, who is not one of "these new tuners of accents."

33. *flies:* implying that they are always buzzing about.

37. *roe:* punning on his name, and perhaps also on "roe," a female deer, i.e., without his lady-love.

39. *numbers:* (lines of) poetry.

41. *Dido:* the first of a list of beautiful lovers famous in classical mythology (and Elizabethan literature derived from it). Dido, Queen of Carthage, killed herself when Aeneas deserted her.

42. *Hero:* whose lover, Leander, swam nightly across Hellespont to see her.

hildings: mean, low women.

Thisbe: lover of Pyramus. In the face of parental opposition, their love ended in a way not unlike that of Romeo and Juliet.

44. *slop:* baggy (sloppy) trousers.

48. *slip:* a term for counterfeit coin. Here it is used with a double meaning.

53. *hams:* knees.

55. *kindly:* suitably.

it: my meaning.

Romeo Pink for flower.

Mercutio Right.

Romeo Why, then is my pump well-flowered.   60

Mercutio Sure wit, follow me this jest now till thou
  has worn out thy pump, that, when the single sole of
  it is worn, the jest may remain, after the wearing,
  solely singular.

Romeo O single-soled jest, solely singular for the   65
  singleness!

Mercutio Come between us, good Benvolio! My wits faint.

Romeo Swits and spurs, swits and spurs! or I'll cry a match.

Mercutio Nay, if our wits run the wild-goose chase, I
  am done; for thou hast more of the wild goose in one
  of thy wits than, I am sure, I have in my whole five.   70
  Was I with you there for the goose?

Romeo Thou wast never with me for anything when
  thou wast not there for the goose.

Mercutio I will bite thee by the ear for that jest.

Romeo Nay, good goose, bite not!   75

Mercutio Thy wit is a very bitter sweeting; it is a most
  sharp sauce.

Romeo And is it not, then, well served in to a sweet goose?

Mercutio O, here's a wit of cheveril, that stretches
  from an inch narrow to an ell broad!   80

Romeo I stretch it out for that word 'broad,' which,
  added to the goose, proves thee far and wide a broad goose.

Mercutio Why, is not this better now than groaning
  for love? Now art thou sociable, now art thou Romeo;
  now art thou what thou art, by art as well as by nature.   85
  For this drivelling love is like a great natural that runs
  lolling up and down to hide his bauble in a hole.

Benvolio Stop there, stop there!

Mercutio Thou desirest me to stop in my tale against
  the hair.

---

58.   *flower:* referring to the phrase, "The flower of courtesy."

60.   *pump:* court shoe (taking up "courtesy"). A "pinked" shoe was punched with holes in patterns, "flowered": decorated.

62.   *single sole:* A pump was made with a single sole, for lightness in dancing (not with a sole added to the shoe, which could be replaced when worn).

64.   *solely singular:* the bare (soles of the) feet.

66.   *My wits faint:* at Romeo's cleverness. (He is being sarcastic, of course).

67.   *match:* contest. By a metaphor from horse racing Romeo says, "Let's carry on with the contest—even if your wits faint—or I'll challenge you."

68.   *the wild-goose chase:* my following you. The term "wild-goose chase" was applied to a contest where two riders started together and, as soon as one obtained the lead, the other had to follow over the same ground. If the second rider could overtake the first, then the position was reversed. The name is taken from the way a flock of geese flies in a line. The phrase has a rather different meaning now.

71.   *Was I with you there:* Did you see my point?

73.   *not there for the goose:* not there to play the part of, to act as silly as, a goose. Romeo replies taking "with me" literally.

74.   *bite thee by the ear:* a term of endearment, not of assault.

76.   *sweeting:* a very sweet kind of apple. The word was used metaphorically as a term of endearment.

77.   *sauce:* referring to the applesauce usually served with roast goose.

79.   *cheveril:* kid leather.

81.   *it:* my wit.

87.   *bauble:* short stick, or baton, of the clown.

89.   *against the hair:* or, as we say, "against the grain," a metaphor from brushing the hair of an animal the opposite way to which it lies. The pun on "tale" (tail) is obvious.

Benvolio Thou wouldst else have made thy tale   90
large.

Mercutio O, thou art deceived! I would have made it
short; for I was come to the whole depth of my tale,
and meant indeed to occupy the argument no longer.

Romeo Here's goodly gear!   95

[Enter NURSE and her Man PETER]

Mercutio A sail, a sail!

Benvolio Two, two! a shirt and a smock.

Nurse Peter!

Peter Anon.

Nurse My fan, Peter.   100

Mercutio Good Peter, to hide her face; for her fan's
the fairer face.

Nurse God ye good morrow, gentlemen.

Mercutio God ye good-den, fair gentlewoman.

Nurse Is it good-den?   105

Mercutio 'Tis no less, I tell ye; for the bawdy hand of
the dial is now upon the prick of noon.

Nurse Out upon you! What a man are you!

Romeo One, gentlewoman, that God hath made for
himself to mar.   110

Nurse By my troth, it is well said. 'For himself to mar,'
quoth 'a? Gentlemen, can any of you tell me where I
may find the young Romeo?

Romeo I can tell you; but young Romeo will be older
when you have found him than he was when you sought   115
him. I am the youngest of that name, for fault of a worse.

Nurse You say well.

Mercutio Yea, is the worst well? Very well took, i' faith!
wisely, wisely.

Nurse If you be he, sir, I desire some confidence with you.   120

Benvolio She will endite him to some supper.

91.	*large:* punning on the sense "vulgar," "broad."
95.	*goodly gear:* said in reference to the Nurse, who, as she comes, looks like a bundle of clothes.
97.	*a shirt and a smock:* a man and a woman.
99.	*Anon:* coming presently.
100.	*fan:* fans were very large in those days and it was not uncommon for them to be carried by a servant.
103.	*God ye:* God give you.
104.	*God ye good-den:* God give you good evening.
105.	*Is it good-den?:* Is it as late as that (after mid-day)?
112.	*'a:* he.
113-115.	*will . . . sought him:* Romeo thinks that she will be wordy.
120.	*confidence:* malapropism (she means "conference").
121.	*endite:* malapropism (he means "invite"). Benvolio mimics the Nurse.

Mercutio A bawd, a bawd, a bawd! So ho!

Romeo What hast thou found?

Mercutio No hare, sir; unless a hare, sir, in a
lenten pie, that is something stale and hoar ere it be spent.₁₂₅
[He walks by them and sings]
An old hare hoar,
And an old hare hoar,
Is very good meat in Lent;
But a hare that is hoar
Is too much for a score   130
When it hoars ere it be spent.
Romeo, will you come to your father's? We'll to
dinner thither.

Romeo I will follow you.

Mercutio Farewell, ancient lady. Farewell. *[Sings]* lady, lady,
lady. *[Exeunt MERCUTIO, BENVOLIO]*   135

Nurse I pray you, sir, what saucy merchant was this
that was so full of his ropery?

Romeo A gentleman, nurse, that loves to hear himself
talk and will speak more in a minute than he will
stand to in a month.   140

Nurse An 'a speak anything against me, I'll take
him down, an 'a were lustier than he is, and twenty
such Jacks; and if I cannot, I'll find those that shall.
Scurvy knave! I am none of his flirt-gills; I am none
of his skains-mates. And thou must stand by too, and   145
suffer every knave to use me at his pleasure!

Peter I saw no man use you at his pleasure. If I had, my
weapon should quickly have been out, I warrant you.
I dare draw as soon as another man, if I see occasion in
a good quarrel, and the law on my side.   150

Nurse Now, afore God, I am so vexed that every part
about me quivers. Scurvy knave! Pray you, sir, a word;
and, as I told you, my young lady bid me inquire you
out. What she bid me say, I will keep to myself; but
first let me tell ye, if ye should lead her into a fool's   155
paradise, as they say, it were a very gross kind of
behaviour, as they say; for the gentlewoman is young;

---

122. *bawd:* a go-between for a man and a woman.

124. *hare:* a rabbit, and a woman of loose character.

125. *lenten pie:* a poor sort of a pie.
hoar: mouldy.

136. *merchant:* fellow—in a disparaging sense. Still so used in Warwickshire, England.

137. *ropery:* roguery.

143. *Jacks:* knaves.

144. *flirt-gills:* loose women. "Gill" (Jill) was a familiar or contemptuous term for a girl (as "Jack" was for a boy).

145. *skains-mates:* loose women.

and therefore, if you should deal double with her,
truly it were an ill thing to be offered to any
gentlewoman, and very weak dealing.   160

Romeo Nurse, commend me to thy lady and mistress.
I protest unto thee—

Nurse Good heart, and i' faith I will tell her as much.
Lord, Lord! she will be a joyful woman.

Romeo What wilt thou tell her, nurse? Thou dost not   165
mark me.

Nurse I will tell her, sir, that you do protest, which, as
I take it, is a gentlemanlike offer.

Romeo Bid her devise
Some means to come to shrift this afternoon;   170
And there she shall at Friar Laurence' cell
Be shrived and married. Here is for thy pains.

Nurse No, truly, sir; not a penny.

Romeo Go to! I say you shall.   174

Nurse This afternoon, sir? Well, she shall be there.   175

Romeo And stay, good nurse, behind the abbey wall.
Within this hour my man shall be with thee
And bring thee cords made like a tackled stair,
Which to the high topgallant of my joy
Must be my convoy in the secret night.   180
Farewell. Be trusty, and I'll quit thy pains.
Farewell. Commend me to thy mistress.

Nurse Now God in heaven bless thee! Hark you, sir.

Romeo What say'st thou, my dear nurse?

Nurse Is your man secret? Did you ne'er hear say,   185
Two may keep counsel, putting one away?

Romeo I warrant thee my man's as true as steel.

Nurse Well, sir, my mistress is the sweetest lady. Lord,
Lord! when 'twas a little prating thing—O, there is a
nobleman in town, one Paris, that would fain   190
lay knife aboard; but she, good soul, had as lieve see
a toad, a very toad, as see him. I anger her sometimes,
and tell her that Paris is the properer man; but I'll
warrant you, when I say so, she looks as pale as any clout

---

160. *and very weak dealing:* This anti-climax is typical of a "weak" intelligence and a wordy tongue—going on for the sake of it.

161. *commend me:* corresponding to our "remember me" (literally "recommend me").

163. *Good heart:* my good fellow.

165. *thou:* Notice that generally (but not invariably) Romeo addresses the Nurse as "thou" and she addresses him as "you."

170. *shrift:* confession (where she would receive shrift, or absolution).

172. *shrived:* absolved from her sins and forgiven.

174. *Go to:* nonsense.

178. *tackled stair:* roped ladder.

179. *topgallant:* highest sail on the mast; hence, summit.

181. *quit:* requite, reward (thee for).

186. *Two may keep counsel . . .:* Two can keep a secret, but not three.

putting one away: if there is only one there.

189. *prating:* empty foolish talking.

191. *lay knife aboard:* possess her.

as lieve: as soon.

193. *properer:* more handsome.

194. *clout:* a piece of cloth.

in the versal world. Doth not rosemary and Romeo   195
begin both with a letter?

Romeo Ay, nurse; what of that? Both with an R.

Nurse. Ah, mocker! That's the dog's name. R is for the—
No; I know it begins with some other letter; and she
hath the prettiest sententious of it, of you and rosemary,   200
that it would do you good to hear it.

Romeo Commend me to thy lady

Nurse Ay, a thousand times. *[Exit ROMEO]* Peter!

Peter Anon.

Nurse Peter, take my fan, and go before, and apace.   205

[Exit after PETER]

195.   *versal:* universal (whole).

rosemary: the flower symbolic of remembrance, and hence used at weddings and at funerals.

a letter: a common letter, "R."

198.   *dog's name:* dog's letter or sound, known as *littera canina* because, when rolled, "r" sounds like a dog's growling.

200.   *sententious:* She means sentences. The nurse often uses words with the wrong sense (malapropisms).

205.   *before:* go before me.

apace: quickly.

COMMENTARY

In this scene, Mercutio and Benvolio search for Romeo in a public square in Verona. Benvolio knows that Romeo didn't make it home the previous night and that Tybalt sent a letter to Romeo, presumably challenging him to a duel. Mercutio claims that Romeo is already dead—killed by blind Cupid's arrow of love. Because love has left Romeo weak-willed and melancholy, Mercutio wonders if Romeo will have much success dueling with masterful Tybalt.

Tybalt is nicknamed the "Prince of Cats" because of his expert fencing ability (19). He is the cat who kills all the mice. In deftly describing Tybalt's duelling style, Mercutio shows that he's also an expert fencer, familiar with such terms as *punto reverso* and *passado*. Benvolio, on the other hand, isn't well-versed in the language of fencing, and he replies to Mercutio's list of duelling terms with the dumbfounded question, "The what?" (27). Once again, we're reminded that Benvolio is a lover, not a fighter.

Defining masculinity

Although Mercutio has some respect for Tybalt's fencing skills, he also makes fun of Tybalt, who speaks with a fake inflection in his voice and is overly interested in the newest fashions and styles. Shakespeare depicts Tybalt as a fashionable courtier who worries more about style than substance, while Mercutio prefers a more old-fashioned brand of masculinity.

Mercutio's criticism of Tybalt's stylish ways, together with his critique of Romeo's melancholy, suggests that Mercutio doesn't like men who show signs of effeminacy. Mercutio prefers a more stereotypical brand of masculinity—men who have a zest for life, who are unsentimental, humorous, unfashionable, and violent. While the play questions the nature of true love, it also questions the nature of masculinity—what does it mean to be a man?

This scene is one of many that raise questions about Shakespeare's views on how a man should behave. Clearly the play criticizes Lord Capulet's capricious and violent mood swings, but does it offer a better model of masculinity? For example, does the play valorize Tybalt and Mercutio's fiery masculinity? Or does it suggest that Romeo's more subdued ways are preferable? Does Prince Escalus provide a good role model for someone trying to become an honourable man?

This scene seems to suggest that Mercutio's way is best. Only here does Romeo achieve Mercutio's brilliance and intensity; only in this scene is Romeo the dramatic equal of Mercutio. However, a later scene of the play shows another side of Mercutio, when he deliberately provokes a fight with Tybalt. The respect we have for his wit and passion will be tempered by his propensity for violence.

Matching wits

When Romeo encounters his friends, Mercutio again makes fun of his "drivelling love" (86). Mercutio puns on Romeo's name; without the "roe," his name becomes *meo* or *O me,* the cry of a melancholy lover (37). Mercutio criticizes famous literary lovers, such as Cleopatra and Petrarch's Laura, claiming that they were all lowborn or unchaste women. The opening section of this scene involves a series of witty, punning remarks between the three young men. These witty exchanges are important because they remind us that the play isn't only about love; the play also focuses on the dexterity of language.

Punning is possible only because words have more than one meaning. Because a word rarely has a singular meaning, you can never know exactly what other people mean when they communicate. For example, in saying that Romeo's wit is "very bitter sweeting; it is a most / sharp sauce," Mercutio refers to applesauce, a traditional accompaniment for goose (76–77). In the lines preceding this reference to applesauce, the men were playing with the idea of a wild-goose chase (see the note to line 68), and Romeo had called Mercutio a goose. Mercutio's words also apply to Romeo's saucy or sharp wit, with which Romeo is able to answer Mercutio jab for jab.

During their witty exchange, Mercutio is elated that Romeo has become his old, sociable self again: "[N]ow art thou Romeo; / now art thou what thou art, by art as well as by nature" (84–85). Romeo's Petrarchan melancholy has vanished because he has found true love with Juliet. However, recalling Juliet's earlier request that Romeo not be Romeo, we know that the question of identity is ambiguous in this play. Mercutio says "now art thou Romeo," but who is Romeo? A self-absorbed adolescent? The lover on the balcony with Juliet? The jester playing with Mercutio? A member of the Montague family?

A message for Juliet

In the midst of Romeo and Mercutio's conversation, the Nurse bustles into the scene, arriving with her man, Peter. Immediately, Mercutio capitalizes on the comic potential of her appearance. He mocks the Nurse's absurdly pompous demeanor, and a vulgar, witty conversation develops. Mercutio's bawdiness doesn't bother the Nurse—she is able to match him sexual innuendo for sexual innuendo. However, she doesn't enjoy being belittled, so, to pacify her, Romeo claims that Mercutio talks for the sake of hearing himself talk and often takes his jests too far.

The Nurse enhances Mercutio's wit and the general humour of the scene by peppering her conversation with malapropisms, words that are used inappropriately. For example, the Nurse says that she desires "some confidence" with Romeo, meaning that she wants to have a private conversation with him (120). As soon as Mercutio leaves, the Nurse reverts to her typical earthy and familiar tone, berating Mercutio for his coarse behaviour.

The Nurse warns Romeo not to mislead Juliet, who is young and innocent. But the Nurse doesn't need to worry—Romeo has serious intentions toward Juliet. He tells the Nurse to send Juliet to Friar Laurence's cell that afternoon so they can marry. Romeo also plans to send Juliet a rope ladder so he can sneak into her bedroom during the night and consummate their marriage. Romeo refers to this ladder as a "tackled stair" and claims that it'll bring him to the "high topgallant" of joy, another of the many nautical references used throughout the play

(178–179). Romeo will use the ladder to climb into Juliet's bedroom in "the secret night," emphasizing that these lovers share a private and secret relationship (180).

The Nurse tells Romeo about Paris's offer of marriage but adds that Juliet has no more interest in Paris than in a toad. The Nurse admits that she finds Paris the "properer man," but Juliet, of course, disagrees (193). Juliet links Romeo's name with rosemary because they both begin with an "R." The Nurse begins to say that a dog's name also begins with "R," but

Rosemary for remembrance.

stops herself, probably in a show of modesty before saying the word "arse." By linking Romeo's name with rosemary, traditionally the herb of remembrance, Juliet creates new meanings for his name. Juliet's choice of rosemary is interesting, because rosemary is one of the ambiguous herbs that the Friar mentions in the previous scene. Rosemary is used at both weddings and funerals and is, therefore, associated with both love and death.

The carnivalesque

Russian literary critic Mikhail Bakhtin identified a literary styling that he called *carnivalesque*. His ideas provide interesting insights on *Romeo and Juliet*. Bakhtin felt that many literary texts contain a double message—one that reflects the official culture and another that reflects popular or folk culture. Bakhtin associated the second message with carnival—not only Pre-Lenten celebrations such as Mardi Gras, but also other social occasions such as theatrical performances, fairs, and public executions. Because the language of carnival is the language of the lower classes, it often concerns issues of survival and, therefore, contains many images related to the body, eating, sex, and death.

Carnivalesque language often treats matters relating to the body or sex in a humorous manner. In addition, carnival language is often grotesque because it mixes sex and death, comedy and tragedy, and festivity and mourning in ways that are improper according to a society's official culture. The language that Mercutio, the Nurse, and many of the servants in the play use can be considered carnivalesque because it emphasizes vulgar or socially unacceptable views of the body and sex. Think back to the opening scene of the play, for example, when the servants Sampson and Gregory exchange bawdy dialogue about having sex with the Montague women.

Because its central characters experience a tragic love, *Romeo and Juliet* seems serious on its surface; however, many comic episodes punctuate its story line. Many readers of the play (and even the fictional Holden Caulfield in *The Catcher in the Rye*) believe that Mercutio and the Nurse are the play's two most interesting characters. The play suggests that the social values of the lower classes are more important than the official values that a society holds. In *Romeo and Juliet*, comedy and vulgarity seem as exciting as the more serious love plot.

A whirlwind courtship

This scene serves many functions. It continues the emphasis on language, both in the opening witticisms and with the final conversation between Romeo and the Nurse. The vulgar comic exchanges between Mercutio and Nurse contrast the seriousness of Romeo and Juliet's love talk in Act II, Scene 3. By alternating between sexual joking and serious conversations, *Romeo and Juliet* emphasizes that love balances the physical and the spiritual.

This scene reintroduces several characters we've seen before. Mercutio criticizes Tybalt for his fiery temper, but consider whether there are key similarities between the two men. Romeo is good friends with Mercutio, but the two men seem very different; what might be the source of their friendship?

This scene presents a new side of Romeo's personality: his sociable side. Although the previous scenes in the play showed Romeo's growing isolation from his friends and family, he renews his friendship with Mercutio in the first part of this scene. At the same time, Romeo's conversation with the Nurse reminds us that his secret relationship with Juliet ultimately will separate him from his friends.

Shakespeare also reminds us of the speed of Romeo and Juliet's courtship here—they have known each other for less than a day, yet they'll soon marry. Remember that Shakespeare shortened the play's time frame from several months (as it was portrayed in his sources) to several days. What effect does this condensation have on the meaning of the play? Why might Shakespeare want to emphasize speed? How does the emphasis on time's swift movement relate to other themes in the play?

Act II, Scene 5

Juliet impatiently awaits the return of the Nurse with word from Romeo. After much delay, the Nurse tells an exasperated Juliet that she is to wed Romeo at Friar Laurence's cell, and later that night, Romeo will climb through her bedroom window to celebrate their nuptials.

ACT II, SCENE 5
The same. Capulet's garden.

[Enter JULIET]

Juliet The clock struck nine when I did send the nurse;
In half an hour she promised to return.
Perchance she cannot meet him. That's not so.
O, she is lame! Love's heralds should be thoughts,
Which ten times faster glide than the sun's beams   5
Driving back shadows over low'ring hills.
Therefore do nimble-pinioned doves draw Love,
And therefore hath the wind-swift Cupid wings.
Now is the sun upon the highmost hill
Of this day's journey, and from nine till twelve   10
Is three long hours; yet she is not come.
Had she affections and warm youthful blood,
She would be as swift in motion as a ball;
My words would bandy her to my sweet love,
And his to me.   15
But old folks, many feign as they were dead—
Unwieldly, slow, heavy and pale as lead.
[Enter NURSE and PETER].
O God, she comes! O honey nurse, what news?
Hast thou met with him? Send thy man away.

Nurse Peter, stay at the gate. *[Exit PETER]*   20

Juliet Now, good sweet nurse—O Lord, why
      lookest thou sad?
Though news be sad, yet tell them merrily;
If good, thou shamest the music of sweet news
By playing it to me with so sour a face.

Nurse I am aweary, give me leave awhile.   25
Fie, how my bones ache! What a jaunce have I had!

NOTES

4.   *lame:* figuratively speaking, of course.

6.   *low'ring:* dark and threatening.

7.   *nimble-pinioned doves:* nimble-winged doves.

     doves: the Chariot of Venus was drawn by doves, which were sacred to her.

14. *bandy:* toss or hit (her).

18. *honey:* sweet.

26. *jaunce:* trudging about.

Juliet I would thou hadst my bones, and I thy news.
Nay, come, I pray thee speak. Good, good nurse, speak.

Nurse Jesu, what haste! Can you not stay awhile?
Do you not see that I am out of breath?   30

Juliet How art thou out of breath when thou hast breath
To say to me that thou art out of breath?
The excuse that thou dost make in this delay
Is longer than the tale thou dost excuse.
Is thy news good or bad? Answer to that.   35
Say either, and I'll stay the circumstance.
Let me be satisfied, is't good or bad?

Nurse Well, you have made a simple choice; you know
not how to choose a man. Romeo? No, not he. Though
his face be better than any man's, yet his leg excels all   40
men's; and for a hand and a foot, and a body, though
they be not to be talked on, yet they are past compare.
He is not the flower of courtesy, but, I'll warrant him,
as gentle as a lamb. Go thy ways, wench; serve God.
What, have you dined at home?   45

Juliet No, no. But all this did I know before.
What says he of our marriage? What of that?

Nurse Lord, how my head aches! What a head have I!
It beats as it would fall in twenty pieces.
My back a t' other side—ah, my back, my back!   50
Beshrew your heart for sending me about
To catch my death with jauncing up and down!

Juliet I' faith, I am sorry that thou art not well.
Sweet, sweet, sweet nurse, tell me, what says my love?

Nurse Your love says, like an honest gentleman,   55
and a courteous, and kind, and handsome,
and, I warrant, a virtuous—Where is your mother?

Juliet Where is my mother? Why, she is within.
Where should she be? How oddly thou repliest!
'Your love says, like an honest gentleman,   60
"Where is your mother?" '

Nurse   O God's Lady dear!
Are you so hot? Marry come up, I trow.
Is this the poultice for my aching bones?
Henceforward do your messages yourself.

---

34. *excuse:* excuse thyself from telling.

36. *circumstance:* details.

38. *simple:* stupid, foolish.

42. *compare:* comparison.

44. *serve God:* enough of that.

50. *a t' other:* on the other.

51. *Beshrew:* curse.

62. *God's Lady dear!:* The Virgin Mary.

63. *hot:* eager

come up, I trow: a colloquial expression of impatience, such as, "Come, come."

Juliet Here's such a coil! Come, what says Romeo?   65

Nurse Have you got leave to go to shrift today?

Juliet I have.

Nurse Then hie you hence to Friar Laurence' cell;
There stays a husband to make you a wife.
Now comes the wanton blood up in your cheeks: 70
They'll be in scarlet straight at any news.
Hie you to church; I must another way,
To fetch a ladder, by the which your love
Must climb a bird's nest soon when it is dark.
I am the drudge, and toil in your delight;   75
But you shall bear the burden soon at night.
Go; I'll to dinner; hie you to the cell.

Juliet Hie to high fortune! Honest nurse farewell.

[Exeunt]

65.   *coil:* trouble, fuss.

68.   *hie:* hasten.

71.   *be in scarlet:* blush (because Juliet has a guilty conscience).

COMMENTARY

As this scene begins, Juliet waits impatiently for the Nurse to return from her meeting with Romeo. Juliet sent the Nurse to find Romeo at 9 a.m., but she didn't meet with him until noon. We never learn what the Nurse did during the three hours, but we can speculate that she was probably bantering with friends along the way.

Juliet's impatience

Juliet's anxiety shows throughout her opening soliloquy. She wishes that the Nurse could complete her tasks more quickly. Lovers shouldn't have to suffer such delays at the hands of old, lame messengers such as the Nurse. Instead, Juliet thinks that lovers' thoughts should fly "ten times faster" than the sun's rays, so that Romeo's words could come directly to her and hers to him (5). In the Friar's garden, we saw how impatient Romeo was for the wedding when he insisted that the Friar perform the ceremony that day. We now see that Juliet's impatience equals Romeo's.

Like Romeo, who was forced to listen to the Friar's moralizing before he agreed to perform the marriage, Juliet must suffer through the Nurse's rambling complaints about her aching body before she learns of the wedding plans. Together, by emphasizing Romeo and Juliet's anxiety and impatience, these scenes provide you with a sense of their love's urgency. The frenzied and secretive nature of their courtship, combined with the immediacy of their plans, generates a feeling of suspense in both Juliet and the audience.

The Nurse teases Juliet by withholding what she knows about the wedding arrangements. Another comic scene results when the Nurse claims that she can't talk because her bones ache and she's out of breath. Juliet becomes more and more frustrated as the Nurse toys with her curiosity. The Nurse isn't being malicious—she realizes how eager Juliet is to see her lover again—but she likes playfully teasing her young charge.

When Juliet insists on being told the news, whether good or bad, the Nurse catalogues Romeo's attractive appearance in response. Always attentive to a man's looks, the Nurse jokes that Juliet doesn't know how to choose a man. Yet the Nurse finds his face, legs, hands, feet, and body beyond compare. The Nurse's list of Romeo's attributes provides an ironic echo of Juliet's analysis of Romeo's body when she wondered which body part identified him as a Montague (II.2.40–47). Similarly, the Nurse's suggestion in line 43 that Romeo isn't "the flower of courtesy" parallels Juliet's suggestion that both a rose and Romeo "by any other word would smell as sweet" (II.2.44).

The marriage message

When Juliet asks about the wedding, the Nurse responds that her head aches. After much delay on the Nurse's part, she finally realizes that Juliet is becoming angry, so she ends her game and delivers Romeo's message. In a succinct manner that contrasts with her previous verbosity, she tells Juliet that Romeo awaits her at Friar Laurence's cell where he's ready to marry her. She also tells Juliet that while the ceremony is under way, the Nurse will fetch a rope ladder to allow Romeo to climb into the "bird's nest," or Juliet's bedroom, that night (74).

This scene ends with typically comic and earthy jesting by the Nurse. The Nurse first teasingly complains about her responsibility for preparing both the wedding and the honeymoon. Although the Nurse toils to prepare the lovers' delight, Juliet will ultimately "bear the burden" of this pleasure, meaning that she'll bear Romeo's weight in bed and that she'll soon be pregnant (76). This parting jest provides another comic interlude that contrasts with the tragic scenes that soon follow.

Act II, Scene 6

Juliet arrives at Friar Laurence's cell to find an elated Romeo revelling in his unbounded vigour. Juliet expresses a reserved excitement, and the Friar is fearful that such an impulsive marriage could result in doom.

ACT II, SCENE 6
The same. Friar Laurence's cell.

[Enter FRIAR LAURENCE and ROMEO]

Friar So smile the heavens upon this holy act
That after-hours with sorrow chide us not!

Romeo Amen, amen! But come what sorrow can,
It cannot countervail the exchange of joy
That one short minute gives me in her sight.   5
Do thou but close our hands with holy words,
Then love-devouring death do what he dare—
It is enough I may but call her mine.

Friar These violent delights have violent ends
And in their triumph die, like fire and powder,   10
Which, as they kiss, consume. The sweetest honey
Is loathsome in his own deliciousness
And in the taste confounds the appetite.
Therefore love moderately: long love doth so;
Too swift arrives as tardy as too slow.   15
[Enter JULIET]
Here comes the lady. O, so light a foot
Will ne'er wear out the everlasting flint.
A lover may bestride the gossamer
That idles in the wanton summer air,
And yet not fall; so light is vanity.   20

Juliet Good even to my ghostly confessor.

Friar Romeo shall thank thee, daughter, for us both.

Juliet As much to him, else is his thanks too much.

Romeo Ah, Juliet, if the measure of thy joy
Be heaped like mine, and that thy skill be more   25
To blazon it, then sweeten with thy breath
This neighbour air, and let rich music's tongue
Unfold the imagined happiness that both
Receive in either by this dear encounter.

NOTES

1.   *smile the heavens:* may heaven favour.

2.   *after-hours:* the future.

4.   *countervail:* outweigh.

     the exchange of joy: the joy for which it is taken in return.

12. *Is loathsome in his own deliciousness:* It is so sweet that it soon becomes sickly.

14. *doth so:* that is, love moderately.

15. *Too swift . . . slow:* in the words of the proverb, "more haste, less speed."

17. *wear out:* outlast.

18. *gossamer:* long, single thread of a spider's web.

20. *vanity:* emptiness.

21. *confessor:* priest who listens to confessions.

22. *thank thee:* return your greeting. The Friar says that he will leave Romeo to say good evening (or thank you), implying that Romeo is anxious to speak to her.

23. *As much:* refers back to "good even"—as much as to say "good evening."

26. *blazon it:* spread it abroad, broadcast it.

27. *neighbour:* neighbouring.

     rich music's tongue: Juliet's voice.

28. *imagined happiness:* mental, imaginative happiness.

Juliet Conceit, more rich in matter than in words,   30
Brags of his substance, not of ornament.
They are but beggars that can count their worth;
But my true love is grown to such excess
I cannot sum up sum of half my wealth.

Friar Come, come with me, and we will make short work;   35
For, by your leaves, you shall not stay alone
Till Holy Church incorporate two in one.

[Exeunt]

30.   *Conceit:* thought, fancy, imagination.

31.   *ornament:* show. Juliet says that the real thing means more to her than any words can say.

36.   *by your leaves:* if you will obey my orders.

COMMENTARY

Romeo and Juliet's wedding hour has finally arrived. As this scene opens, Romeo waits impatiently in Friar Laurence's room. The Friar prophetically prays that the heavens will smile on the marriage, no matter what sorrow later befalls the couple. Rather than presenting a carefree image of marriage in this scene, Shakespeare intertwines images of death with love and sorrow with joy.

Although tragedy waits in the wings of his marriage, Romeo isn't worried about sorrow. He feels that nothing can diminish the joy he feels in Juliet's presence, even if it lasts for only "one short minute" (5). Romeo ominously challenges "love-devouring death" to do what it dare; he feels that nothing can take Juliet from him (7).

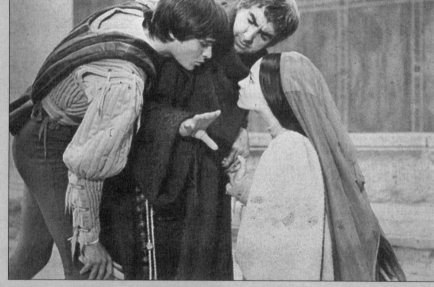

Leonard Whiting and Olivia Hussey star as Romeo and Juliet in the 1968 film.
Everett Collection

Romeo's bravado and bold statements once again upset the Friar. The Friar fears that only violence can result from Romeo's excessive delight. In fact, the Friar predicts that a quickly ignited love like Romeo and Juliet's will "die, like fire and powder, / Which, as they kiss, consume" (10–11). According to the Friar, too much of a good thing ultimately becomes "loathsome" (12). Opposing the impetuosity of youth, the older and wiser Friar counsels cautious and moderate love. But the Friar's cautions are not necessarily reflected in his own actions; after all, the marriage can occur only with his aid.

When Juliet arrives at the Friar's room, the Friar predicts that Juliet's lightness will result in an early death. Romeo uses rich imagery to describe his love for Juliet, which "blazon[s]" and unfolds "imagined happiness" (26, 28). But Juliet is unimpressed with his verbal displays. Like the Friar, she thinks Romeo's verbal excess connotes fake, literary love rather than true, deep love. She believes that "substance" is more important than "ornament"; she prefers a plainer speech that contains more meaning (31). Indeed, silence best captures the spiritual significance of this moment for Juliet. Her own love has grown so excessive that she can't express it with words. Language is limited and can't always capture the truth of our feelings.

In this scene, Romeo is again chided for trying to be too poetic—an affectation that Juliet believes reveals Romeo's superficiality. Although Juliet tried to describe her "true-love passion" in words earlier in the play, she now believes that words are inadequate to set boundaries on the "wealth" of her feelings (34).

Notes

Notes

COLES NOTES TOTAL STUDY EDITION

ROMEO AND JULIET
ACT III

Juliet *'Romeo is banished'—to speak that word*
Is father, mother, Tybalt, Romeo, Juliet,
All slain, all dead. 'Romeo is banished'—
There is no end, no limit, measure, bound,
In that word's death; no words can that woe sound.

Act III, Scene 1

Mercutio and Tybalt fight in the public square, and Romeo, who has secretly married Juliet, tries to stop them. Tybalt kills Mercutio, and Romeo exacts revenge by taking Tybalt's life. The Prince, along with Montague, Capulet, and their wives, arrives and hears accounts of what happened. The Prince banishes Romeo under penalty of death.

ACT III, SCENE 1
Verona. A public place.

[Enter MERCUTIO, BENVOLIO, and Men]

Benvolio I pray thee, good Mercutio, let's retire.
The day is hot, the Capulets abroad,
And, if we meet, we shall not 'scape a brawl,
For now, these hot days, is the mad blood stirring.

Mercutio Thou are like one of these fellows that, when 5
he enters the confines of a tavern, claps me his sword
upon the table and says 'God send me no need of thee!'
and by the operation of the second cup draws him on the
drawer, when indeed there is no need.

Benvolio Am I like such a fellow?   10

Mercutio Come, come, thou art as hot a Jack in thy
mood as any in Italy; and as soon moved to be moody,
and as soon moody to be moved.

Benvolio And what to?

Mercutio Nay, and there were two such, we should 15
have none shortly, for one would kill the other. Thou!
why, thou wilt quarrel with a man that hath a hair
more or a hair less in his beard than thou hast. Thou
wilt quarrel with a man for cracking nuts, having no
other reason but because thou hast hazel eyes. What 20
eye but such an eye would spy out such a quarrel? Thy
head is as full of quarrels as an egg is full of
meat; and yet thy head hath been beaten as addle as
an egg for quarrelling. Thou hast quarrelled with a man for
coughing in the street, because he hath wakened thy 25
dog that hath lain asleep in the sun. Didst thou not fall
out with a tailor for wearing his new doublet before
Easter? With another for tying his new shoes with old
riband? And yet thou wilt tutor me from quarrelling!

NOTES

1. *retire:* go away from the crowds.
2. *abroad:* out and about.
4. *blood:* temper, fury.
6. *me:* let me tell you.
8. *by the operation of the second cup:* by the time the second cup of liquor has worked upon him.
9. *drawer:* waiter or barman.
11. *Jack:* fellow.
12. *moved:* provoked or incited.
    moody: bad tempered.
14. *what to?:* provoked to what?
15. *two:* Mercutio interprets Benvolio's "to" as "two."
20. *hazel:* the colour of hazel nuts.
23. *meat:* food, not necessarily flesh. (As in the phrase "meat and drink.")
    addle: mixed up and, perhaps, rotten.
26. *fall out with:* quarrel with a friend.
27. *doublet:* close-fitting body garment, with or without sleeves, worn by men from the 14th to the 18th century.
29. *tutor me from quarrelling:* teach me how to avoid getting into quarrels.

Benvolio An I were so apt to quarrel as thou art, any   30
man should buy the fee simple of my life for an hour
and a quarter.

Mercutio The fee simple? O simple!

[Enter TYBALT and others]

Benvolio By my head, here come the Capulets.

Mercutio By my heel, I care not.   35

Tybalt Follow me close, for I will speak to them.
Gentlemen, good-den. A word with one of you.

Mercutio And but one word with one of us?
Couple it with something; make it a word and a blow.

Tybalt You shall find me apt enough to that, sir, an   40
you will give me occasion.

Mercutio Could you not take some occasion
without giving?

Tybalt Mercutio, thou consortest with Romeo.

Mercutio Consort? What, dost thou make us minstrels?   45
An thou make minstrels of us, look to hear
Nothing but discords. Here's my fiddlestick; here's
that shall make you dance. Zounds, consort!

Benvolio We talk here in the public haunt of men.
Either withdraw unto some private place,   50
Or reason coldly of your grievances,
Or else depart. Here all eyes gaze on us.

Mercutio Men's eyes were made to look, and let them gaze.
I will not budge for no man's pleasure, I.

[Enter ROMEO]

Tybalt Well, peace be with you, sir. Here comes my man.   55

Mercutio But I'll be hanged, sir, if he wear your livery.
Marry, go before to field, he'll be your follower!
Your worship in that sense may call him man.

Tybalt Romeo, the love I bear thee can afford
No better term than this: thou art a villain.   60

Romeo Tybalt, the reason that I have to love thee
Doth much excuse the appertaining rage

---

31.   *fee simple:* complete legal rights over (by purchase).

31-32.   *for an hour and a quarter:* implying that by the end of that time he would be dead (dramatic irony).

33.   *simple!:* foolish!

37.   *good-den:* good evening (means good afternoon).

41.   *occasion:* excuse.

43.   *giving:* being given one.

44.   *consortest:* keep company with, or keep in tune with.

45.   *Consort?:* the regular word for harmony among players or for an actual group of fiddlers. Looking for a quarrel, Mercutio gives the word its worst sense—wandering fiddler.

45.   *make us minstrels:* call us vagabond fiddlers.

47.   *fiddlestick:* his sword.

48.   *Zounds:* a contraction of the oath, "By God's wounds" (i.e., on the cross).

51.   *reason coldly:* work out the solution without passion.

56.   *wear your livery:* be your manservant.

57.   *field:* battleground.

58.   *Your worship:* said with great sarcasm.

59.   *love:* used ironically, because Tybalt thinks Romeo is a villain.

      afford: allow.

61.   *the reason . . . thee:* his marriage to one of Tybalt's family.

62.   *excuse the appertaining rage:* excuse me from the rage which would become such a greeting.

To such a greeting. Villain am I none.
Therefore farewell. I see thou knowest me not.

Tybalt Boy, this shall not excuse the injuries   65
That thou hast done me; therefore turn and draw.

Romeo I do protest I never injured thee,
But love thee better than thou canst devise
Till thou shalt know the reason of my love;
And so, good Capulet, which name I tender   70
As dearly as mine own, be satisfied.

Mercutio O calm, dishonourable, vile submission!
Alla stoccata carries it away. *[Draws]*
Tybalt, you ratcatcher, will you walk?

Tybalt What wouldst thou have with me?   75

Mercutio Good King of Cats, nothing but one of your
nine lives. That I mean to make bold withal, and,
as you shall use me hereafter, dry-beat the rest of the eight.
Will you pluck your sword out of his pilcher by the ears?
Make haste, lest mine be about your ears ere it be out.   80

Tybalt I am for you. *[Draws]*

Romeo Gentle Mercutio, put thy rapier up.

Mercutio Come, sir, your passado! *[They fight]*

Romeo Draw, Benvolio; beat down their weapons.
Gentlemen, for shame! forbear this outrage!   85
Tybalt, Mercutio, the Prince expressly hath
Forbid this bandying in Verona streets.
Hold Tybalt! Good Mercutio!

*[TYBALT under ROMEO'S arm thrusts MERCUTIO in,
and flies with his Followers]*

Mercutio   I am hurt.
A plague o' both your houses! I am sped.
Is he gone and hath nothing?

Benvolio   What, art thou hurt?   90

Mercutio Ay, ay, a scratch, a scratch. Marry, 'tis enough.
Where is my page? Go, villain, fetch a surgeon.
[Exit Page]

Romeo Courage, man. The hurt cannot be much.

---

64. *knowest me not:* do not know my feelings towards you.

65. *Boy:* here a term of contempt.

injuries: insults (by coming to the mask uninvited—as Tybalt thinks).

68. *devise:* make out, imagine.

73. *Alla stoccata carries it away:* The sword gets away with it. (Alla stoccata is Italian for "with the stoccado"; the stoccado is a thrust in fencing.)

74. *ratcatcher:* because he has a name often given to cats.

will you walk?: to a quiet place where we may fight a duel.

77. *make bold withal:* take, make free with.

78. *as you shall use me hereafter:* according to the way in which you treat me after I have taken one of your nine lives, i.e., the way I feel after fighting with you.

dry-beat: beat hard without drawing blood (liquid).

79. *his pichler:* its case, scabbard.

ears: hilt. "By the ears" was a contemptuous expression in Shakespeare's day.

81. *for:* ready for.

83. *passado:* forward thrust with the sword, one foot being advanced at the same time (*pas* is French for footstep).

87. *bandying:* exchanging blows.

89. *sped:* finished with.

90. *hath nothing:* is unhurt.

92. *villain:* affectionate use of the term among friends.

Mercutio No, 'tis not so deep as a well, nor so wide as
a church door; but 'tis enough, 'twill serve. Ask for   95
me to-morrow, and you shall find me a grave man. I am
peppered, I warrant, for this world. A plague o' both
your houses! Zounds, a dog, a rat, a mouse, a cat, to
scratch a man to death! a braggart, a rogue, a villain,
that fights by the book of arithmetic! Why the devil   100
came you between us? I was hurt under your arm.

Romeo I thought all for the best.

Mercutio Help me into some house, Benvolio,
Or I shall faint. A plague o' both your houses!
They have made worms' meat of me. I have it,   105
And soundly too. Your houses!

[Exit, supported by BENVOLIO]

Romeo This gentleman, the Prince's near ally,
My very friend, hath got this mortal hurt
In my behalf—my reputation stained
With Tybalt's slander—Tybalt, that an hour   110
Hath been my cousin. O sweet Juliet,
Thy beauty hath made me effeminate
And in my temper soft'ned valour's steel!

[Enter BENVOLIO]

Benvolio O Romeo, Romeo, brave Mercutio is dead!
That gallant spirit hath aspired the clouds,   115
Which too untimely here did scorn the earth.

Romeo This day's black fate on moe days doth depend;
This but begins the woe others must end.

[Enter TYBALT]

Benvolio Here comes the furious Tybalt back again.

Romeo Alive in triumph, and Mercutio slain?   120
Away to heaven respective lenity,
And fire-eyed fury be my conduct now!
Now, Tybalt, take the 'villain' back again
That late thou gavest me; for Mercutio's soul
Is but a little way above our heads,   125
Staying for thine to keep him company.
Either thou or I, or both, must go with him.

Tybalt Thou, wretched boy, that didst consort him here,

97.	*peppered:* done for.
100.	*by the book of arithmetic:* according to a set plan. Mercutio has previously said in his fight with Tybalt that he "keeps time, distance, and proportion."
105.	*I have it:* I've had it.
107.	*ally:* kinsman.
108.	*very:* (adjective) true.
110.	*With Tybalt's slander:* "Thou art a villain."
113.	*temper:* temperament, punning on the "temper" of steel.
115.	*aspired:* soared to, risen to.
117.	*on moe days doth depend:* hangs over other days (in the future).
118.	*others:* other woes.
121.	*respective lenity:* tolerance that respects the difference between persons.
122.	*conduct:* guide.
123.	*take the 'villain' back again:* take back the word 'villain'.

Shalt with him hence.

Romeo   This shall determine that.

[They fight. TYBALT falls]

Benvolio Romeo, away, be gone!   130
The citizens are up, and Tybalt slain.
Stand not amazed. The Prince will doom thee death
If thou art taken. Hence, be gone, away!

Romeo O, I am fortune's fool!

Benvolio   Why dost thou stay?

[Exit ROMEO. Enter Citizens]

Citizen Which way ran he that killed Mercutio?   135
Tybalt, that murderer, which way ran he?

Benvolio There lies that Tybalt.

Citizen   Up, sir, go with me.
I charge thee in the Prince's name obey.

*[Enter PRINCE (attended), old MONTAGUE, CAPULET,
their WIVES, and all]*

Prince Where are the vile beginners of this fray?

Benvolio O noble Prince, I can discover all   140
The unlucky manage of this fatal brawl.
There lies the man, slain by young Romeo,
That slew thy kinsman, brave Mercutio.

Capulet's Wife Tybalt, my cousin! O my brother's child!
O Prince! O husband! O, the blood is spilled   145
Of my dear kinsman! Prince, as thou art true,
For blood of ours shed blood of Montague.
O cousin, cousin!

Prince Benvolio, who began this bloody fray?

Benvolio Tybalt, here slain, whom Romeo's hand did slay. 150
Romeo, that spoke him fair, bid him bethink
How nice the quarrel was, and urged withal
Your high displeasure. All this—uttered
With gentle breath, calm look, knees humbly bowed—
Could not take truce with the unruly spleen   155
Of Tybalt deaf to peace, but that he tilts
With piercing steel at bold Mercutio's breast;

---

131.   *up:* in arms, in a rabble.

132.   *amazed:* stupefied.

134.   *fortune's fool:* the plaything of luck.

141.   *manage:* course or management.

152.   *nice:* trivial.

      withal: in addition.

155.   *unruly spleen:* uncontrolled anger.

156.   *but that he tilts:* so that he should not tilt (tilt meaning to thrust at).

Who, all as hot, turns deadly point to point,
And, with a martial scorn, with one hand beats
Cold death aside and with the other sends   160
It back to Tybalt, whose dexterity
Retorts it. Romeo he cries aloud,
'Hold, friends! friends, part!' and swifter than his tongue,
His agile arm beats down their fatal points,
And 'twixt them rushes; underneath whose arm   165
An envious thrust from Tybalt hit the life
Of stout Mercutio, and then Tybalt fled;
But by and by comes back to Romeo,
Who had but newly entertained revenge,
And to't they go like lightning; for, ere I   170
Could draw to part them, was stout Tybalt slain;
And, as he fell, did Romeo turn and fly.
This is the truth, or let Benvolio die.

Capulet's Wife He is a kinsman to the Montague;
Affection makes him false, he speaks not true.   175
Some twenty of them fought in this black strife,
And all those twenty could but kill one life.
I beg for justice, which thou, Prince, must give.
Romeo slew Tybalt; Romeo must not live.

Prince Romeo slew him; he slew Mercutio   180
Who now the price of his dear blood doth owe?

Montague Not Romeo, Prince; he was Mercutio's friend;
His fault concludes but what the law should end,
The life of Tybalt.

Prince   And for that offense
Immediately we do exile him hence.   185
I have an interest in your hate's proceeding,
My blood for your rude brawls doth lie a-bleeding;
But I'll amerce you with so strong a fine
That you shall all repent the loss of mine.
I will be deaf to pleading and excuses;   190
Nor tears, nor prayers shall purchase out abuses.
Therefore use none. Let Romeo hence in haste,
Else, when he is found, that hour is his last.
Bear hence this body, and attend our will.
Mercy but murders. pardoning those that kill.   195

[Exit, with others]

---

158. *hot:* hot-tempered.

160. *Cold death:* Tybalt's sword.

162. *Retorts it:* turns it back.

166. *envious:* spiteful, malicious.

169. *newly entertained:* recently thought of.

181. *Who now the price of his dear blood doth owe?:* Who must pay for Tybalt's death?

183. *concludes:* brings to an end (by killing).

186. *your hate's proceeding:* the consequences of your feud.

187. *My blood:* Mercutio was the Prince's kinsman.

188. *amerce:* punish.

191. *purchase out:* buy a pardon for.

194. *attend our will:* wait on "us" to do what "we" require. Or, perhaps, pay attention to what "we" have decided.

195. *Mercy . . . kill:* Giving pardon to murderers only causes more murders to take place.

COMMENTARY

While many of the scenes in Act II have a comic tone, the mood of the play shifts in Act III. The juxtaposition between the peaceful wedding ceremony of Act II, Scene 6 and the violence of this scene is shocking.

As this scene begins, Benvolio, Mercutio, and several of Romeo's other friends walk through the streets. It's a hot Monday afternoon and Benvolio wants to go inside to avoid a fight with the Capulets, because he believes that the hot weather sets people's "mad blood stirring" (4). Mercutio ironically teases Benvolio for being a moody man who easily gets into fights for the most inconsequential reasons (because someone has hazel eyes or too much hair in his beard). Of course, Mercutio is only joking. As we see later in this scene, Mercutio is the real hothead, while Benvolio is the calmest and most diplomatic of Romeo's friends.

"A word and a blow"

In the middle of this playful conversation, Tybalt, and his friends enter. Tybalt immediately confronts Romeo's friends, and Mercutio responds antagonistically. In fact, Mercutio introduces the idea of violence, demanding that Tybalt give them "a word and a blow" after Tybalt civilly asks for "a word" with one of Romeo's friends (39, 37).

This scene mixes the language and imagery of fencing with that of music as Mercutio quibbles with Tybalt's statement that Mercutio "consortest with Romeo" (44). Mercutio purposely misinterprets Tybalt, suggesting that the word "consort" implies that Romeo and his friends are lower-class minstrels. Because minstrels were often homeless wanderers in Early Modern England, they were not viewed as stable or respectable. Therefore, Mercutio is suggesting that Tybalt has insulted both him and Romeo by linking them with these disreputable characters.

Mercutio then plays with images of fencing and music (a combination of images that continues from II.4.20–23), telling Tybalt that his "fiddlestick" (his sword) will surely make Mercutio "dance" (47–48). Benvolio

tries to calm Mercutio down by saying that they shouldn't fight in a public place; he urges Mercutio to "reason coldly"(51). As we know, Mercutio's "mercurial" name associates him with passion and energy; he is a man more interested in hot verbal play than in cold logic. Not surprisingly, Mercutio refuses to follow Benvolio's advice, not caring if everyone in the square looks at them. The significance of this scene is that Tybalt doesn't pursue the fight with Mercutio; instead, Mercutio is the first to reach for his "fiddlestick" and provoke violence.

Romeo arrives, and Tybalt immediately focuses on him, saying politely to Mercutio, "Well, peace be with you sir. Here comes my man" (55). Tybalt has a strict code of honour; he wants revenge on Romeo for his actions at the Capulet party but doesn't want to participate in a random fight with Mercutio. Again, Mercutio purposely misinterprets the meaning of Tybalt's words. Mercutio says, "I'll be hanged, sir, if he wear your livery," indicating that he interpreted Tybalt's use of "man" to mean "manservant" (56). Tybalt continues to ignore Mercutio's baiting but calls Romeo a "villain" (60).

Romeo attempts peace

For Romeo, the entry into this infraction must be jarring. Just returning from his peaceful marriage to Juliet, Romeo doesn't want to fight. In fact, he can't be angry with his new kinsman. Romeo says to Tybalt, "[T]he reason that I have to love thee / Doth much excuse the appertaining rage / To such a greeting," and he says that Tybalt "knowest [him] not" (61–64). Because neither Tybalt nor Romeo's friends know about the secret wedding ceremony between Romeo and Juliet, they don't know how to interpret Romeo's puzzling speech.

Here again is a clash between appearance and reality; while Tybalt looks at Romeo and sees an enemy, Romeo knows that they are now linked by his recent marriage to Juliet. Romeo's identity as enemy has changed, but Tybalt doesn't know it. As Juliet suggested in the balcony scene (Act II, Scene 2), identities constantly shift. Romeo feels he is no longer a "Montague" because his identity is now merged with Juliet's; therefore, he no longer wants to feud with the Capulets, who are now legally his kinsmen. Tybalt insists upon fighting, but Romeo states that he loves Tybalt "better than [he] canst devise" and that "Capulet" is now a name which he loves as dearly as his own (68).

Mercutio becomes angry with Romeo's "vile submission" to Tybalt; he sees Romeo's kindness as proof that his friend's character has become feminized through obsession with love (72). Like Tybalt, Mercutio knows nothing about Romeo's recent marriage to Juliet; therefore, he is also unaware of the truth of Romeo's statement.

Always the jester, Mercutio calls Tybalt a "rat-catcher," referring to his title as "Prince of Cats" (II.4.19), and claims that he wants one of Tybalt's nine lives (74). Mercutio says that depending on how he feels after taking one life, he may spare the other eight or he may thrash them all. This exchange emphasizes Mercutio's wit and also shows the violence of his temper as he finally goads Tybalt into fighting. The exchange also emphasizes the extreme difference in mood between Romeo and his friend; Mercutio wants to "[m]ake haste" and fight, but Romeo urges "[g]entle Mercutio" to put away his sword (80, 82). Mercutio rejects Romeo's suggestion and instead asks for Tybalt's "passado," the fencing move for which he is famous (83).

Romeo tries to break up the fight, reminding the men of the Prince's orders and stepping between Tybalt and Mercutio. Tybalt thrusts his sword under Romeo's arm and into Mercutio. Tybalt and his friends run away, but Mercutio is hurt. Mercutio curses both Tybalt and Romeo with a "plague" on their houses, refusing to recognize his own role in causing this fatal mishap (88). His curse foreshadows the impending tragedy soon to befall both the Montagues and Capulets.

Mercutio's death

Although Mercutio believes that his downfall has been caused by someone else's ancient feud, his death actually results directly from his own hatred for Tybalt. Mercutio wasn't forced to quarrel with Tybalt because of the feud. Instead, he deliberately provoked Tybalt. In *Romeo and Juliet,* tragedy often befalls characters because of

the mysterious and unreasonable working of fate. However, in Mercutio's case, death is the direct result of personal action; neither fate nor the feud plays a significant role.

Even on the brink of death, Mercutio maintains his sense of humour, saying that tomorrow he'll be "a grave man" (96). He argues that Tybalt "fights by the book of arithmetic" (the book of fencing), just as Romeo, according to Juliet in Act I, kissed "by th' book" and Paris is a book that Lady Capulet wants Juliet to read (100). Mercutio, like Juliet, believes in the powers of imagination and in creating your own rules. This aspect of his personality is fundamental to his criticism of Romeo; not knowing about Romeo's new, boundary-breaking love for Juliet, Mercutio believes that Romeo is still following the rules of Petrarchanism. The dual aspects of Mercutio's character—his passionate creativity and equally passionate violence—suggest that both social and personal transformations are often accompanied by turmoil.

Mercutio claims that Romeo caused his death by stepping between him and Tybalt. Romeo accepts the guilt for Mercutio's death and believes, as Mercutio would probably argue, that love has made him "-effeminate / And in [his] temper soft'ned valour's steel" (112–113). He feels deeply ashamed of his failure to defend Mercutio, and the play again questions what it means to be a man. Was Romeo's attempt to reconcile with Tybalt valorous? Or should he have fought the duel with Tybalt?

Earlier in the play, Mercutio seemed more interesting than Romeo: he was witty and exciting while Romeo was dull and depressed. Yet this scene presents a dark side of Mercutio's personality. Many critics wonder if Mercutio's death serves a necessary purpose in the play. Did Shakespeare kill him off because of his exceptional vitality, which threatened to make Mercutio (rather than Romeo or Juliet) the centre of the play? That doesn't seem probable.

Mercutio's death serves as a reminder that extreme and random violence isn't acceptable. Romeo's friends and elders imply that fighting and violence are the marks of true masculinity, but the play questions this notion and suggests that it needs to change. Just as the

Friar asks Romeo to subdue his violent love for Juliet, the play asks its viewers (and readers) to seek moderation in all things rather than passionately pursuing violence. The fact that calm, diplomatic Benvolio survives this scene while fiery Mercutio and Tybalt die is significant. Perhaps the Prince, who is even more powerfully opposed to civil violence than Benvolio, is the true exemplar of masculinity in the play. He tries to create positive change in Verona with the least amount of bloodshed.

As Romeo continues to wonder if he has done the right thing by not fighting Tybalt, Benvolio reenters the scene to announce that Mercutio is dead. The day, which began with the happy union of Juliet and Romeo, has quickly taken a dark turn. Romeo recognizes that the day's "black fate" hasn't yet ended; Mercutio's

death has simply begun "the woe others must end" (117–118). Like his friend, Romeo believes that this tragedy was driven by fate rather than by Mercutio's personal choices.

Romeo's revenge

Tybalt returns and Romeo vows to forget his leniency, even for his new cousin; his mood is now "fire-eyed fury" (122). Romeo and Tybalt fight, and Tybalt dies. Benvolio urges Romeo to leave before the Prince arrives and sentences him to death. Romeo again claims to be "fortune's fool"; he's become the victim of fate, just as the first prologue to the play announces (134).

Romeo runs away and the Prince, the Montagues, and the Capulets enter. Benvolio explains to the Prince what has happened. He blames Tybalt for beginning the fight, selectively forgetting that Mercutio provoked Tybalt. He also lets the Prince know that Romeo tried to stop the fight by reminding his friends of the Prince's warning. Lady Capulet champions Tybalt and argues that Benvolio is lying to defend Romeo because they are both Montagues.

Banishment

Rather than asking for Romeo's life, the Prince leniently exiles him. Each family must also pay a large fine, which is not subject to appeal. The Prince is personally hurt by the feud, because Mercutio was the Prince's kinsman. Nothing can change the Prince's mind about Romeo's sentence. He declares that if Romeo is found within the city's walls, he'll be killed.

Tybalt's body remains on the stage throughout the speeches by Benvolio and the Prince and is removed only when the Prince leaves. The body's presence on stage throughout this scene reminds us sharply of the tragic turn that the play has taken.

This scene marks the turning point in the play. While many previous scenes were lighthearted and even comical, events have now turned tragic with the deaths of Tybalt and Mercutio and the banishment of Romeo. Before these events, a happy solution to Romeo and Juliet's situation may have been found. If the secret marriage between Romeo and Juliet were publicly announced, perhaps the Montagues and Capulets would have put aside their warring ways.

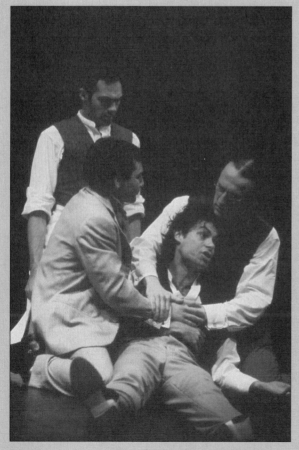

Dermot Kerrigan as Tybalt in 1995 Royal Shakespeare Company production. Henrietta Butler/PAL

While many readers wish that Shakespeare had plotted the play in a more hopeful way, these changes would completely alter his message. As the Friar has suggested, sometimes seemingly bad things can result in positive change. In Verona, tragedy seems to be the only thing that will create a lasting societal transformation, because the feud has become so deeply engrained.

The foreshadowing of even more ominous events continues in this scene. Juliet, Romeo, and Friar Laurence all intuited in Act II, Scene 6 that "love-devouring death" may result from their marriage. Mercutio's curse on the houses of both Montague and Capulet only heightens our sense of approaching doom.

Shakespeare creates much sympathy for Romeo in this scene. Although the audience may have distrusted Romeo's quick love for Juliet earlier in the play, the depth of his affection for her is now obvious. He is willing to stain his own reputation to maintain peace with Tybalt. Unlike his friend Mercutio, Romeo attempts to avoid violence. When he kills Tybalt, he does so only because he feels he must revenge Mercutio's death.

Act III, Scene 2

The Nurse brings tragic news to Juliet, and Juliet at first believes that Romeo has been killed. When she learns about Tybalt's death and Romeo's banishment, she is filled with grief. She sends the Nurse to the Friar's cell to ask Romeo to see her one last time.

ACT III, SCENE 2
The same. Capulet's orchard.

[Enter JULIET alone]

Juliet Gallop apace, you fiery-footed steeds,
　Towards Phoebus' lodging! Such a wagoner
　As Phaeton would whip you to the west
　And bring in cloudy night immediately.
　Spread thy close curtain, love-performing night,　　5
　That runaways' eyes may wink, and Romeo
　Leap to these arms untalked of and unseen.
　Lovers can see to do their amorous rites
　By their own beauties; or, if love be blind,
　It best agrees with night. Come, civil night,　　10
　Thou sober-suited matron, all in black,
　And learn me how to lose a winning match,
　Played for a pair of stainless maidenhoods.
　Hood my unmanned blood, bating in my cheeks,
　With thy black mantle till strange love grow bold,　　15
　Think true love acted simple modesty.
　Come, night; come, Romeo; come, thou day in night;
　For thou wilt lie upon the wings of night
　Whiter than new snow upon a raven's back.
　Come, gentle night; come, loving, black-browed night,　　20
　Give me my Romeo; and, when he shall die,
　Take him and cut him out in little stars,
　And he will make the face of heaven so fine
　That all the world will be in love with night
　And pay no worship to the garish sun.　　25
　O, I have bought the mansion of a love,
　But not possessed it; and though I am sold,
　Not yet enjoyed. So tedious is this day
　As is the night before some festival

NOTES

1.　*steeds:* horses (of the sun).

2.　*Phoebus:* sun-god.
　　wagoner: driver.

3.　*Phaeton:* son of Helios (the sun) who tried to drive his father's chariot; he so nearly set the earth on fire that Zeus had to strike him dead with a thunderbolt.

5.　*love-performing:* making it easy for lovers.

6.　*wink:* close, be unable to see.

10.　*civil:* sober, serious.

12.　*lose a winning match:* gain, by surrendering, a husband for myself.

14.　*Hood my unmanned blood:* a metaphor from falconry. There is a pun on "unmanned."

15.　*strange:* unfamiliar, reserved.

17.　*day:* bright joy.

21.　*when he shall die:* surely Juliet would not think of Romeo's death now. The implication is that when she is gone she does not want any other women to enjoy him, but "all the world."

23.　*fine:* bright.

25.　*garish:* too bright; therefore, tawdry.

27.　*I am sold:* continuing the metaphor of the empty house in reverse. She has sold herself to Romeo, but he has not yet entered into possession.

To an impatient child that hath new robes   30
And may not wear them. O, here comes my nurse,
[Enter NURSE, with cords]
And she brings news; and every tongue that speaks
But Romeo's name speaks heavenly eloquence.
Now, nurse, what news? What hast thou there?
The cords that Romeo bid thee fetch?

Nurse   Ay, ay, the cords.   35
[Throws them down]

Juliet Ay me! what news? Why dost thou wring thy hands?

Nurse Ah, weraday! he's dead, he's dead, he's dead!
We are undone, lady, we are undone!
Alack the day! he's gone, he's killed, he's dead!

Juliet Can heaven be so envious?

Nurse   Romeo can,   40
Though heaven cannot. O Romeo, Romeo!
Who ever would have thought it? Romeo!

Juliet What devil art thou that dost torment me thus?
This torture should be roared in dismal hell.
Hath Romeo slain himself? Say thou but 'I,'   45
And that bare vowel 'I' shall poison more
Than the death-darting eye of cockatrice.
I am not I, if there be such an 'I'
Or those eyes shut that makes the answer 'I.'
If he be slain, say 'I'; or if not, 'no.'   50
Brief sounds determine of my weal or woe.

Nurse I saw the wound, I saw it with mine eyes,
(God save the mark!) here on his manly breast.
A piteous corse, a bloody piteous corse;
Pale, pale as ashes, all bedaubed in blood,   55
All in gore-blood. I swounded at the sight.

Juliet O, break, my heart! poor bankrupt, break at once!
To prison, eyes; ne'er look on liberty!
Vile earth, to earth resign; end motion here,
And thou and Romeo press one heavy bier!   60

Nurse O Tybalt, Tybalt, the best friend I had!
O courteous Tybalt! honest gentleman!
That ever I should live to see thee dead!

37. *weraday:* a corruption of an Old English exclamation of woe. Similar to "alas the day" (an intensified form of "alas") and "alack the day."

45. *I:* the affirmative "Ay," which was spelled "I" in the Elizabethan age.

47. *cockatrice:* a creature fabled to kill by a look, said to be like a serpent with a cock's head; often identified with the basilisk.

49. *Or those eyes shut that make thee answer 'I':* or if Romeo's eyes be shut.

51. *Brief sounds determine of:* let brief sounds decide.

weal: welfare.

53. *God save the mark!:* Pardon me for saying it!

54. *corse:* corpse.

56. *gore:* coagulated.

57. *bankrout:* Juliet's investment in Romeo has come to naught.

59. *Vile earth:* addressing her own body.

resign: submit (reflexive).

60. *heavy:* because it has the weight of two bodies.

Juliet What storm is this that blows so contrary?
　Is Romeo slaught'red, and is Tybalt dead?　　　　　65
　My dearest cousin, and my dearer lord?
　Then, dreadful trumpet, sound the general doom!
　For who is living, if those two are gone?

Nurse Tybalt is gone, and Romeo banished;
　Romeo that killed him, he is banished;　　　　　70

Juliet O God! Did Romeo's hand shed Tybalt's blood?

Nurse It did, it did! alas the day, it did!

Juliet O serpent heart, hid with a flow'ring face!
　Did ever dragon keep so fair a cave?
　Beautiful tyrant! fiend angelical!　　　　　75
　Dove-feathered raven! wolvish-ravening lamb!
　Despised substance of divinest show!
　Just opposite to what thou justly seem'st—
　A damned saint, an honourable villain!
　O nature, what hadst thou to do in hell　　　　　80
　When thou didst bower the spirit of a fiend
　In mortal paradise of such sweet flesh?
　Was ever book containing such vile matter
　So fairly bound? O, that deceit should dwell
　In such a gorgeous palace!

Nurse　　　　　　　　There's no trust,　　　　　85
　No faith, no honesty in men; all perjured,
　All forsworn, all naught, all dissemblers.
　Ah, where's my man? Give me some aqua vitae.
　These griefs, these woes, these sorrows make me old.
　Shame come to Romeo!

Juliet　　　　　　　　Blistered be thy tongue　　　　　90
　For such a wish! He was not born to shame.
　Upon his brow shame is ashamed to sit;
　For 'tis a throne where honour may be crowned
　Sole monarch of the universal earth.
　O, what a beast was I to chide at him!　　　　　95

Nurse Will you speak well of him that killed your cousin?

Juliet Shall I speak ill of him that is my husband?
　Ah, poor my lord, what tongue shall smooth thy name
　When I, thy three-hours wife, have mangled it?

---

64. *so contrary:* in opposite directions.

67. *general doom:* reference to the day of wrath at the end of the world (St. Paul: I Corinthians, XV, 52).

73. *serpent . . . face:* like a serpent under a flower, a comparison Shakespeare uses again in Macbeth.

77. *divinest show:* excellent appearance.

78. *Just:* exactly.
　justly: rightly.

80. *hadst thou to do:* were you about.

81. *bower:* enclose, contain in a bower, embower.

87. *naught:* worthless, good-for-nothing.
　dissemblers: liars.

98. *smooth:* speak well of (with a pun on the literal meaning as opposed to "mangled" in the following line).

But wherefore, villain, didst thou kill my cousin?   100
That villain cousin would have killed my husband.
Back, foolish tears, back to your native spring!
Your tributary drops belong to woe,
Which you, mistaking, offer up to joy.
My husband lives, that Tybalt would have slain;   105
And Tybalt's dead, that would have slain my husband.
All this is comfort; wherefore weep I then?
Some word there was, worser than Tybalt's death,
That murd'red me. I would forget it fain;
But O, it presses to my memory   110
Like damned guilty deeds to sinners' minds
'Tybalt is dead, and Romeo—banished.'
That 'banished,' that one word 'banished,'
Hath slain ten thousand Tybalts. Tybalt's death
Was woe enough, if it had ended there;   115
Or, if sour woe delights in fellowship
And needly will be ranked with other griefs,
Why followed not, when she said 'Tybalt's dead,'
Thy father, or thy mother, nay, or both,
Which modern lamentation might have moved?   120
But with a rearward following Tybalt's death,
'Romeo is banished'—to speak that word
Is father, mother, Tybalt, Romeo, Juliet,
All slain, all dead. 'Romeo is banished'—
There is no end, no limit, measure, bound,   125
In that word's death; no words can that woe sound.
Where is my father and my mother, nurse?

Nurse Weeping and wailing over Tybalt's corse.
Will you go to them? I will bring you thither.

Juliet Wash they his wounds with tears? Mine shall be spent,   130
When theirs are dry, for Romeo's banishment.
Take up those cords. Poor ropes, you are beguiled,
Both you and I, for Romeo is exiled.
He made you for a highway to my bed;
But I a maid, die maiden-widowed.   135
Come, cords; come, nurse I'll to my wedding bed;
And death, not Romeo, take my maidenhead!

Nurse Hie to your chamber. I'll find Romeo

---

101.   *That villain . . . husband:* Her intuition gives her the answer to her own question.

110.   *presses to:* forces itself on.

114.   *Hath slain:* on balance is equal to the death of.

119.   *Thy:* i.e., Juliet's.

120.   *modern:* common (*not* up-to-date).

123.   *Is:* is equal to.

126.   *that word's:* the word "banished."

   sound: utter, or plumb the depth of.

130.   *spent:* shed (*not* exhausted).

132.   *beguiled:* cheated (of your purpose).

136.   *I'll to my wedding bed:* Refer to her speech near the end of I.5.—"My grave is like to be my wedding bed."

To comfort you. I wot well where he is.
Hark ye, your Romeo will be here at night.   140
I'll to him; he is hid at Laurence' cell.

Juliet O, find him! give this ring to my true knight
And bid him come to take his last farewell.

[Exit with NURSE]

139.   *wot:* know.

COMMENTARY

Another quick change in mood occurs between Act III, Scene 1 and this scene. From the fiery violence of the fight, the play switches focus to a dreamy, introspective Juliet. As the scene opens, Juliet wanders through her father's orchard, fantasizing about Romeo. Her speech beginning "Gallop apace, you fiery-footed steeds" poetically expresses her impatience with waiting for the day to end so that she can once again see her lover (1). Juliet's soliloquy is an example of a traditional *epithalamion*, or wedding song, in which a bride looks forward to physical union with her husband. Juliet longs for the "love-performing night" when Romeo will be in her arms (5).

Waiting for Romeo

Using unrhymed verse to emphasize Juliet's impatient, ecstatic mood, this soliloquy juxtaposes many of the images of light and dark that Shakespeare uses throughout the play. Juliet says that because love is blind, it suits the nighttime relationship between Romeo and Juliet, which is associated with dreams and fantasy. Juliet is happy that Romeo will arrive after dark because he won't see her blushing. She asks the darkness, "Hood my unmanned blood," meaning that Juliet would like to hood her face to hide her blushing cheeks (14). The request uses the language of falconry, which we have seen previously in this play: Juliet requires hooding just as an untrained falcon requires hooding so its wings don't flutter.

Juliet also claims that it won't actually be dark when Romeo arrives, because he'll bring "day in night," creating his own light with the beauty of his love (17). In arguing that the "wings of night" will be "[w]hiter than new snow" when they are together, Juliet shows how opposites break down so that white turns to black and night to day when the lovers unite (18–19). Juliet doesn't know how quickly the breakdown of opposites will impact her; the sad news she'll soon receive from the Nurse will turn day into night.

We hear a tragic note even in Juliet's celebratory soliloquy. She says that when she dies, she wants Romeo cut into little stars that will make the heavens "so fine / That all the world will be in love with night " (23–24). Even Juliet's dreams of love are plagued by images of death; for her, and for this play in general, the idea of sexuality is necessarily also a kind of death. But Juliet transforms this death imagery into something beautiful. As Friar Laurence claimed in his first speech (in Act II, Scene 3), bad things often have a good side. Juliet believes that Romeo's death will light up the heavens rather than serve as a reminder of tragedy. In fact, she says, even the sun will seem "garish" in comparison with the beautiful night lit by her lover (25). Juliet's words remind us of Act I, Scene 1, in which Romeo's friends and family associated him with dawn and night—times of solitude, renewal and meditation—rather than with the more active energies of the day.

Like an anxious child waiting for a party so she can wear her new dress, Juliet frets impatiently for Romeo. The imagery of festival in this passage is a reminder of the carnivalesque aspect of this play. Festivals (such as Mardi Gras) are a time to purge sins and prepare for a new life. Juliet's nighttime encounter with Romeo will serve a similar ritual purpose, signalling the beginning of a new phase of her life: her transformation from daughter to wife.

The Nurse brings news

While Juliet daydreams, her Nurse enters the room, obviously upset. In Act II, Scene 5, Juliet impatiently awaited the Nurse's return so that she might hear news of Romeo. In this scene, Juliet again eagerly anticipates the Nurse's news. While in Act II the Nurse comically and purposefully withheld information about Romeo from Juliet, in this scene she stalls out of frustration and anguish because Tybalt is dead. Again, the Nurse confuses Juliet by not presenting her information clearly, which adds to the *dramatic irony* of the scene. The audience knows that Juliet's cousin Tybalt is dead and Romeo banished, but Juliet doesn't know it. Declaring "he's dead, he's dead, he's dead," the Nurse sends Juliet into a panic, thinking that Romeo has been slain (37).

In anguish, Juliet tries to piece together the fragments of the Nurse's story. She wants the Nurse to say "I" if Romeo has been killed. Juliet claims, "I am not I if there be such an 'I'" (48). Punning on the similar sounds of "Ay" and "I," Juliet insists that she can't exist without Romeo. The difference between the short sounds of "ay" and "no" make all the difference to Juliet; for her, they distinguish heaven from hell.

But why is the focus on this short word "I" so important? Just as Mercutio continued punning at the moment of his death, Juliet plays with words at this moment of extreme distress when she believes that her lover may be dead. Punning on the sounds of words— ay, I, eye—Juliet also toys with the idea of identity. Love effectively destroyed her individual ego, so her sense of "I" or identity is now dependent upon Romeo. Without him, she can't see ("eye") herself, so she won't exist. While the Nurse suggested in Act I that love makes a woman bigger, Juliet shows that love can also make a woman smaller. She believes that she'll disappear without Romeo.

Romeo's banishment

The Nurse finally clarifies the situation by saying, "O Tybalt, Tybalt, the best friend I had!" (61). At first Juliet assumes that both Romeo and Tybalt, her lover and her cousin, are dead. But the Nurse explains that Tybalt is dead by Romeo's hand and Romeo has been banished. So shocking is this news to Juliet that, at first, she has difficulty making sense of it. She impulsively denounces Romeo, a response representative of her youth. She plays more with paradox and oxymoron, describing Romeo as "opposite to what [he] justly seem'st— / A damned saint, an honourable villain!" (78–79).

Juliet again finds that distinguishing appearance from reality or categorizing the world in simple black and white is impossible. She describes the complexity of interpretation by using the book/reading images that began earlier in the play. "Was ever book containing such vile matter / So fairly bound?," she wonders (83–84). Reading character, like reading a book, requires that you go beyond the beautiful exterior to examine the words hidden inside. *Romeo and Juliet* questions how you can become a good reader, able to differentiate true and false, when both words and people seem to hold so many contradictory meanings and identities.

When the Nurse asks that shame come to Romeo, Juliet immediately forgets her anger as Capulet and resumes her place as Montague (Romeo's wife). From youthful anger, she moves to mature sympathy, recognizing that she was "a beast . . . to chide at [her husband]" (95). If she doesn't support him, who will? Clearly, her love for Romeo is stronger than anything else in her life—even the families' feud. Although she mourns Tybalt's death, she also realizes that Tybalt would've killed Romeo given the opportunity. Thus, Tybalt's death, like so many things in life, is a mixed blessing.

Suddenly, Juliet remembers that there was some word "worser than Tybalt's death, / That murd'red me" (108–109). That word is "banished." For Juliet, news of Romeo's banishment is worse than the death of "ten thousand Tybalts" (114). For her, there is "no end, no limit, measure, bound, / In that word's death; no words can that woe sound" (125–126). Just as her excessive love for Romeo left her speechless earlier, the word "banished" now causes her so much grief that she's moved beyond speech. Juliet believes that her marriage is now over, that Romeo will not come to her bed that night, and that she'll die a virgin: "[D]eath, not Romeo, take my maidenhead" (137). But the Nurse assures her that Romeo will arrive. In fact, the Nurse knows where he is and will bring him to Juliet's chamber. Juliet gives the Nurse a ring to take to Romeo, her "true knight" (142). A ring, more than a word, proves the substantiality of love.

Act III, Scene 3

At the Friar's cell, Romeo despairs and tries to kill himself. The Friar scolds him for his weakness and points out that banishment is preferable to death. The Friar proposes that Romeo visit Juliet that night and then leave the city before daybreak to travel to Mantua, where he will stay until he can safely return to Verona. Romeo agrees.

ACT III, SCENE 3
The same. Friar Laurence's cell.

[Enter FRIAR LAURENCE]

Friar Romeo, come forth; come forth, thou fearful man.
Affliction is enamoured of thy parts,
And thou art wedded to calamity.

[Enter ROMEO]

Romeo Father, what news? What is the Prince's doom?
What sorrow craves acquaintance at my hand   5
That I yet know not?

Friar   Too familiar
Is my dear son with such sour company.
I bring thee tidings of the Prince's doom.

Romeo What less than doomsday is the Prince's doom?

Friar A gentler judgment vanished from his lips—   10
Not body's death, but body's banishment.

Romeo Ha, banishment? Be merciful, say 'death';
For exile hath more terror in his look,
Much more than death. Do not say 'banishment.'

Friar Hence from Verona art thou banished.   15
Be patient, for the world is broad and wide.

Romeo There is no world without Verona walls,
But purgatory, torture, hell itself.
Hence banished is banished from the world,
And world's exile is death. Then 'banished'   20
Is death mistermed. Calling death 'banished"
Thou cut'st my head off with a golden axe
And smilest upon the stroke that murders me.

Friar O deadly sin! O rude unthankfulness!
Thy fault our law calls death; but the kind Prince,   25
Taking thy part, hath rushed aside the law,

NOTES

1.   *fearful:* frightened (about what is going to happen to him).

2.   *enamoured of:* in love with.

     parts: good qualities.

4.   *doom:* judgment (passed on me).

10. *vanished:* came forth.

20. *world's exile:* Romeo feels exiled from the world.

22. *with a golden axe:* You call it by a more attractive name, but the effect is just as deadly.

25. *death:* as a punishment.

26. *rushed aside:* pushed aside.

And turned that black word 'death' to banishment.
This is dear mercy, and thou seest it not.

Romeo 'Tis torture, and not mercy. Heaven is here,
Where Juliet lives; and every cat and dog   30
And little mouse, every unworthy thing,
Live here in heaven and may look on her;
But Romeo may not. More validity,
More honourable state, more courtship lives
In carrion flies than Romeo. They may seize   35
On the white wonder of dear Juliet's hand
And steal immortal blessing from her lips,
Who, even in pure and vestal modesty,
Still blush, as thinking their own kisses sin;
But Romeo may not, he is banished.   40
Flies may do this but I from this must fly;
They are freemen, but I am banished.
And sayest thou yet that exile is not death?
Hadst thou no poison mixed, no sharp-ground knife,
No sudden mean of death, though ne'er so mean   45
But 'banished' to kill me—'banished'?
O friar, the damned use that word in hell;
Howling attends it! How hast thou the heart,
Being a divine, a ghostly confessor,
A sin-absolver, and my friend professed,   50
To mangle me with that word 'banished'?

Friar Thou fond mad man, hear me a little speak.

Romeo O, thou wilt speak again of banishment.

Friar I'll give thee armour to keep off that word;
Adversity's sweet milk, philosophy,   55
To comfort thee, though thou art banished.

Romeo Yet 'banished'? Hang up philosophy!
Unless philosophy can make a Juliet,
Displant a town, reverse a prince's doom,
It helps not, it prevails not. Talk no more.   60

Friar O, then I see that madmen have no ears.

Romeo How should they, when that wise men have no eyes?

Friar Let me dispute with thee of thy estate.

Romeo Thou canst not speak of that thou dost not feel.
Wert thou as young as I, Juliet thy love,   65

28. *dear mercy:* loving mercy.

34. *courtship:* state suitable to a court (carries also the notion of a lover's courting a mistress).

52. *fond:* foolish.

54. *armour:* protection (in the form of philosophic resignation, or stoicism).

55. *sweet milk:* It makes adversity palatable.

57. *Hang up:* get rid of (as the hangman gets rid of a criminal).

63. *estate:* condition.

An hour but married, Tybalt murdered,
Doting like me, and like me banished,
Then mightst thou speak, then mightst thou tear thy hair,
And fall upon the ground, as I do now,
Taking the measure of an unmade grave.   70

[Enter NURSE and knocks]

Friar Arise; one knocks. Good Romeo, hide thyself.

Romeo Not I: unless the breath of heartsick groans
Mist-like infold me from the search of eyes. *[Knock]*

Friar Hark, how they knock! Who's there? Romeo, arise;
Thou wilt be taken.—Stay awhile!—Stand up;   75
[Knock]
Run to my study.—By and by!—God's will,
What simpleness is this.—I come, I come! *[Knock]*
Who knocks so hard? Whence come you? What's your will?

[Enter NURSE]

Nurse Let me come in, and you shall know my errand.
I come from Lady Juliet.

Friar   Welcome then.   80

Nurse O holy friar, O, tell me, holy friar,
Where is my lady's lord, where's Romeo?

Friar There on the ground, with his own tears made drunk.

Nurse O, he is even in my mistress' case,
Just in her case! O woeful sympathy!   85
Piteous predicament! Even so lies she,
Blubb'ring and weeping, weeping and blubb'ring.
Stand up, stand up! Stand, an you be a man.
For Juliet's sake, for her sake, rise and stand!
Why should you fall into so deep an O?   90

Romeo *[rises]* Nurse—

Nurse Ah sir! ah sir! Death's the end of all.

Romeo Spakest thou of Juliet? How is it with her?
Doth not she think me an old murderer,
Now I have stained the childhood of our joy   95
With blood removed but little from her own?
Where is she? and how doth she! and what says
My concealed lady to our cancelled love?

---

67.   *Doting:* passionately in love.

73.   *infold me:* enfold me, wrap me up.

77.   *simpleness:* folly.

84.   *case:* position.
85.   *sympathy:* identification (empathy) in suffering.
86.   *predicament:* Juliet's condition.

90.   *O:* groan, lament.

94.   *old:* seasoned.

98.   *My concealed lady:* Juliet, who is not known to most others as my wife.

Nurse O, she says nothing, sir, but weeps and weeps;
And now falls on her bed, and then starts up,   100
And Tybalt calls; and then on Romeo cries,
And then down falls again.

Romeo   As if that name,
Shot from the deadly level of a gun,
Did murder her; as that name's cursed hand
Murdered her kinsman. O, tell me, friar, tell me,   105
In what vile part of this anatomy
Doth my name lodge? Tell me, that I may sack
The hateful mansion.

[He offers to stab himself, and Nurse snatches the dagger away]

Friar   Hold thy desperate hand.
Art thou a man? Thy form cries out thou art;
Thy tears are womanish, thy wild acts denote   110
The unreasonable fury of a beast.
Unseemly woman in a seeming man!
And ill-beseeming beast in seeming both!
Thou hast amazed me. By my holy order,
I thought thy disposition better tempered.   115
Hast thou slain Tybalt? Wilt thou slay thyself?
And slay thy lady that in thy life lives,
By doing damned hate upon thyself?
Why railest thou on thy birth, the heaven, and earth?
Since birth and heaven and earth, all three do meet   120
In thee at once; which thou at once wouldst lose.
Fie, fie, thou shamest thy shape, thy love, thy wit,
Which, like a usurer, abound'st in all,
And usest none in that true use indeed
Which should bedeck thy shape, thy love, thy wit.   125
Thy noble shape is but a form of wax,
Digressing from the valour of a man;
Thy dear love sworn but hollow perjury,
Killing that love which thou hast vowed to cherish;
Thy wit, that ornament to shape and love,   130
Misshapen in the conduct of them both,
Like powder in a skilless soldier's flask,
Is set afire by thine own ignorance,
And thou dismemb'red with thine own defense.
What, rouse thee, man! Thy Juliet is alive,   135

103.   *level:* aim.

112.   *Unseemly:* unseemly in a man.

113.   *both:* a man in form and a woman in the way you take misfortune.

118.   *damned hate:* self-murder as an act of hatred.

120.   *heaven and earth:* here meaning soul and body.

120-121.   *meet in thee at once:* have a place in you at the same time.

123.   *which abound'st in all:* all of which abound in you.

126.   *but a form of wax:* no more durable than a figure cast in wax.

127.   *Digressing:* if you depart.

129.   *love:* loved one, i.e., he would kill Juliet (metaphorically speaking) by his own death.

130.   *that ornament:* it is well-suited to his "shape (form) and love."

131.   *conduct:* ruling, governance.

134.   *dismemb'red with:* torn to pieces by.

For whose dear sake thou wast but lately dead.
There art thou happy. Tybalt would kill thee,
But thou slewest Tybalt. There art thou happy too.
The law, that threat'ned death, becomes thy friend
And turns it to exile. There art thou happy.   140
A pack of blessings light upon thy back;
Happiness courts thee in her best array;
But, like a misbehaved and sullen wench,
Thou pout'st upon thy fortune and thy love.
Take heed, take heed, for such die miserable.   145
Go get thee to thy love, as was decreed,
Ascend her chamber, hence and comfort her.
But look thou stay not till the watch be set,
For then thou canst not pass to Mantua,
Where thou shalt live till we can find a time   150
To blaze your marriage, reconcile your friends,
Beg pardon of the Prince, and call thee back
With twenty hundred thousand times more joy
Than thou went'st forth in lamentation.
Go before, nurse. Commend me to thy lady,   155
And bid her hasten all the house to bed,
Which heavy sorrow makes them apt unto.
Romeo is coming.

Nurse O Lord, I could have stayed here all the night
To hear good counsel. O, what learning is!   160
My lord, I'll tell my lady you will come.

Romeo Do so, and bid my sweet prepare to chide.

Nurse Here is a ring she bid me give you, sir.
Hie you, make haste, for it grows very late. *[Exit]*

Romeo How well my comfort is revived by this!   165

Friar Go hence; good night; and here stands all your state:
Either be gone before the watch be set,
Or by the break of day disguised from hence.
Sojourn in Mantua. I'll find out your man,
And he shall signify from time to time   170
Every good hap to you that chances here.
Give me thy hand. 'Tis late. Farewell; good night.

Romeo But that a joy past joy calls out on me,
It were a grief so brief to part with thee.
Farewell. *[Exeunt]*   175

136.   *dead:* ready to die.

144.   *pout'st upon:* treat with contempt.

147.   *Ascend:* It had been arranged that he should ascend to Juliet's room by a rope-ladder.

151.   *blaze:* proclaim.

157.   *heavy sorrow:* on account of Tybalt's death.

162.   *to chide:* to rebuke.

165.   *How well . . . this!:* The fact that Juliet has sent him a ring shows that she still loves him although he has slain her kinsman.

166.   *here stands all your state:* Your entire future depends on this.

COMMENTARY

Juliet's excessive emotion about Tybalt's death and Romeo's banishment are echoed by Romeo's hysteria in this scene. Romeo has just arrived in Friar Laurence's cell, and here they plan Romeo's future. As the scene begins, Friar Laurence suggests that misfortune follows Romeo—that fate has marked him for hardship, and he is "wedded to calamity" (3). Romeo wonders what new sorrows await him, because he hasn't yet heard the Prince's judgment following Tybalt's death.

Romeo learns his fate

The Friar tells Romeo that he's been banished instead of put to death. While the Friar interprets the Prince's punishment as a "gentler judgment," Romeo feels that exile is more terrifying than death, because it means he'll be far from Juliet (10). The Friar tells him to be patient and reminds him that "the world is broad and wide" (16). Romeo claims that "'banished' / Is death, mistermed" (20–21). Like Juliet in the previous scene, here Romeo plays with the meanings of the word, claiming that banishment and death are two words sharing a single meaning.

Fortune's blind justice

The Friar is upset with Romeo's disrespect for his own life and reminds him that the merciful Prince has altered the law to save his life—he's turned the "black word 'death'" into banishment (27). Using his power to alter the laws for a good cause, the Prince characteristically shows more mercy than either the Montagues or Capulets. His behaviour reminds us that perhaps a true leader, like a true man, is merciful. But Romeo isn't comforted by the Friar's logic. For him, heaven is in Verona with Juliet. Every cat, dog, and mouse will be able to see her, but her husband will not. Even "carrion flies" will be able to "steal immortal blessing" from Juliet's lips, while Romeo is banished from her presence (35, 37).

Romeo links banishment with hell and with loss of identity; for example, he claims that Friar Laurence has "mangle[d]" him with the word banished (51). Like Juliet, he believes that his identity is now entwined with hers; without her, he will be dismembered, because the portion of his self that now belongs to her will be cut off.

Melodramatic response

Both Romeo and Juliet are hysterical at the news of his exile. But while Juliet's response is presented as reasonable (partially through Shakespeare's emphasis on the Nurse's bungling, which increases our sympathy for Juliet), Romeo's response to the Prince's sentence seems juvenile and ungrateful. Romeo cowardly asks the Friar for a poison, believing that suicide is an apt substitute for banishment. Although Romeo claims to love Juliet deeply, he ignores how seriously his suicide would wound her. Romeo selfishly neglects to consider Juliet's feelings. As usual, Romeo is melodramatic, emotional, and rash. Just as he quickly fell out of love with Rosaline and into love with Juliet, he now thoughtlessly rushes toward suicide as the solution to his problems.

The Friar offers to provide Romeo with an "armour to keep off that word [banishment]" (54). (In this scene, words have become so powerful, they must be defended against.) The Friar offers philosophy as Romeo's defense. But Romeo doesn't believe that philosophy can combat his troubles. In fact, he doesn't think that an old man like the Friar can understand the troubles of youths in love. In Romeo's opinion, the Friar has lived a holy and meditative life and, therefore, can know nothing about the intensity of romantic love. Reminding us again of the contrast between youth and age, this scene presents Romeo as impetuous and unreasonable while the Friar is calm and wise. As the scene progresses, Romeo, like Juliet in the previous scene, becomes somewhat more mature and less impulsive.

The Nurse brings hope

The mood in the Friar's cell changes when the Nurse arrives with Juliet's message. Like the Friar, the Nurse disapproves of Romeo's childish behaviour and reminds him that "[d]eath's the end of all"—unlike banishment, death is absolute (92). She insists that Romeo "be a man" so he can help Juliet (88).

In the conversation that follows, the three discuss the power of language, arguing once more that words have the strength to harm, in fact to murder. For example, Romeo says his name is like a shot from a gun that has murdered Juliet, "as that name's cursed hand / Murdered her kinsman" (104–105). Tybalt was murdered because of his name, and Romeo killed for his name. Shakespeare never reveals the cause of the Montague-Capulet feud, suggesting that the original reason for the fighting has been long forgotten. Now, the families feud over names.

Paralleling Juliet's meditation about "[w]hat's Montague" (II.2.38–51), Romeo wonders in "what vile part of this anatomy / Doth my name lodge?" (106–107). With this question, the play continues to explore the meaning of identity. If identity is so easily changed by falling in love and marrying, for example, how can it be the source of so much violence? How can something as arbitrary as someone's last name be the cause of so much suffering?

Romeo wants to "sack / The hateful mansion," meaning to hurt himself in order to destroy the source of his identity that led him to murder Tybalt (107–108). His language parallels Juliet's statement in Act II, Scene 2 that, in marrying Romeo, she's "bought the mansion of a love / But not possess'd it" (meaning her marriage hasn't been consummated). Romeo's body, once the mansion of Juliet's love, is now hateful to him as the source of his violence against Tybalt. This parallel between scenes emphasizes the ways that Shakespeare exploits language's plasticity. The meanings of phrases and ideas (such as "mansion" or "love") are constantly modified throughout the play. At the end of this conversation, Romeo tries to stab his body, which he now sees as a corrupt mansion of love.

Defining masculinity

The Friar stops Romeo from killing himself. Just as the Nurse earlier questioned Romeo's masculinity, the Friar now says that Romeo's tears are "womanish" and that his wild acts are like the "unreasonable fury of a beast" (110–111). Romeo has become both an "[u]nseemly woman" and an "ill-beseeming beast" rather than a true man (112–113). Indeed, following the death of Tybalt, Romeo seems to have regressed into adolescence. The Friar compares Romeo to a "usurer," who has many goods but doesn't put them to proper use (123). Romeo's also a "form of wax"—the figure of a real man, but one that lacks a true man's "valour" (126–127).

In trying to define masculinity, this scene juxtaposes it with femininity; therefore, Juliet can weep and blubber because she's a woman, but Romeo cannot imitate that behaviour without seeming inappropriate. The play asks us to questions the true meaning of names, identity and gender: Why is it appropriate for a woman to cry, but not a man? Why are Juliet's tears reasonable, while Romeo's are hysterical, and even bestial? Of course, the play doesn't actually depict Juliet as a weak woman. In many scenes, she proves herself far more courageous than Romeo. Just the fact that she chose her own lover rather than marrying for convenience indicates her strength.

The Friar claims that Romeo acts like a "misbehaved and sullen wench" when he should be thankful for his many blessings: Juliet is alive, Tybalt could have easily killed Romeo, and the Prince could have sentenced him to death instead of exile (143).

The Friar urges Romeo to rush to Juliet's chamber and comfort her. He devises a plan to send Romeo to Mantua until the situation in Verona changes. The Friar sends the Nurse back to the Capulet mansion to hasten the household to bed so that Romeo can sneak into Juliet's bedroom. The Nurse is impressed with the Friar's advice and promises to follow it. Before leaving, she gives Romeo Juliet's ring, the symbol of her love, which assures him that Juliet isn't angry over Tybalt's death.

While words can lie because their meanings are so multiple, the ring indicates a single meaning: Juliet still loves Romeo.

In the course of this scene, Romeo moves between extremes, from absolute despair to absolute ecstasy. As he leaves the Friar's room with Juliet's ring, he feels "joy past joy" (173). Ironically, his love for her will soon be "past joy." From now on, Romeo must be disguised when he's in Verona. Despite the unpleasant reminder of Romeo's banishment, this scene ends happily. Unlike the Friar's previous speech, which hinted at impending doom, his words here seem hopeful, uplifting, and logical.

In its structure, this scene parallels Act III, Scene 2. In the previous scene, Juliet received the news of Romeo's banishment, and here Romeo learns of his fate. In the previous scene, the Nurse was Juliet's confidant, and in this scene, Romeo speaks with the Friar. But while the Nurse was upset and incoherent, the Friar is calm and philosophical. And although Juliet's mood changes from impulsive anger to calm courage as she reminds herself of her loyalty to her husband, Romeo remains mired in an adolescent, unproductive rage until he receives Juliet's ring.

This scene continues the attempt to define the attributes of true masculinity. Both the Nurse and the Friar are upset by Romeo's "womanish" tears and hysteria, but Romeo's response to news of his banishment seems to denote his youth more than his manhood. While Juliet finds courage and strength through love, Romeo's narcissism makes him unable to fully understand his lover's needs. Although Romeo seems to have matured following his relationship with Rosaline, he still has much growing up to do.

Act III, Scene 4

Paris discusses with Capulet and Lady Capulet his proposed marriage to Juliet. The Capulets at first protest that Tybalt's death had made it impossible to think of marriage for the near future. But Capulet quickly changes his mind and tells Paris that he and Juliet will be married on Thursday.

ACT III, SCENE 4
The same. A room in Capulet's house.

[Enter old CAPULET, his WIFE, and PARIS]

Capulet Things have fall'n out, sir, so unluckily
  That we have had no time to move our daughter.
  Look you, she loved her kinsman Tybalt dearly,
  And so did I. Well, we were born to die.
  'Tis very late; she'll not come down to-night.   5
  I promise you, but for your company,
  I would have been abed an hour ago.

Paris These times of woe afford no times to woo.
  Madam, good night. Commend me to your daughter.

Lady I will, and know her mind early to-morrow;   10
  To-night she's mewed up to her heaviness.

Capulet Sir Paris, I will make a desperate tender
  Of my child's love. I think she will be ruled
  In all respects by me; nay more, I doubt it not.
  Wife, go you to her ere you go to bed;   15
  Acquaint her here of my son Paris' love
  And bid her (mark you me?) on Wednesday next—
  But soft! what day is this?

Paris   Monday, my lord.

Capulet Monday! ha, ha! Well, Wednesday is too soon.
  A Thursday let it be—a Thursday, tell her,   20
  She shall be married to this noble earl.
  Will you be ready? Do you like this haste?
  We'll keep no great ado—a friend or two;
  For hark you, Tybalt being slain so late,
  It may be thought we held him carelessly,   25
  Being our kinsman, if we revel much.
  Therefore we'll have some half a dozen friends,
  And there an end. But what say you to Thursday?

NOTES

2.   *move:* persuade, sway.

10.   *know:* find out, discover.

11.   *mewed up to her heaviness:* engaged in her grief.

12.   *desperate tender:* bold offer.

19.   *ha,ha!:* does not mean laughter. Denotes a pause for reflection: h'm, h'm.

23.   *keep no great ado:* make no big fuss.

25.   *held him carelessly:* thought little of him.

Paris My lord, I would that Thursday were tomorrow.

Capulet Well, get you gone. A Thursday be it then.   30
Go you to Juliet ere you go to bed;
Prepare her, wife, against this wedding day.
Farewell, my lord.—Light to my chamber, ho!
Afore me, it is so very very late
That we may call it early by and by.   35
Good night.

[Exeunt]

34. *Afore me:* before me, a pretty oath, weakened from "Afore God!" He is politely telling Paris to go before him as they leave.

35. *by and by:* soon.

COMMENTARY

Between scenes 3 and 4 of Act III, Romeo leaves the Friar's cell and climbs the rope ladder to Juliet's bedroom. Neither scene shows this action. Scene 4 begins later on Monday evening, when Romeo is in Juliet's room and the Capulets speak with Paris about his marriage proposal to their daughter. The dramatic irony is obvious; while Romeo and Juliet enjoy the consummation of their marriage, the unsuspecting Capulets plan to marry her to Paris.

Lord Capulet explains to Paris that they haven't had time to discuss the proposal with Juliet because of Tybalt's recent death. She loved Tybalt dearly, but, as Capulet flippantly declares, "[W]e were born to die" (4). Capulet's response to Tybalt's death is expectedly callous. His views of death contrast with the Nurse's words ("death is the end of all") in the previous scene. While the Nurse sensitively emphasized the finality of death to renew Romeo's interest in life, Capulet's hard words have a different meaning: because everyone dies, it isn't very important and shouldn't require excessive mourning. Even powerful words like "death" don't have a singular or stable meaning: for the Nurse death is the end of all things, while for Capulet it is just another stop on the wheel of life.

Paris realizes that this isn't a good time to pursue his courtship, but Capulet promises to make his best attempt to convince Juliet to marry. Revelling in his parental authority, he declares that she'll be ruled by her father and marry Paris whether she wants to or not. Little does Lord Capulet know that Juliet has already defied him: Not only has she married the man of her dreams rather than a parentally sanctioned suitor, but she has married the enemy—a Montague. Becoming more excited by the idea of Juliet's alliance with Paris, Capulet urges his wife to go to Juliet that very night and inform her that she'll marry Paris on Thursday. The ceremony will be small out of respect for Tybalt's death.

This scene emphasizes Capulet's arbitrariness. Although earlier he felt that Juliet was too young for marriage and didn't want his only child "marr'd," he now quickly (and without apparent reason) changes his mind. Like many of the decisions in this play, he makes his with neither forethought nor moderation—not only will Juliet marry Paris, but she'll marry him immediately.

This scene adds another twist to the plot, reminding us how thoroughly fate is against the lovers. In a stunning example of dramatic irony, the audience knows that Juliet is already married, but her family doesn't. Just as Romeo and Juliet were impatient to marry, Paris is almost unbearably anxious to wed Juliet; he wishes "that Thursday were tomorrow" (29). Even though Paris's affections for Juliet seem honest and real, he bases his marriage proposal on convenience rather than love. By choosing to marry Romeo, Juliet picks passion over propriety.

Act III, Scene 5

The morning after Romeo and Juliet's first night of married life, the Nurse enters Juliet's chamber to warn her that Lady Capulet is coming. Romeo escapes down the rope ladder. Lady Capulet informs Juliet of her upcoming marriage to Paris, and Capulet enters to share the same news. When Juliet refuses to marry Paris, Capulet becomes violently angry and threatens to send Juliet out to live in the street. Lady Capulet and Nurse side with Capulet, so Juliet determines to seek the Friar's help.

ACT III, SCENE 5
The same. Juliet's chamber.

[Enter ROMEO and JULIET aloft, at the window]

Juliet Wilt thou be gone? It is not yet near day.
  It was the nightingale, and not the lark,
  That pierced the fearful hollow of thine ear.
  Nightly she sings on yond pomegranate tree.
  Believe me, love, it was the nightingale.   5

Romeo It was the lark, the herald of the morn;
  No nightingale. Look, love, what envious streaks
  Do lace the severing clouds in yonder East.
  Night's candles are burnt out, and jocund day
  Stands tiptoe on the misty mountain tops.   10
  I must be gone and live, or stay and die.

Juliet Yond light is not daylight; I know it, I.
  It is some meteor that the sun exhales
  To be to thee this night a torchbearer
  And light thee on thy way to Mantua.   15
  Therefore stay yet; thou need'st not to be gone.

Romeo Let me be ta'en, let me be put to death.
  I am content, so thou wilt have it so.
  I'll say yon grey is not the morning's eye,
  'Tis but the pale reflex of Cynthia's brow;   20
  Nor that is not the lark whose notes do beat
  The vaulty heaven so high above our heads.
  I have more care to stay than will to go.
  Come, death, and welcome! Juliet wills it so.
  How is't, my soul? Let's talk; it is not day.   25

Juliet It is, it is! Hie hence, be gone, away!
  It is the lark that sings so out of tune,
  Straining harsh discords and unpleasing sharps.

Some say the lark makes sweet division;
This doth not so, for she divideth us.   30
Some say the lark and loathed toad change eyes;
O, now I would they had changed voices too,
Since arm from arm that voice doth us affray,
Hunting thee hence with hunts-up to the day.
O, now be gone! More light and light it grows.   35

Romeo More light and light—more dark and dark our woes.

[Enter NURSE, hastily]

Nurse Madam!

Juliet Nurse?

Nurse Your lady mother is coming to your chamber.
The day is broke; be wary, look about. *[Exit]*   40

Juliet Then, window, let day in, and let life out.

Romeo Farewell, farewell! One kiss, and I'll descend.
[He goeth down]

Juliet Art thou gone so, love-lord, ay husband-friend?
I must hear from thee every day in the hour,
For in a minute there are many days.   45
O, by this count I shall be much in years
Ere I again behold my Romeo!

Romeo Farewell!
I will omit no opportunity
That may convey my greetings, love, to thee.   50

Juliet O, think'st thou we shall ever meet again?

Romeo I doubt it not; and all these woes shall serve
For sweet discourses in our times to come.

Juliet O God, I have an ill-divining soul!
Methinks I see thee, now thou art so low,   55
As one dead in the bottom of a tomb.
Either my eyesight fails, or thou lookest pale.

Romeo And trust me, love, in my eye so do you.
Dry sorrow drinks our blood. Adieu, adieu!
[Exit]

Juliet O Fortune, Fortune! all men call thee fickle.   60
If thou art fickle, what dost thou with him

NOTES

1.   *Wilt:* must.

3.   *fearful:* Sounds make him fearful because he dreads discovery by day.

9.   *Night's candles:* the stars.

10.   *tiptoe:* ready to spring forth.

13.   *meteor that the sun exhales:* Meteors were thought to be caused by the rays of the sun igniting vapours drawn up ("exhaled") from the earth by the sun's warmth.

18.   *so:* if, provided that.

20.   *reflex:* reflection.
      Cynthia's: the moon's.

That is renowned for faith? Be fickle, Fortune,
For then I hope thou wilt not keep him long
But send him back.

[She goeth down from the window. Enter Mother]

Lady Ho, daughter! are you up?   65

Juliet Who is't that calls? It is my lady mother.
  Is she not down so late, or up so early?
  What unaccustomed cause procures her hither?

Lady Why, how now, Juliet?

Juliet   Madam, I am not well.

Lady Evermore weeping for your cousin's death?   70
  What, wilt thou wash him from his grave with tears?
  An if thou couldst, thou couldst not make him live.
  Therefore have done. Some grief shows much of love;
  But much of grief shows still some want of wit.

Juliet Yet let me weep for such a feeling loss.   75

Lady So shall you feel the loss, but not the friend
  Which you weep for.

Juliet   Feeling so the loss,
  I cannot choose but ever weep the friend.

Lady Well, girl, thou weep'st not so much for his death
  As that the villain lives which slaughtered him.   80

Juliet What villain, madam?

Lady   That same villain Romeo.

Juliet *[aside]* Villain and he be many miles asunder.—
  God pardon him! I do, with all my heart;
  And yet no man like he doth grieve my heart.

Lady That is because the traitor murderer lives.   85

Juliet Ay, madam, from the reach of these my hands.
  Would none but I might venge my cousin's death!

Lady We will have vengeance for it, fear thou not.
  Then weep no more. I'll send to one in Mantua,
  Where that same banished runagate doth live,   90
  Shall give him such an unaccustomed dram
  That he shall soon keep Tybalt company;
  And then I hope thou wilt be satisfied.

29.   *division:* a quick run of notes.

31.   *the lark . . . eyes:* a rustic fancy because the toad's eyes are beautiful and the lark's small and unattractive.

32.   *I would . . . too:* for the toad's croak would not be herald of the morn.

33.   *arm from arm that voice doth us affray:* frighten us out of one another's arms.

34.   *hunts-up:* Originally the sound that roused huntsmen, this expression means any morning greeting.

41.   *life:* Romeo.

46.   *count:* reckoning.
       in years: older.

54.   *ill-divining:* foreboding evil.

59.   *Dry sorrow drinks our blood:* another old belief, that sorrow caused people to go pale through lack of blood.

61.   *dost thou:* is your concern.

Juliet Indeed I never shall be satisfied
With Romeo till I behold him—dead—   95
Is my poor heart so for a kinsman vexed.
Madam, if you could find out but a man
To bear a poison, I would temper it;
That Romeo should, upon receipt thereof,
Soon sleep in quiet. O, how my heart abhors   100
To hear him named and cannot come to him,
To wreak the love I bore my cousin
Upon his body that hath slaughtered him!

Lady Find thou the means, and I'll find such a man.
But now I'll tell thee joyful tidings, girl.   105

Juliet And joy comes well in such a needy time.
What are they, beseech your ladyship?

Lady Well, well, thou hast a careful father, child;
One who, to put thee from thy heaviness,
Hath sorted out a sudden day of joy   110
That thou expects not nor I looked not for.

Juliet Madam, in happy time! What day is that?

Lady Marry, my child, early next Thursday morn
The gallant, young, and noble gentleman,
The County Paris, at Saint Peter's Church,   115
Shall happily make thee there a joyful bride.

Juliet Now by Saint Peter's Church, and Peter, too,
He shall not make me there a joyful bride!
I wonder at this haste, that I must wed
Ere he that should be husband comes to woo.   120
I pray you tell my lord and father, madam,
I will not marry yet; and when I do, I swear
It shall be Romeo, whom you know I hate,
Rather than Paris. These are news indeed!

Lady Here comes your father. Tell him so yourself,   125
And see how he will take it at your hands.

[Enter CAPULET and NURSE]

Capulet When the sun sets the earth doth drizzle dew,
But for the sunset of my brother's son
It rains downright.
How now? a conduit, girl? What, still in tears?   130

67. *down:* gone to bed—to lie down.

68. *procures:* brings (with overtones of "procuring" or of "being procured.")

69. *how now:* What's the matter?

73. *Some:* a little.

74. *still:* always.

75. *feeling:* deeply felt. She really means Romeo, though she knows Lady Capulet will take it to refer to Tybalt.

76. *but not:* but not feel, i.e., your grief will not bring back the friend whom you mourn.

90. *runagate:* vagabond (runaway).

91. *unaccustomed dram:* dram to which he is unaccustomed (poison).

Evermore show'ring? In one little body
Thou counterfeit'st a bark, a sea, a wind:
For still thy eyes, which I may call the sea,
Do ebb and flow with tears; the bark thy body is,
Sailing in this salt flood; the winds, thy sighs,   135
Who, raging with thy tears and they with them,
Without a sudden calm will overset
Thy tempest-tossed body. How now, wife?
Have you delivered to her our decree?

Lady Ay, sir; but she will none, she gives you thanks.   140
I would the fool were married to her grave!

Capulet Soft! take me with you, take me with you, wife.
How? Will she none? Doth she not give us thanks?
Is she not proud? Doth she not count her blest,
Unworthy as she is, that we have wrought   145
So worthy a gentleman to be her bride?

Juliet Not proud you have, but thankful that you have.
Proud can I never be of what I hate,
But thankful even for hate that is meant love.

Capulet How, how, how, how, chopped-logic? What is this?150
'Proud'—and 'I thank you'—and 'I thank you not'—
And yet 'not proud'? Mistress minion you,
Thank me no thankings, nor proud me no prouds,
But fettle your fine joints 'gainst Thursday next
To go with Paris to Saint Peter's Church,   155
Or I will drag thee on a hurdle thither.
Out, you green-sickness carrion! out, you baggage!
You tallow-face!

Lady   Fie, fie! what, are you mad?

Juliet Good father, I beseech you on my knees,
Hear me with patience but to speak a word.   160

Capulet. Hang thee, young baggage! disobedient wretch!
I tell thee what—get thee to church a Thursday
Or never after look me in the face.
Speak not, reply not, do not answer me!
My fingers itch. Wife, we scarce thought us blest   165
That God had lent us but this only child;
But now I see this one is one too much,

95.   *dead:* Romeo is dead, and so is Juliet's heart.

98.   *temper:* mix.

102.   *wreak:* pay.

108.   *careful:* one who cares for you.

110.   *sorted out a sudden day:* arranged an unexpected day (as in the next line).

112.   *in happy time:* for heaven's sake (expresses impatience).

124.   *These are news:* said sarcastically, referring to the "joyful tidings."

126.   *at your hands:* from you yourself (from your own lips).

130.   *conduit:* fountain.

And that we have a curse in having her.
Out on her, hilding!

Nurse   God in heaven bless her!
You are to blame, my lord, to rate her so.   170

Capulet And why, my Lady Wisdom? Hold your tongue,
Good Prudence. Smatter with your gossips, go!

Nurse I speak no treason.

Capulet   O, God-i-god-en!

Nurse May not one speak?

Capulet   Peace, you mumbling fool!
Utter your gravity o'er a gossip's bowl,   175
For here we need it not.

Lady   You are too hot.

Capulet God's bread! it makes me mad.
Day, night; hour, tide, time; work, play;
Alone, in company; still my care hath been
To have her matched; and having now provided   180
A gentleman of noble parentage,
Of fair demesnes, youthful, and nobly trained,
Stuffed, as they say, with honourable parts,
Proportioned as one's thought would wish a man—
And then to have a wretched puling fool,   185
A whining mammet, in her fortune's tender,
To answer 'I'll not wed, I cannot love;
I am too young, I pray you pardon me'!
But, an you will not wed, I'll pardon you!
Graze where you will, you shall not house with me.   190
Look to't, think on't; I do not use to jest.
Thursday is near; lay hand on heart, advise:
An you be mine, I'll give you to my friend;
An you be not, hang, beg, starve, die in the streets,
For, by my soul, I'll ne'er acknowledge thee,   195
Nor what is mine shall never do thee good.
Trust to't. Bethink you. I'll not be forsworn.
[Exit]

Juliet Is there no pity in the clouds
That sees into the bottom of my grief?
O sweet my mother, cast me not away!   200

142.   *Soft! Take me with you:* Don't go so quickly; slow down so that I may understand you.

144.   *proud:* of such a marriage.

        her: herself.

145.   *wrought:* arranged for.

147.   *thankful:* insofar as you have done it out of love for me.

149.   *meant:* meant for, or as.

150.   *chopped-logic:* one who bandies logic; one who exchanges trivial points of logic.

152.   *minion:* hussy, as employed here (ironic form of "darling").

153.   *Thank . . . prouds:* Do not argue with me. A common method of rebuff in Shakespeare's time.

154.   *fettle:* make ready.

156.   *hurdle:* a wooden framework in which prisoners were taken to punishment.

157.   *carrion:* no better than dead flesh.

        baggage: hussy or minx.

158.   *are you mad?:* Lady Capulet may be joining in the attack on Juliet or (in view of her next speech) she may think that her husband is going too far.

165.   *itch:* to hit you.

Delay this marriage for a month, a week;
Or if you do not, make the bridal bed
In that dim monument where Tybalt lies.

Lady Talk not to me, for I'll not speak a word.
Do as thou wilt, for I have done with thee.   205
[Exit]

Juliet O God!—O nurse, how shall this be prevented?
My husband is on earth, my faith in heaven.
How shall that faith return again to earth
Unless that husband send it me from heaven
By leaving earth? Comfort me, counsel me.   210
Alack, alack, that heaven should practise stratagems
Upon so soft a subject as myself!
What say'st thou? Hast thou not a word of joy?
Some comfort, nurse.

Nurse   Faith, here it is.
Romeo is banished; and all the world to nothing   215
That he dares ne'er come back to challenge you;
Or if he do, it needs must be by stealth.
Then, since the case so stands as now it doth,
I think it best you married with the County.
O, he's a lovely gentleman!   220
Romeo's a dishclout to him. An eagle, madam,
Hath not so green, so quick, so fair an eye
As Paris hath. Beshrew my very heart,
I think you are happy in this second match,
For it excels your first; or if it did not,   225
Your first is dead—or 'twere as good he were
As living here and you no use of him.

Juliet Speak'st thou from thy heart?

Nurse And from my soul too; else beshrew them both.

Juliet Amen!   230

Nurse What?

Juliet Well, thou hast comforted me marvellous much.
Go in; and tell my lady I am gone,
Having displeased my father, to Laurence' cell,
To make confession and to be absolved.   235

169. *hilding:* good-for-nothing fellow.

170. *rate:* scold.

172. *Smatter:* onomatopoetic word for gossip (parallel to chatter).

173. *God-i-god-en:* God give you good evening—used here to dismiss the Nurse abruptly.

176. *hot:* hot-tempered.

177. *God's bread:* in the Sacrament.

178. *tide:* time.

185. *puling:* whining.

186. *mammet:* puppet or doll.

      in her fortune's tender: when a good chance (of marriage) is offered her.

189. *pardon you:* give you back your pardon (sarcastic).

191. *do not use:* am not in the habit of.

197. *Trust to't:* I mean it, you can rely on what I say.

      forsworn: made to break my word to Paris.

Nurse Marry, I will; and this is wisely done.
[*Exit*]

Juliet Ancient damnation! O most wicked fiend!
Is it more sin to wish me thus forsworn,
Or to dispraise my lord with that same tongue
Which she hath praised him with above compare   240
So many thousand times? Go, counsellor!
Thou and my bosom henceforth shall be twain.
I'll to the friar to know his remedy.
If all else fail, myself have power to die.
[*Exit*]

204.   *I'll not speak a word:* in your favour to your father.

207.   *my faith:* all I believe in. The general idea is very simple—there is no solution so long as Romeo remains alive.

COMMENTARY

Romeo and Juliet are together in her room the morning after their wedding. In Act III, Scene 3 the Friar instructed Romeo to be gone from Juliet's chamber before dawn so Romeo could begin his journey to Mantua without the watchmen seeing him. As the scene begins, Juliet begs Romeo to stay, arguing that the bird they hear is a nightingale, a bird of night, rather than a lark, which signals the dawn. But Romeo sees the first signs of morning, streaks of dawn that "lace" the clouds (8). Juliet argues that this isn't daylight but a meteor, acting as "torchbearer" to light Romeo's journey to Mantua (14). Romeo says that he'll gladly die if "Juliet wills it so" (24).

The beauty of the poetry in this conversation links it with the lovers' first sonnet and with the balcony scene. Many critics argue that because of the beauty of their language, Romeo and Juliet's relationship is not an ordinary adolescent crush. When Romeo invokes death, Juliet changes her mind, recognizing that the lark has indeed sung and Romeo must leave quickly. Juliet finds the lark's song discordant and unpleasant. Although some people say that larks make "sweet division," meaning a beautiful melody, Juliet argues that this isn't true because the lark divides her from Romeo (29). According to Juliet, the lark has become a hunter, driving Romeo from his haven. The lighter the day becomes, the darker their woes grow. In this play, daylight consistently marks the end of their time together, because their relationship can only flourish in the darkness.

"The day is broke"

The Nurse signals the end of Romeo and Juliet's wedding night, just as the Nurse signalled the end of their first meeting at the Capulet's party and the end of their conversation on the balcony. The Nurse enters to let Juliet know that Lady Capulet is on her way. Even the Nurse's lines are prophetic in this scene; "The day is broke," she says, foreshadowing the tragedy that will soon result (40).

Romeo climbs down the rope ladder, and, saddened, Juliet asks, "O, think'st thou we shall ever meet again?" (51). Romeo assures her that they'll surely meet again and laugh about all the problems they've had, but Juliet knows better. In a prophetic moment, she imagines Romeo "dead in the bottom of a tomb" (56). The hand of fortune enters the lives of these "star-crossed lovers" again, because Juliet astutely recognizes that death will be the outcome of their time together. The next time Juliet sees Romeo, he will, in fact, be dead in a tomb. Their one night together was beautiful, but their parting conversation seems filled with dark presentiments. Love and death, light and dark have become almost inextricable.

Lady Capulet enters Juliet's room. Juliet is crying, and Lady Capulet naturally assumes that she's still weeping for her cousin's death. Lady Capulet feels that her daughter's mourning for Tybalt is too heavy, showing a "want of wit" (74). She assures Juliet that all of her weeping will not bring Tybalt back from the grave.

Thinking that Juliet will want to avenge her cousin's death, Lady Capulet proposes a plan to have Romeo poisoned. Juliet's replies to her mother's proposition exemplify dramatic irony, because she tries to answer truthfully while keeping her affection for Romeo a secret from her mother. Although Lady Capulet thinks that Juliet's responses demonstrate her grief at Tybalt's death, the audience knows that Juliet demonstrates her despair following Romeo's banishment and recent departure. For example, in saying that she "never shall be satisfied / With Romeo till I behold him—dead— / Is my poor heart," Juliet means that her poor heart is dead until she sees Romeo again (94–96). Her mother, however, interprets the sentence to mean that Juliet won't be satisfied until she sees Romeo dead. Shakespeare adds a further irony to this sentence because Juliet actually never again sees Romeo alive.

Juliet's engagement

In an attempt to relieve her daughter's despair, Lady Capulet changes the subject by telling Juliet of the planned marriage with Paris. Justifying this sudden and capricious marriage, Lady Capulet argues that Juliet has "a careful father" who has arranged this wedding to help Juliet overcome her grief at Tybalt's death (108). Of course, the reader sees the irony in this statement, because Capulet is anything but careful. No logical explanation seems to exist for his sudden change of mind regarding Juliet's marriage. Capulet's moods shift suddenly and violently, and his actions are equally unpredictable.

Juliet tells her mother that she won't marry Paris; he has never courted her, and she doesn't want to marry a stranger. Ironically, Juliet says that she would rather marry Romeo (whom her mother thinks she hates) than Paris. This scene again emphasizes the dexterity of language, which can contain many meanings at the same time depending on the listeners' context and background. The scene also emphasizes the difference between marrying for love and marrying for convenience. The interaction between Romeo and Juliet that opens the scene is filled with love and gentleness, while the conversation surrounding the proposed marriage of convenience leads to anger and arguments.

Capulet's rage

The volume of the scene gets turned up a notch when Lord Capulet and the Nurse enter Juliet's room. Continuing with the sea imagery used throughout the play, Capulet compares his daughter to "a bark, a sea, a wind" all in one because of her nonstop tears (132). Her eyes full of tears are the sea; her body, sailing in salt water, is the ship ("bark"); and her sighs, raging with the tears, are the wind. Unless she stops crying, she'll overturn her "tempest-tossed body" (138). The imagery presented in this speech parallels the sea imagery Romeo will use in the final scene of the play.

An English National Opera production of Romeo and Juliet *at The Coliseum, 1983.*
Clive Barda/PAL

When Lady Capulet tells her husband that Juliet refuses to marry Paris, her anger is brutal, even murderous; not merely upset, she wishes that Juliet "were married to her grave" (141). Earlier in the play, Lady Capulet seemed like a model of propriety, coldly convincing Juliet of Paris's charms. She now seems ferocious. In just a few lines, Lady Capulet essentially plots the deaths of Romeo and Juliet. Sadly, her careless wish will soon become reality.

Lord Capulet echoes his wife's anger, asking how an unworthy daughter could turn down such a worthy offer. Juliet's reply, full of playful, paradoxical logic, augments his anger: "Proud can I never be of what I hate, / But thankful even for hate that is meant love" (148–149). Infuriated by Juliet's "chopped-logic," Lord Capulet resorts to nasty name-calling (150). He tells his daughter that she's "carrion," and "baggage," and he then informs her that she'll marry on Thursday even if he has to drag her to St. Peter's Church against her will (157).

This scene demonstrates the Capulets' lack of sympathy for their daughter and the extreme violence of their tempers. Juliet's parents are unreasonable and reckless people, whose moods change suddenly and without warning. The scene also emphasizes Juliet's courage; although she's not willfully disobedient, Juliet does what she knows is the right thing, instead of giving in to her parents. We can guess that Juliet has probably dealt with her parents' anger often in her short lifetime.

In a rage, Lord Capulet tells Juliet to either be at the church on Thursday or "never after look [him] in the face" (163). He claims that he was cursed in having her. From this episode, we can see how the source of the feud between families could easily have resulted from Capulet's unreasonable temper, which quickly prompts him to say inappropriate and vicious things.

The Nurse's betrayal

The Nurse tries to intervene on Juliet's behalf, but Capulet tells her to be quiet, calling her a "mumbling fool" in the process (174). Even Lady Capulet, backing away from her own anger, recognizes her husband is "too hot" (176). Capulet tries to explain his rage, stating that he has focused his entire life on finding an appropriate match for Juliet, and Juliet rejects the proper gentleman that he's found. Juliet seems to be an object instead of a human being in her father's eyes. His frustration may be understandable, but his vow to kick Juliet out of the house and watch her die in the streets if she doesn't wed is not. He claims that not only will he refuse to help her, but he'll make sure that "what is [his]" does not help her either (196). As in Act I, Scene 1, the anger that feeds the feud has infiltrated all aspects of society; the fighting takes place not only in Verona's streets, but also in its bedrooms.

Although Romeo's interaction with the Friar in Act III, Scene 3 suggests that impetuous youth should listen to the wise words of the elders, this scene presents the opposite message. In comparison with her parents' uncontrollable anger, Juliet's calm and patience seem astonishing, especially because she is only 13 years old. The play again confounds our ability to make a firm value judgment; sometimes youth is wiser than age, and at other times, age is wiser than youth. The play's only truth seems to be that no singular or lasting truth exists.

Capulet leaves the room, and Juliet is left to ponder her fate. Juliet asks her mother to help her by at least delaying the marriage, but Lady Capulet refuses and, returning to her earlier anger with Juliet, says that she's done with her daughter. The Capulets seem prepared to disinherit their only (supposedly beloved) daughter. One by one the members of Juliet's support system desert her. Lady Capulet leaves the room, and Juliet tries to discuss the situation with her Nurse. Juliet feels that heaven is playing tricks on her. Fate, rather than personality, seems to drive this tragedy, as Juliet astutely recognizes. Only fate could influence her parents to decide upon this hasty marriage to Paris.

Rather than supporting Juliet in this difficult situation, the Nurse urges her to marry Paris. She indicates that Romeo would be powerless to stop the marriage; he's been banished and wouldn't dare return to Verona to challenge Paris. The Nurse also feels that Paris is "a lovely gentleman" and that Romeo could never compare with him (220). Like the Capulets, the Nurse proves herself prone to sudden changes in mood and opinion. In Act II, Scene 5, the Nurse orchestrated Juliet's marriage and honeymoon. Here, she decides that she doesn't like

Romeo. This episode shows the fickleness in the Nurse's character and her lack of understanding for the passion that exists between Romeo and Juliet. From the Nurse's perspective, physical attraction is the most important quality of love. She finds Paris more handsome than Romeo, so she insists that Juliet forget about Romeo and marry Paris.

Although the Nurse's responses to Juliet are callous, they also reflect her position as a servant in the Capulet home. Her job requires her to support the authority of Juliet's parents. Realizing the trouble she will face if her role in Juliet's secret marriage is discovered, the Nurse now tries to control the damage. (By helping the Capulets convince Juliet to marry Paris, she may be able to cover up her role in the previous wedding.) Juliet pretends to accept the Nurse's advice and leaves for Friar Laurence's cell, supposedly to confess her sins and absolve herself. In reality, she goes to seek the Friar's advice. Both Romeo and Juliet are dependent upon the Friar's support as their situation becomes more dire.

When the Nurse leaves, Juliet calls her a "wicked fiend" and vows never to trust the old woman again (237). Juliet is understandably upset by the Nurse's sudden shift in opinion about Romeo. The Friar is Juliet's only confidante from now on, because both her parents and the Nurse betrayed her. Juliet vows that she will not trust the Nurse's counsel ever again. She decides that if Friar Laurence cannot devise a way out of the marriage to Paris, she will choose suicide rather than forced marriage.

A strong contrast is created in this scene between the idyllic and secluded realm of Romeo and Juliet and the angry world of her parents. The limitations of arranged marriages (the source of the Capulets' union, we can assume) are clearly shown: Without true love, domestic space becomes the source of discord and anger that spreads from the bedroom to the streets. The Nurse's view of love is also critiqued here. Based primarily on physical attraction, this type of love leaves no room for the spiritual intimacy that supposedly exists between Romeo and Juliet. How is that intimacy depicted in this scene? What makes Romeo and Juliet's relationship special or different from other relationships? The scene also asks us to question the proper relations between parents and children: Is Juliet correct to disobey her parents when they are so unreasonable?

Notes

Notes

COLES NOTES TOTAL STUDY EDITION
ROMEO AND JULIET
ACT IV

Capulet *O son, the night before thy wedding day*
Hath Death lain with thy wife. There she lies,
Flower as she was, deflowered by him.
Death is my son-in-law, Death is my heir;
My daughter he hath wedded. I will die
And leave him all. Life, living, all is Death's.

Act IV, Scene 1

Paris visits the Friar's cell to tell him that he and Juliet will marry on Thursday. Juliet arrives at the cell, and after Paris leaves, she tells the Friar that she believes death is the only solution for her and Romeo. The Friar convinces her that a remedy is possible, and Juliet agrees to consume an herb on Wednesday night that will trick her family into believing she is dead so she can be laid in the family vault and rescued by Romeo.

ACT IV, SCENE 1
Verona. Friar Laurence's cell.

[Enter FRIAR LAURENCE and COUNTY PARIS]

Friar On Thursday, sir? The time is very short.

Paris My father Capulet will have it so,
And I am nothing slow to slack his haste.

Friar You say you do not know the lady's mind.
Uneven is the course; I like it not.   5

Paris Immoderately she weeps for Tybalt's death,
And therefore have I little talked of love;
For Venus smiles not in a house of tears.
Now, sir, her father counts it dangerous
That she do give her sorrow so much sway,   10
And in his wisdom hastes our marriage
To stop the inundation of her tears,
Which, too much minded by herself alone,
May be put from her by society.
Now do you know the reason of this haste.   15

Friar *[aside]* I would I knew not why it should be slowed.—
Look, sir, here comes the lady toward my cell.

[Enter JULIET]

Paris Happily met, my lady and my wife!

Juliet That may be, sir, when I may be a wife.

Paris That 'may be' must be, love, on Thursday next.   20

Juliet What must be shall be.

Friar   That's a certain text.

Paris Come you to make confession to this father?

NOTES

3.   *I am . . . haste:* I will not delay his hurry.

13.   *Which, too much minded by herself alone:* She gives too much attention to her grief when she is by herself.

14.   *society:* the company of another.

16.   *I would I knew not why:* I would prefer not to have such good reasons for the delay.

20.   *That 'may be' must be:* i.e., you must be mine.

21.   *certain text:* true saying.

Juliet To answer that, I should confess to you.

Paris Do not deny to him that you love me.

Juliet I will confess to you that I love him.   25

Paris So will ye, I am sure, that you love me.

Juliet If I do so, it will be of more price,
    Being spoke behind your back, than to your face.

Paris Poor soul, thy face is much abused with tears.

Juliet The tears have got small victory by that,   30
    For it was bad enough before their spite.

Paris Thou wrong'st it more than tears with that report.

Juliet That is no slander, sir, which is a truth;
    And what I spake, I spake it to my face.

Paris Thy face is mine, and thou hast sland'red it.   35

Juliet It may be so, for it is not mine own.
    Are you at leisure, holy father, now,
    Or shall I come to you at evening mass?

Friar My leisure serves me, pensive daughter, now.
    My lord, we must entreat the time alone.   40

Paris God shield I should disturb devotion!
    Juliet, on Thursday early will I rouse ye.
    Till then, adieu, and keep this holy kiss. *[Exit]*

Juliet O, shut the door! and when thou hast done so,
    Come weep with me—past hope, past cure, past help!   45

Friar Ah, Juliet, I already know thy grief;
    It strains me past the compass of my wits.
    I hear thou must, and nothing may prorogue it,
    On Thursday next be married to this County.

Juliet Tell me not, friar, that thou hearest of this,   50
    Unless thou tell me how I may prevent it.
    If in thy wisdom thou canst give no help,
    Do thou but call my resolution wise
    And with this knife I'll help it presently.
    God joined my heart and Romeo's, thou our hands;   55
    And ere this hand, by thee to Romeo's sealed,
    Shall be the label to another deed,
    Or my true heart with treacherous revolt

---

32.   *Thou:* Notice that when Paris starts to speak in tender fashion to Juliet he addresses her as "thou."

34.   *And what I spake, I spake it to my face:* not slanderously because openly.

36.   *it is not mine own:* Her hidden meaning is that it is Romeo's.

37-38.   *Are you . . . mass?:* a polite hint to Paris that she wishes to be alone with the Friar.

40.   *entreat the time alone:* pray to be left alone for the time being.

41.   *shield:* forbid.

48.   *prorogue:* put off.

53.   *resolution:* i.e., to commit suicide.

54.   *help it:* i.e., "help my resolution."

    presently: in the present, now.

57.   *be the label to:* seal.

    deed: euphemism.

Turn to another, this shall slay them both.
Therefore, out of thy long-experienced time,   60
Give me some present counsel; or, behold,
'Twixt my extremes and me this bloody knife
Shall play the umpire, arbitrating that
Which the commission of thy years and art
Could to no issue of true honour bring.   65
Be not so long to speak. I long to die
If what thou speak'st speak not of remedy.

Friar Hold, daughter. I do spy a kind of hope,
Which craves as desperate an execution
As that is desperate which we would prevent.   70
If, rather than to marry County Paris,
Thou hast the strength of will to slay thyself,
Then is it likely thou wilt undertake
A thing like death to chide away this shame,
That cop'st with death himself to scape from it;   75
And, if thou darest, I'll give thee remedy.

Juliet O, bid me leap, rather than marry Paris,
From off the battlements of any tower,
Or walk in thievish ways, or bid me lurk
Where serpents are; chain me with roaring bears,   80
Or hide me nightly in a charnel house,
O'ercovered quite with dead men's rattling bones,
With reeky shanks and yellow chapless skulls;
Or bid me go into a new-made grave
And hide me with a dead man in his shroud—   85
Things that, to hear them told, have made me tremble—
And I will do it without fear or doubt,
To live an unstained wife to my sweet love.

Friar Hold, then. Go home, be merry, give consent
To marry Paris. Wednesday is tomorrow.   90
Tomorrow night look that thou lie alone;
Let not the nurse lie with thee in thy chamber.
Take thou this vial, being then in bed,
And this distilling liquor drink thou off;
When presently through all thy veins shall run   95
A cold and drowsy humour; for no pulse
Shall keep his native progress, but surcease;
No warmth, no breath, shall testify thou livest;
The roses in thy lips and cheeks shall fade

59.	*both:* i.e., heart and hand.
62.	*extremes:* desperate position.
63.	*play the umpire:* i.e., decide between them.
63-65.	*arbitrating . . . bring:* deciding that which the authority of your years and knowledge could not honourably settle.
68.	*Hold:* Notice that the Friar's next two speeches after this one also begin with this word.
69.	*as desperate an execution:* as much desperation in putting the plan into effect.
73.	*is it:* it is.
74.	*chide away:* drive away.
75.	*That cop'st with:* a thing that has to do with producing a death-like state.
78.	*any:* i.e., however tall.
79.	*thievish:* i.e., where thieves abound.
83.	*reeky shanks:* smelly legs (between knee and ankle).
	chapless: fleshless, literally jawless.
91.	*look:* see.
	lie: sleep.
96.	*cold and drowsy humour:* moisture carrying cold and sleeplessness.
97.	*native:* own.
	surcease: cease.

To wanny ashes, thy eyes' windows fall   100
Like death when he shuts up the day of life;
Each part, deprived of supple government,
Shall, stiff and stark and cold, appear like death;
And in this borrowed likeness of shrunk death
Thou shalt continue two-and-forty hours,   105
And then awake as from a pleasant sleep.
Now, when the bridegroom in the morning comes
To rouse thee from thy bed, there art thou dead.
Then, as the manner of our country is,
In thy best robes uncovered on the bier   110
Thou shalt be borne to that same ancient vault
Where all the kindred of the Capulets lie.
In the mean time, against thou shalt awake,
Shall Romeo by my letters know our drift;
And hither shall he come; and he and I   115
Will watch thy waking, and that very night
Shall Romeo bear thee hence to Mantua.
And this shall free thee from this present shame,
If no inconstant toy nor womanish fear
Abate thy valour in the acting it.   120

Juliet Give me, give me! O, tell not me of fear!

Friar Hold! Get you gone, be strong and prosperous
In this resolve. I'll send a friar with speed
To Mantua, with my letters to thy lord.

Juliet Love give me strength! and strength shall help afford. 125
Farewell, dear father. *[Exit with Friar]*

---

100.   *eyes' windows:* eyelids (shutters).

102.   *supple government:* control that keeps limbs supple.

103.   *stark:* rigid, stiff.

     appear like death: No such drug is known to medicine or science.

105.   *two-and-forty hours:* Actually the period of Juliet's "sleep" does not tally with the Friar's estimate.

109.   *as the manner of our country is:* stated because this was an Italian, not an English, custom.

110.   *uncovered on the bier:* not in a coffin.

113.   *against thou shalt awake:* in readiness for thy awakening.

114.   *drift:* what we are driving at.

119.   *inconstant toy:* whimsical streak.

125.   *help:* i.e., the "remedy."

COMMENTARY

Earlier in the play, Romeo went to Friar Laurence's cell to plan his wedding to Juliet. In this scene, Paris is at the Friar's cell with the same mission. Friar Laurence is shocked first to learn about the proposed wedding and then to discover that it's planned for Thursday, a mere two days away. Immediately, the Friar understands the desperation of Juliet's situation. Paris admits that Juliet isn't necessarily enthusiastic about the marriage, but he blames this on her sorrow over Tybalt's death. The Friar wonders if the wedding could be delayed, but Paris explains that Lord Capulet is rushing the marriage because of Juliet's excessive mourning over Tybalt's death—he hopes that the wedding festivities will help her overcome her grief.

The Friar's counsel

Juliet appears at the Friar's cell, and she meets and talks to Paris for the first time. Paris's affection for Juliet seems genuine; he asks her to confess to the Friar that she loves him. She responds to his flirtatious remarks with short, carefully worded phrases that effectively defer his compliments and show, once again, her skill with punning and double entendre. For example, Paris doesn't fully understand her meaning when she says of her face, "[I]t is not mine own" (36). However, both the audience and Friar Laurence realize that Juliet's face, like the rest of her, belongs to Romeo. When Paris leaves, Juliet entreats the Friar's assistance.

This scene parallels two prior scenes in the play. Paris's conference with the Friar is similar to Romeo's prenuptial planning session, and Juliet's meeting with the Friar is reminiscent of Romeo's interview with this holy man following Tybalt's death. Neither Romeo nor Juliet can turn to family members for help, so they both find the Friar to be their most faithful source of good advice.

Discussing her situation with the Friar, Juliet declares that "[w]hat must be shall be," reiterating the belief in fate or fortune that's present throughout the play (21). Her comment echoes the idea of tragic inevitability that is a fundamental aspect of Greek dramas. The characters in Greek tragedy are punished because of a fatal character flaw; Juliet's tragedy, however, results solely from fate rather than character defect.

The Friar, of course, has already heard the bad news, and Juliet argues that her love for Romeo was divinely sanctioned: "God joined my heart and Romeo's" (55). Because of the holy sanctity of their vows, Juliet would rather kill herself than give her hand or her heart to another man. She hopes for a solution that will bring "true honour" (65). She offers to kill herself if no other solution exists. But, unlike Romeo, who could think only of suicide when he sought advice from the Friar following Tybalt's death, Juliet isn't fixated on her own death; instead, she's willing to listen to the Friar's ideas and hopes that he can help her find another remedy to her problems.

A living death

The Friar thinks of an imaginative option; rather than killing herself, Juliet will "undertake / A thing like death . . . / That cop'st with death himself to scape from it" (73–75). Like most things in this play, the Friar's solution breaks the boundaries between life and death. Similar to a zombie, Juliet will become living death. Earlier in

the play, the Friar remarked upon the dual powers of herbs and of nature, philosophizing that the earth "that's nature's mother is her tomb" (II.3.9). To help Romeo and Juliet, the Friar plans to use herbs to create a false tomb for Juliet so she can be reborn in her new life with Romeo. The Friar's theory that vice can become virtue, just as virtue can become vice, appropriately describes his actions in the play. His "virtuous" plan for Juliet results in "vice," because both lovers end up dead.

Juliet declares that she would do anything rather than marry Paris: jump from a tower, walk down a path infested with thieves, or hide in a grave with a corpse. Her final two lines—"bid me go into a new-made grave / And hide me with a dead man in his shroud"—are sadly prophetic (84–85). By play's end, she'll lay in a "new-made grave" along with Paris and Romeo, next to Tybalt "in his shroud." Although Juliet was previously afraid of these things, she'll now do any of them—"without fear or doubt"—to maintain the sanctity of her marriage to Romeo (87). The scene shows Juliet's growing courage and moral strength and proves that the play is about feminine (as well as masculine) identity. Instead of weeping, Juliet is courageously ready to take whatever remedy is necessary, even if it frightens her. Notice that the imagery in this scene is based almost completely in death.

The Friar's plan

The Friar gives his advice: Juliet should go home and give her consent to marry Paris. The Friar will prepare a vial of potion for Juliet to drink on Wednesday night. This potion will cause Juliet to fall into a trance-like state in which her pulse and breath stop and the "roses in [her] lips and cheeks shall fade" (99). Juliet's "bud of love" is wilting, a movement toward death. In other words, she'll appear dead. Juliet will remain in this "borrowed likeness of shrunk death" for 42 hours (104). When her family discovers her body, they'll place her in the Capulet burial vault.

In the meantime, the Friar will send a letter to Romeo informing him of the plan. Romeo will then arrive at the vault to watch her wake from her false sleep and will take her with him to Mantua. Consider why the Friar advocates this dangerous, complicated plan rather than going to the Capulets with the truth. Does Shakespeare's representation of the Capulets' personalities make the Friar's decision more understandable?

The Friar reminds Juliet that the plan won't work if any inconstancy or "womanish fear" interferes with her courage (119). Juliet assures him that she'll remain strong, because love has given her strength and resolution. Like Romeo, Juliet needs to relinquish all signs of "womanish" behaviour, suggesting that both men and women should be, and are, courageous. Consider how the play critiques traditional ideas of femininity. What does the Friar's statement about "womanish fear" imply about his views of femininity, for example? How does Juliet defy those traditional expectations?

By the end of this scene, the final transformation in Juliet's character has occurred. No longer a timid and fearful girl, she's now a strong and resolute woman willing to risk complete isolation from her family and community to remain with Romeo. Love (not God) has given her strength, in the same way that Romeo's fortitude grew when he received Juliet's ring. Romantic love is the new religion, replacing faith in God.

Shakespeare creates coherence in this scene both through the parallels with Romeo's earlier meetings with the Friar and through the reintroduction of the Friar's medicinal powers. In making Juliet's potion, the Friar puts his knowledge of herbs to use. The Friar creates a living death for Juliet, breaking down the boundaries between life and death and dangerously usurping God's power. Unfortunately, the Friar's plan comes too close to death; although the medicine works, his plan doesn't. Fate's powers are stronger than the Friar's, and the strange series of mishaps in the following scenes of the play fulfill its tragic destiny, leaving both Romeo and Juliet in a "new-made grave."

The Friar's plan shows his imaginative ability but leaves us wondering if even this wise, old man has intellectual limitations. Wouldn't it be more appropriate for the Friar to tell Juliet's parents about the first marriage or to arrange for Juliet's escape to Mantua in disguise? Does he have Juliet's best interests in mind? Will he benefit by Juliet's move to Mantua?

Act IV, Scene 2

Juliet goes home, where everyone is busy preparing for her wedding feast, and tells her father that she will be ruled by his wishes. Thrilled at this change of heart, Capulet decides to move the wedding day up to Wednesday, the very next day.

ACT IV, SCENE 2
The same. Hall in Capulet's house.

[Enter CAPULET, MOTHER, NURSE, and Servingmen, two or three]

Capulet So many guests invite as here are writ.
[Exit a Servingman]
Sirrah, go hire me twenty cunning cooks.

Servingman You shall have none ill, Sir; for I'll
try if they can lick their fingers.

Capulet How canst thou try them so?   5

Servingman Marry, sir, 'tis an ill cook that cannot
lick his own fingers. Therefore he that cannot lick
his fingers goes not with me.

Capulet Go, begone. *[Exit Servingman]*
We shall be much unfurnished for this time.   10
What, is my daughter gone to Friar Laurence?

Nurse Ay, forsooth.

Capulet Well, he may chance to do some good on her.
A peevish self-willed harlotry it is.

[Enter JULIET]

Nurse See where she comes from shrift with merry look.   15

Capulet How now, my headstrong? Where have you been
gadding?

Juliet Where I have learnt me to repent the sin
Of disobedient opposition
To you and your behests, and am enjoined   20
By holy Laurence to fall prostrate here
To beg your pardon. Pardon, I beseech you!
Henceforward I am ever ruled by you.

NOTES

2.   *cunning:* skillful.

7.   *lick his own fingers:* taste his own products.

10.   *much unfurnished:* not ready.

14.   *peevish:* irritable to perversity.

      harlotry: wantonness.

15.   *shrift:* confession.

Capulet Send for the County. Go tell him of this.
I'll have this knot knit up tomorrow morning.   25

Juliet I met the youthful lord at Laurence' cell
And gave him what becomed love I might,
Not stepping o'er the bounds of modesty.

Capulet Why, I am glad on't. This is well. Stand up.
This is as't should be. Let me see the County.
Ay, marry, go, I say, and fetch him hither.   30
Now, afore God, this reverend holy friar,
All our whole city is much bound to him.

Juliet Nurse, will you go with me into my closet
To help me sort such needful ornaments
As you think fit to furnish me tomorrow?   35

Mother No, not till Thursday. There is time enough.

Capulet Go, nurse, go with her. We'll to church tomorrow.

[Exeunt JULIET and NURSE]

Mother We shall be short in our provision.
'Tis now near night.

Capulet   Tush, I will stir about,
And all things shall be well, I warrant thee, wife.   40
Go thou to Juliet, help to deck up her.
I'll not to bed tonight; let me alone.
I'll play the housewife for this once. What, ho!
They are all forth; well, I will walk myself
To County Paris, to prepare up him   45
Against tomorrow. My heart is wondrous light,
Since this same wayward girl is so reclaimed.

[Exit with MOTHER]

---

25. *this knot:* the marriage tie.

26. *becomed:* fitting.

33. *closet:* room.

35. *furnish me:* prepare me for.

38. *provision:* all the arrangements for the wedding, not just food.

39. *stir about:* get moving.

42. *let me alone:* i.e., leave things to me.

44. *They:* the servants.
     forth: i.e., out.

47. *reclaimed:* another metaphor from falconry—to *reclaim* a hawk was to recall it, or entice it back.

COMMENTARY

As this scene opens, the Capulets are planning Juliet and Paris's wedding banquet. Capulet tells a servant to hire "twenty cunning cooks," even though the family won't be ready for such a large festival (2). Earlier in the play, Capulet wanted a small wedding to show his respect for Tybalt; however, he's now preparing a grand event. As always, Capulet is impulsive, unreasonable, and mean. In this scene, he continues his defamation of Juliet, calling her, for example, a model of "peevish self-willed harlotry" (14). Consider why Shakespeare focuses so much on Capulet's meanness. How does this characterization influence other actions in the play?

As the wedding preparations continue, Juliet returns from her meeting with the Friar. Throughout this scene, Juliet's words and actions reflect dramatic irony. She tells her parents that she was at Friar Laurence's cell and that he has urged her to marry Paris. In addition, she says that she repents her disobedience toward her parents and begs her father's forgiveness. She says that from now on, she'll always allow him to rule her. She also tells her father that she saw Paris at the Friar's and "gave him what becomed love I might, / Not stepping o'er the bounds of modesty" (26–27).

Juliet's display of deference to her parents throughout the scene shows much duplicity. While Juliet pretends to prepare for her marriage to Paris, she's actually designing the "death" that will lead her to Romeo. Giving credit to Friar Laurence for Juliet's new submissiveness, Capulet doesn't realize that the holy man is actually plotting against him.

We have little sympathy for Juliet's father, though, because he shows his unpredictability again. At Juliet's show of humility, he decides to move the wedding forward to Wednesday, the very next day. Fate is obviously working against the lovers, because this change in the wedding date will disrupt the timing of the Friar's plan. Lady Capulet argues that Thursday is soon enough for the wedding, but her husband insists that the wedding take place on Wednesday, even though the family won't have sufficient time to prepare for the feast.

Capulet revels in the disorder, and his wife has no power or authority over him. Her weakness makes Juliet's disobedience appear even more courageous. Unlike her mother, Juliet controls her own life, even if the results are doomed. What does this scene show us about the proper role of women and wives? Is Lady Capulet a good role model for her daughter?

Capulet sends his wife to help Juliet prepare her clothing for the wedding while he agrees to "play the housewife for this once" and prepare the food and decorations for the wedding banquet (43). Does it seem odd that Capulet is taking the role of "housewife" or does it fit with other aspects of his personality?

In this scene, Capulet shows his typical moodiness. Both his good and bad moods are excessive. Now that his daughter is following his instructions, Capulet becomes almost unnaturally joyful. In his happiness, he (inappropriately) rules his wife's domestic domain. Shakespeare demonstrates again how little respect Capulet has for his wife and daughter.

Act IV, Scene 3

The night before her wedding, Juliet begs the Nurse and Lady Capulet to leave her alone in her chamber. She considers the fate that awaits her if the Friar's plan is not successful. Filled with foul images of death, she drinks the poisonous liquid.

ACT IV, SCENE 3
The same. Juliet's chamber.

[Enter JULIET and NURSE]

Juliet Ay, those attires are best; but, gentle nurse,
I pray thee leave me to myself tonight;
For I have need of many orisons
To move the heavens to smile upon my state,
Which, well thou knowest, is cross and full of sin.   5

[Enter MOTHER]

Mother What, are you busy, ho? Need you my help?

Juliet No, madam; we have culled such necessaries
As are behoveful for our state tomorrow.
So please you, let me now be left alone,
And let the nurse this night sit up with you;   10
For I am sure you have your hands full all
In this so sudden business.

Mother   Good night.
Get thee to bed, and rest; for thou hast need.

[Exeunt MOTHER and NURSE]

Juliet Farewell! God knows when we shall meet again.
I have a faint cold fear thrills through my veins   15
That almost freezes up the heat of life.
I'll call them back again to comfort me.
Nurse!—What should she do here?
My dismal scene I needs must act alone.
Come, vial.   20
What if this mixture do not work at all?
Shall I be married then tomorrow morning?
No, no! This shall forbid it. Lie thou there.
[Lays down a dagger]
What if it be a poison which the friar

NOTES

1.   *attires:* dresses

3.   *orisons:* prayers (from the French *oraisons*).

4.   *state:* i.e., of heart and mind.

5.   *cross:* perverse, wayward.

7.   *culled:* picked out; gathered (from the French *cueillir*, to pluck).

8.   *behoveful:* necessary.

     state: pomp.

11. *all:* entirely.

18. *What should she do:* i.e., what good would she be?

19. *dismal:* disastrous.

Subtly hath minist'red to have me dead,   25
Lest in this marriage he should be dishonoured
Because he married me before to Romeo?
I fear it is; and yet methinks it should not,
For he hath still been tried a holy man.
How if, when I am laid into the tomb,   30
I wake before the time that Romeo
Come to redeem me? There's a fearful point!
Shall I not then be stifled in the vault,
To whose foul mouth no healthsome air breathes in,
And there die strangled ere my Romeo comes?   35
Or, if I live, is it not very like
The horrible conceit of death and night,
Together with the terror of the place—
As in a vault, an ancient receptacle
Where for this many hundred years the bones   40
Of all my buried ancestors are packed;
Where bloody Tybalt, yet but green in earth,
Lies fest'ring in his shroud; where, as they say,
At some hours in the night spirits resort—
Alack, alack, is it not like that I,   45
So early waking—what with loathsome smells,
And shrieks like mandrakes torn out of the earth,
That living mortals, hearing them, run mad—
O, if I wake, shall I not be distraught,
Environed with all these hideous fears,   50
And madly play with my forefathers' joints,
And pluck the mangled Tybalt from his shroud,
And, in this rage, with some great kinsman's bone
As with a club dash out my desp'rate brains?
O, look! methinks I see my cousin's ghost   55
Seeking out Romeo, that did spit his body
Upon a rapier's point. Stay, Tybalt, stay!
Romeo, I come! this do I drink to thee.

[She falls upon her bed within the curtains]

---

25.   *minist'red:* prepared, provided.

28.   *should not:* is not likely to (be a poison).

29.   *tried:* found by experience.

35.   *strangled:* suffocated.

37.   *conceit:* imaginings, nightmares.

39.   *As:* (being) as it is.

42.   *green:* fresh (freshly placed).

43.   *fest'ring:* rotting.

47.   *mandrakes torn:* The mandrake is an herb with a forked root, in popular imagination supposed to resemble a man or a duck (man-drake). Because it was used as a sleep-inducing drug, a number of superstitions clung about it. One was that it shrieked if torn out of the ground, and the person who had pulled it went mad at the sound.

55.   *my cousin's:* Tybalt's.

56.   *spit:* i.e., transfix, pierce through, as meat for roasting in the fire was impaled on a spit.

57.   *stay:* stop, do not do it.

58.   *this do I drink to thee:* She takes the Friar's potion as if drinking to Romeo's health thinking, in her imagination, to go to him when he needs her.

The Friar's potion.

COMMENTARY

This scene opens on Tuesday night, when Juliet and the Nurse are in Juliet's bedroom preparing for bed. Tonight, Juliet will drink the Friar's herbal potion. Juliet needs to consume the potion as soon as possible, so she begs the Nurse to leave, claiming that she wants time alone for her prayers. Lady Capulet enters and asks if she can help Juliet prepare for her wedding the next day. Juliet replies that she is ready and urges her mother to take care of her own preparations. Both Lady Capulet and the Nurse leave, and Juliet is alone. Unbeknownst to any of them, this is the last time that Juliet will see either her mother or Nurse.

During the long, grisly soliloquy that follows, Juliet tries to prepare herself mentally for the hardships she'll soon endure. Shakespeare powerfully depicts the fears of an imaginative teenage girl who faces her own mortality at too young an age. Juliet first feels "a faint cold fear" go through her veins, almost freezing the heat of life out of her body (15). (Even before drinking the Friar's potion, her life is already moving toward death.) For a moment, Juliet thinks about calling her mother and nurse back so they can comfort her, but she knows that she must act alone. Compare Juliet's isolation with Romeo's: does her trial here require more or less courage than his banishment?

Juliet's courage reaches its peak during this episode, because she solitarily lifts the vial to her lips. Before she swallows it, she experiences a variety of doubts. "What if this mixture do not work at all?" she wonders (21). Juliet sets a dagger beside her bed as an alternative, because suicide is preferable to marrying Paris. Next, Juliet worries that the Friar may

Juliet sets a dagger beside her in case the potion doesn't work.

have given her poison instead of the sleeping potion. If he feels guilty for marrying her to Romeo, this potion is one way for him to hide his responsibility in the plot. Do Juliet's fears about the Friar seem justified?

Juliet also worries that if she wakes before Romeo arrives, she may be asphyxiated in the vault. She then imagines the ghosts of her "buried ancestors" and Tybalt who "[l]ies fest'ring in his shroud" (41, 43). Working herself into hysteria, she finally thinks that she may grab the bones of one of her ancestors and, using them as a club, "dash out [her] desp'rate brains" (54). Juliet only calms down when she thinks she sees Tybalt's ghost searching for Romeo to get revenge. At the sight of Romeo's image, she calls out "Romeo, I come!" and drinks the potion, falling within the curtains on her bed (58).

In depicting the ghastly horrors of the tomb, this scene emphasizes Juliet's bravery. All of her fears are justified, yet she manages to drink down the contents of the vial. She takes this step alone, with neither help nor comfort, except from the ghostly image she sees of Romeo. How does the imagery in Juliet's soliloquy foreshadow the play's tragic ending? Do we see any signs or images of hope in this scene?

The hands of fate are conspiring against the two lovers: Juliet hasn't told the Friar about the change in the wedding date, so he hasn't informed Romeo. This lack of communication will prove disastrous. Consider other places in the play where miscommunication has led to problems. How might lack of communication be seen as a theme in this play?

Act IV, Scene 4

In the wee hours of Wednesday morning, Capulet hears music and knows that Paris is approaching the household. He sends the Nurse to awaken Juliet.

ACT IV, SCENE 4
The same. Hall in Capulet's house.

[Enter LADY of the House and NURSE]

Lady Hold, take these keys and fetch more spices, nurse.

Nurse They call for dates and quinces in the pastry.

[Enter old CAPULET]

Capulet Come, stir, stir, stir! The second cock hath crowed,
The curfew bell hath rung, 'tis three o'clock.
Look to the baked meats, good Angelica;   5
Spare not for cost.

Nurse   Go, you cot-quean, go,
Get you to bed! Faith, you'll be sick tomorrow
For this night's watching.

Capulet No, not a whit. What, I have watched ere now
All night for lesser cause, and ne'er been sick.   10

Lady. Ay, you have been a mouse-hunt in your time;
But I will watch you from such watching now.

[Exit LADY and NURSE]

Capulet A jealous hood, a jealous hood!
[Enter three or four Fellows with spits and logs and baskets]
Now, fellow, What is there?

First Fellow Things for the cook, sir; but I know not what. 15

Capulet Make haste, make haste. *[Exit first Fellow]*
Sirrah, fetch drier logs.
Call Peter; he will show thee where they are.

Second Fellow I have a head, sir, that will find out logs
And never trouble Peter for the matter.

Capulet Mass, and well said; a merry whoreson, ha!   20
Thou shalt be loggerhead. *[Exit second Fellow, with the others]*
Good Father! 'tis day.

NOTES

2. *pastry:* the place where pastry was made.

4. *curfew bell:* the alarm to wake the servants.

5. *baked meats:* meat pies.

6. *cot-quean:* man that busies himself unduly with matters belonging to the housewife's province ("quean," or hussy, of the cottage).

8. *watching:* keeping awake, as in "watch and pray."

11. *mouse-hunt:* one who runs after women.

12. *watch you from such watching now:* prevent you from running after women now by keeping watch on you.

13. *a jealous hood:* jealous.

20. *whoreson:* fellow.

21. *loggerhead:* blockhead.

The Country will be here with music straight,
For so he said he would. *[Play music]* I hear him near.
Nurse! Wife! What, ho! What, nurse, I say!
[Enter NURSE]
Go waken Juliet; go and trim her up.   25
I'll go and chat with Paris. Hie, make haste,
Make haste! The bridegroom he is come already:
Make haste, I say. *[Exit]*

22. *music straight:* i.e., musicians straightway. In Old England, the bride and bridegroom did not meet at the church. It was the custom for the bridegroom to call early for the bride to take her to church—with music in well-to-do families.

23. *For . . . would:* He said so to Juliet, too (IV.1.42), assuming that the wedding would be on Thursday.

26. *Hie:* away.

COMMENTARY

This scene begins at three o'clock on Wednesday morning, when the newly jovial Capulets are still in their kitchen preparing for that day's wedding feast. Throughout these happy, trivial preparations, Juliet lies in her bedroom drugged by the Friar's potion. As Juliet moves closer toward death, the Capulet household fills with life. Shakespeare emphasizes speed: The family rushes to prepare for this unplanned wedding. Capulet orders everyone to "Come stir, stir, stir!" as they scurry to find spices, dates, and quinces for the wedding pastries (3). Only Juliet rests as she hastens toward tragedy.

The Nurse and Capulet banter throughout the scene, and the Nurse speaks freely to her boss. For example, she urges Capulet to get some sleep so he won't be sick the next day, calling him a "cot-quean," or a man who intrudes in domestic affairs (6). Critics wonder if these lines are correctly attributed to the Nurse, because it seems odd that a servant should speak so freely with her master. Earlier in the play, Capulet told his wife that he would, indeed, be the "housewife just this once" in preparing for the wedding, so the Nurse's comments on his domestic interference may ring true (IV.2.43). The lines' vulgarity also seems consistent with the Nurse's character, and the informality of this household may allow the Nurse to speak her mind, especially when Capulet is in such a good mood.

In answer to the Nurse's comment, Capulet assures her that he's stayed up all night in the past for lesser reasons, and he's never become sick from lack of sleep. We gain further insight into the character of the Capulets' marriage when Lady Capulet says that her husband was a "mouse-hunt" in his younger days, meaning that he was a lady's man, but that she now keeps him from such nefarious pursuits (11). Capulet seems happy with his wife's jealous response, and there seems to be a playful tension in their relationship. The changes in the Capulets' moods are dizzying; the household has switched from grief for Tybalt's death to anger with Juliet's disobedience to joy at preparing for the wedding, all within a few hours.

With the sound of music, Paris nears the Capulet house. Juliet's father urges the Nurse to wake his daughter while he goes to speak with Paris. The joviality here provides an emotional respite between Juliet's grisly soliloquy in the previous scene and the equally somber discovery soon to take place. From scene to scene, *Romeo and Juliet* juxtaposes life and death and festival and funeral, creating a feeling of carnival.

The interactions between the servants and Capulets in this scene show the boundaries between upper and lower classes breaking down, which also contributes to the carnivalesque impulse of the play. Moments such as this demonstrate that distinctions between classes are laughable just as the feud between Montague and Capulet, which is based simply on name differences, is laughable. The fact that Juliet lies near death and is officially married to a Montague while her family revels in this festivity adds to the farce, reminding us that death and change will ultimately overcome tradition and stasis.

Act IV, Scene 5

The Nurse tries to awaken Juliet and finds her lying senseless in her bed. She believes that Juliet is dead and calls for help. Capulet, his wife, and Paris lament her death until the Friar tells them to be glad that Juliet is in heaven. Capulet orders that the wedding preparations be converted to funeral preparations.

ACT IV, SCENE 5
The same. Juliet's chamber.

[NURSE goes to curtains]

Nurse Mistress! what, mistress! Juliet! Fast, I warrant her, she.
  Why, lamb! why, lady! Fie, you slug-abed.
  Why, love, I say! madam! sweetheart! Why, bride!
  What, not a word? You take your pennyworths now;
  Sleep for a week; for the next night, I warrant,   5
  The County Paris hath set up his rest
  That you shall rest but little. God forgive me!
  Marry, and amen. How sound is she asleep!
  I needs must wake her. Madam, madam, madam!
  Ay, let the County take you in your bed;   10
  He'll fright you up, i' faith. Will it not be?
  [Draws aside the curtains]
  What, dressed, and in your clothes, and down again?
  I must needs wake you. Lady! lady! lady!
  Alas, alas! Help, help! my lady's dead!
  O weraday that ever I was born!   15
  Some aqua vitae, ho! My lord! my lady!

[Enter MOTHER]

Mother What noise is here?

Nurse   O lamentable day!

Mother What is the matter?

Nurse   Look, look! O heavy day!

Mother O me, O me! My child, my only life!
  Revive, look up, or I will die with thee!   20
  Help, help! Call help.

[Enter CAPULET]

NOTES

1. *what:* a loud call.
    Fast: fast asleep.

2. *slug-abed:* literally slug in a bed, i.e., lazy creature.

4. *pennyworths:* small quantities (of sleep), pronounced *pennorths.*

11. *fright you up:* scare you awake.
    Will it not be?: i.e., will you not wake up?

15. *weraday:* alas the day.

16. *aqua vitae:* brandy, a favourite remedy.

19. *my only life:* life itself to me.

Capulet For shame, bring Juliet forth; her lord is come.

Nurse She's dead, deceased; she's dead, alack the day!

Mother Alack the day, she's dead, she's dead, she's dead!

Capulet. Ha! let me see her. Out alas! she's cold,   25
   Her blood is settled, and her joints are stiff;
   Life and these lips have long been separated.
   Death lies on her like an untimely frost
   Upon the sweetest flower of all the field.

Nurse O lamentable day!

Mother   O woeful time!   30

Capulet Death, that hath ta'en her hence to make me wail,
   Ties up my tongue and will not let me speak.

*[Enter FRIAR LAURENCE and the COUNTY PARIS, with
   Musicians]*

Friar Come, is the bride ready to go to church?

Capulet Ready to go, but never to return.
   O son, the night before thy wedding day   35
   Hath Death lain with thy wife. There she lies,
   Flower as she was, deflowered by him.
   Death is my son-in-law, Death is my heir;
   My daughter he hath wedded. I will die
   And leave him all. Life, living, all is Death's.   40

Paris Have I thought long to see this morning's face,
   And doth it give me such a sight as this?

Mother Accursed, unhappy, wretched, hateful day!
   Most miserable hour that e'er time saw
   In lasting labour of his pilgrimage!   45
   But one, poor one, one poor and loving child,
   But one thing to rejoice and solace in,
   And cruel Death hath catched it from my sight.

Nurse O woe! O woeful, woeful, woeful day!
   Most lamentable day, most woeful day   50
   That ever ever I did yet behold!
   O day, O day, O day! O hateful day!
   Never was seen so black a day as this.
   O woeful day! O woeful day!

25.   *Out:* intensified "alas!"
26.   *settled:* congealed.

37.   *deflowered by:* having surrendered her maiden-head to him.

40.   *living:* means of life, possessions.
41.   *thought long to see this morning's face:* looked forward to seeing for a long time.

45.   *lasting:* i.e., the long unending.

Paris Beguiled, divorced, wronged, spited, slain!   55
Most detestable Death, by thee beguiled,
By cruel, cruel thee quite overthrown.
O love! O life! not life, but love in death!

Capulet Despised, distressed, hated, martyred, killed!
Uncomfortable time, why cam'st thou now   60
To murder, murder our solemnity?
O child, O child! my soul, and not my child!
Dead art thou—alack, my child is dead,
And with my child my joys are buried!

Friar Peace, ho, for shame! Confusion's cure lives not   65
In these confusions. Heaven and yourself
Had part in this fair maid—now heaven hath all,
And all the better is it for the maid.
Your part in her you could not keep from death,
But heaven keeps his part in eternal life.   70
The most you sought was her promotion,
For 'twas your heaven she should be advanced;
And weep ye now, seeing she is advanced
Above the clouds, as high as heaven itself?
O, in this love, you love your child so ill   75
That you run mad, seeing that she is well.
She's not well married that lives married long,
But she's best married that dies married young.
Dry up your tears and stick your rosemary
On this fair corse, and, as the custom is,   80
In all her best array bear her to church;
For though fond nature bids us all lament,
Yet nature's tears are reason's merriment.

Capulet All things that we ordained festival
Turn from their office to black funeral—   85
Our instruments to melancholy bells,
Our wedding cheer to a sad burial feast;
Our solemn hymns to sullen dirges change;
Our bridal flowers serve for buried corse;
And all things change them to the contrary.   90

Friar Sir, go you in; and, madam, go with him;
And go, Sir Paris. Every one prepare
To follow this fair corse unto her grave.

---

59. *Despised:* i.e., by fate.

60. *Uncomfortable:* with no comfort.

62. *not:* i.e., not now.

65. *Confusion's:* destruction's. In the next line the word has more its modern sense.

70. *in eternal life:* in the life she now enjoys.

72. *heaven:* i.e., idea of what was best.

73. *advanced:* i.e., in life.

76. *well:* i.e., in heaven.

82. *fond nature:* foolish natural feeling.

83. *reason's merriment:* laughable when considered from the viewpoint of reason.

86. *instruments:* musical instruments.

90. *them:* themselves.

The heavens do low'r upon you for some ill;
Move them no more by crossing their high will.   95

[Exeunt casting rosemary on her and shutting the
curtains. Manet the Nurse with Musicians]

First Musician Faith, we may put up our pipes and be gone.

Nurse Honest good fellows, ah, put up, put up!
For well you know this is a pitiful case. *[Exit]*

First Musician Ay, by my troth, the case may be amended.

[Enter PETER]

Peter Musicians, O, musicians, 'Heart's ease,' 'Heart's   100
ease'! O, an you will have me live, play 'Heart's ease.'

First Musician Why 'Heart's ease'?

Peter O, musicians, because my heart itself plays 'My
heart is full of woe.' O, play me some merry dump to
comfort me.   105

First Musician Not a dump we! 'Tis no time to play now.

Peter You will not then?

First Musician No.

Peter I will then give it you soundly.

First Musician What will you give us?   110

Peter No money, on my faith, but the gleek. I will give
you the minstrel.

First Musician Then will I give you the serving-creature.

Peter Then will I lay the serving-creature's dagger on
your pate. I will carry no crotchets. I'll re you, I'll fa   115
you. Do you note me?

First Musician An you re us and fa us, you note us.

Second Musician Pray you put up your dagger, and
put out your wit.

Peter Then have at you with my wit! I will dry-beat   120
you with an iron wit, and put up my iron dagger.
Answer me like men.
'When griping grief the heart doth wound,
And doleful dumps the mind oppress,

---

94.   *ill:* i.e., evil deed that you have done.

95.   *Move:* anger.

s.d.   *Manet:* stay, remain.

96.   *put up our pipes:* pack up.

98.   *pitiful case:* sad state of affairs.

99.   *case:* musical instrument case.

100-104. *Heart's ease; My heart is full of woe:* both popular English songs at the end of the sixteenth century. The second is the chorus of a ballad called "A Pleasant New Ballad of Two Lovers," by Richard Edwards. It is quoted later in the scene.

106. *dump:* tune (a sad one).

109. *give it you soundly:* let you have it thoroughly. The pun on the word "sound" is obvious.

111. *gleek:* jest, mock.

112. *give you the minstrel:* call you "minstrel."

113. *give you the serving-creature:* call you a servant. "Creature" adds a note of contempt. Notice that to call anyone a minstrel was as insulting as to call him a serving creature.

115. *carry:* endure.
       crochets: whims.

117. *re . . . fa:* terms from the tonic solfa (system of musical tones).

119. *put out:* extinguish.

120. *have at you:* I challenge you.
       dry-beat: refer to note to III.1.78.

Then music with her silver sound'—   125
Why 'silver sound'? Why 'music with her silver
sound'? What say you, Simon Catling?

First Musician Marry, sir, because silver hath a sweet sound.

Peter Pretty! What say you, Hugh Rebeck?

Second Musician I say 'silver sound' because musicians sound
     for silver.   130

Peter Pretty too! What say you, James Soundpost?

Third Musician Faith, I know not what to say.

Peter O, I cry you mercy, you are the singer. I will say
for you. It is 'music with her silver sound' because   135
musicians have no gold for sounding.
'Then music with her silver sound
With speedy help doth lend redress.' *[Exit]*

First Musician What a pestilent knave is this same!

Second Musician Hang him, Jack! Come, we'll in here, tarry 140
for the mourners, and stay dinner.

[Exit with others]

127.	*Catling:* catgut.
129.	*Rebeck:* A three-stringed fiddle.
131.	*for silver:* i.e., to be paid.
132.	*Soundpost:* the name of the piece of wood fixed near the bridge of a violin to keep the back and the belly apart.
134.	*cry you mercy:* beg your pardon.
	you are the singer: and therefore cannot "say." Peter is still playing with words.
136.	*sounding:* i.e., the music they make.
137-138.	*Then music . . . redress:* He completes the stanza he started above.
140.	*Jack:* refer to II.4.143.

COMMENTARY

This scene takes place later on Wednesday morning, shortly before the planned wedding celebration. Paris has just arrived at the Capulet house for his wedding celebration, so the Nurse rushes to wake Juliet, who she assumes is fast asleep. The dramatic irony of the play is paramount in this scene because the audience knows that Juliet is merely in a trance while all the characters in the play, except the Friar, believe that she's really dead. Entering Juliet's bedroom, the Nurse jokes that Juliet should get her sleep now, because her honeymoon night won't be restful. The Nurse then apologizes for her rude joke. The irony is acute, because Juliet will soon be "bedded" with death.

Juliet's living death

After trying desperately to wake Juliet, the Nurse comes to the conclusion that Juliet is dead. The Nurse calls for *aqua vitae*, or brandy, just as she did following Tybalt's death, and Lady Capulet rushes into the room, wondering what the fuss is about. Lady Capulet seemed to lack concern for her daughter earlier in the play, but she now feels truly stricken with grief. She says, "My child, my only life! / Revive, look up, or I will die with thee! / Help, help! Call help" (19–21).

Lord Capulet enters Juliet's bedchamber. He checks her vital signs and determines that Juliet, "the sweetest flower of all the field," is dead (29). Juliet has blossomed from a "bud of love" into "the sweetest flower" as she hoped that she would, but hers was a flower soon blighted. Lord Capulet claims death has taken away his usual excessive capacity for speech. He observes, literally, a moment of silence before rushing into more speech.

Friar Laurence, Paris, and the musicians are the next to enter Juliet's bedchamber. Not long silenced, Capulet continues his flower imagery, stating that death has "deflowered" Juliet (37). He says that death is not only Juliet's rapist, but death is also his son-in-law and heir: "[L]ife, living, all is Death's" (40). Lady Capulet's wish to see Juliet "married to her grave" in Act III, Scene 5 seems to have been fulfilled, because Juliet now appears to lie dead dressed in her wedding attire. Lady Capulet laments that her only child, the one thing she had "to rejoice and solace in," has been taken from her (47). Although her despair seems appropriate, the Capulets' lack of compassion for their daughter earlier in the play lessens some of the audience's sympathy for them now.

Competing grief

Again emphasizing the carnivalesque aspects of this play, the characters' expressions of grief seem gruesomely insincere and almost comical in this scene. For example, when describing his despair at Juliet's death, Paris says that he's been "[b]eguiled, divorced, wronged, spited, slain!" (55). Wouldn't one adverb have been more effective? Paris's long list of wrongs seems artificial—too much ornament combined with too little substance, much like Romeo's wedding speech earlier in the play that drew soft criticism from Juliet.

Ironically, Paris's words are also a wedding speech, so Juliet's criticism applies to both of her potential mates. In addition, Shakespeare doesn't specify if Paris's list of ills is even a lamentation for Juliet; instead, his words seem to bemoan his own feeling of betrayal by "detestable Death" (56). Paris's speech is reminiscent of Romeo's earlier speeches about Rosaline. Overly intellectualized and flowery, his words lack substance and sincerity. Note later how Romeo's words at the news of Juliet's death will contrast with Paris's.

Capulet's response, "Despised, distressed, hated, martyred, killed!," seems designed to outdo his almost son-in-law by stringing together a more powerful list of grievances (59). Both men pile words on top of each other to try to create meaning. However, both of their lamentations lack true feeling. Capulet seems upset that death has ruined his party. He wants to know why death

has arrived at this "[u]ncomfortable time" to "murder our solemnity" (60–61).

The Nurse's response to the sight of Juliet—"O day, O day! O hateful day"—shows her inability to articulate her feelings over Juliet's death (52). Her lines, considered along with Paris's and Capulet's, indicate a general lack of sincerity among the mourners. The response to Juliet's death makes the vows between Romeo and Juliet seem even more genuine in contrast. Some critics suggest a different interpretation: that the mourners use language as a barricade so they won't have to acknowledge the reality of death. Which interpretation makes more sense, especially in relation to what we already know about these characters?

The Friar takes control

The Friar asks everyone to calm down, because their crying doesn't help the situation. In a speech that lacks compassion, the Friar tells the mourners to be happy that Juliet is now in heaven, because heaven will give her eternal life. The Friar argues that they love Juliet poorly by lamenting her death, because they should rejoice that she's in heaven. The Friar urges everyone to stop crying and put rosemary, the symbol of remembrance, on her body. His use of rosemary here echoes the Nurse's earlier association of Romeo with rosemary (II.4.202–203). An herb of remembrance that plays a part in both weddings and funerals, rosemary's use in this scene seems especially appropriate because Juliet is essentially wedded to her grave.

As soon as the Friar finishes his speech, Capulet asks that all of the festival foods be turned into funeral meats—"all things change them to the contrary" (90). Just as virtue quickly turns to vice in this play, celebration changes quickly into mourning.

Friar Laurence tells the family to prepare for the funeral, and then he ominously warns them that the "heavens do low'r upon you for some ill" (94). As usual, the Friar's statement is prophetic, because fate is, indeed, lowering upon them. At this point, the Friar doesn't know that his plan has gone fatally wrong; he still hopes that Romeo and Juliet's marriage will mend the feud between the warring families.

Comic relief

From this dark display of mourning, the scene shifts to a much lighter discussion between the musicians and the Nurse's servant, Peter. Peter asks the musicians to play the song "Heart's ease," because his heart is so heavy that it needs lightening (100). This playful conversation elevates the mood of the previously depressing scene. Because the musicians won't play the song he requested, Peter vows that he'll give them the *minstrel,* a term of disrespect as Mercutio noted earlier during his fight with Tybalt (III.1.45–48). The musicians, punning (as members of the serving class in *Romeo and Juliet* always do), vow to give Peter "the serving-creature" just as he will give them "the minstrel" (113, 112). Peter responds that he'll "lay the serving-creature's dagger" on them and will "re you, I'll fa you. Do you note me?" (114–116). Peter wittily plays with the terminology of music as he jokes with the musicians.

The musicians for Paris's and Juliet's wedding.

The servants and minor characters in this play serve primarily as comics, brilliantly jesting with language. Peter quotes part of a poem and asks the musicians to interpret the line "music with her silver sound" (126–127). Why, Peter wonders, does music have a "silver sound"? After the musicians provide a variety of answers, Peter argues that music has a silver sound "because musicians have no gold for sounding" (136). The musicians then wait for the mourners so they can have dinner.

Critics suggest that Shakespeare introduces the musicians at this point in the play because their awkward presence is a reminder of the untimeliness of death. The musicians also create continuity of action, making the transition between the mourning over Juliet's death in this scene and Romeo's light-hearted mood in Act V, Scene 1 less jarring. A final suggestion is that Shakespeare wrote the part of Peter for one of his favourite comic actors and wanted to give this actor some extra lines! Have we seen similar sudden mood shifts elsewhere in the play?

Notes

Notes

Notes

ROMEO AND JULIET
ACT V

Prince *Where be these enemies? Capulet, Montague,*
  See what a scourge is laid upon your hate,
  That heaven finds means to kill your joys with love.
  And I, for winking at your discords too,
  Have lost a brace of kinsmen. All are punished.

Act V, Scene 1

Romeo's servant, Balthasar, tells him that Juliet is dead. Romeo resolves to return to Verona, and then he visits an apothecary to request some poison. The apothecary at first refuses to sell the illegal substance, but Romeo offers him a large sum of money, so he agrees.

ACT V, SCENE 1
Mantua. A street.

[Enter ROMEO]

Romeo If I may trust the flattering truth of sleep,
 My dreams presage some joyful news at hand.
 My bosom's lord sits lightly in his throne,
 And all this day an unaccustomed spirit
 Lifts me above the ground with cheerful thoughts.   5
 I dreamt my lady came and found me dead
 (Strange dream that gives a dead man leave to think!)
 And breathed such life with kisses in my lips
 That I revived and was an emperor.
 Ah me! How sweet is love itself possessed,   10
 When but love's shadows are so rich in joy!
 [Enter Romeo's Man BALTHASAR, booted]
 News from Verona! How now, Balthasar?
 Dost thou not bring me letters from the friar?
 How doth my lady? Is my father well?
 How fares my Juliet? That I ask again,   15
 For nothing can be ill if she be well.

Balthasar Then she is well, and nothing can be ill.
 Her body sleeps in Capel's monument,
 And her immortal part with angels lives.
 I saw her laid low in her kindred's vault   20
 And presently took post to tell it you.
 O, pardon me for bringing these ill news,
 Since you did leave it for my office, sir.

Romeo Is it e'en so? Then I defy you, stars!
 Thou knowest my lodging. Get me ink and paper   25
 And hire posthorses. I will hence to-night.

Balthasar I do beseech you, sir, have patience.
 Your looks are pale and wild and do import
 Some misadventure.

NOTES

1. *trust the flattering truth of sleep:* trust the pictures which we see in dreams, but which are seldom realized in life.

3. *bosom's lord:* love.

 his throne: the heart.

6. *I dreamt . . . dead:* a reversal of the actual. Amongst all his happiness this gives a presentiment of evil without telling us just how things are going to happen.

7. *gives:* permits.

9. *an emperor:* lord of all.

10. *possessed:* enjoyed.

11. *but love's shadows:* merely dreams of love.

12. *How now:* corresponding to our exclamation, "What now?"

13-15. *Dost . . . again:* The way in which Romeo fires question after question at Balthasar without waiting for answer is very natural: it shows the excitement of a lonely banished man on seeing someone with news. Notice that Romeo addresses his servant as "thou," but Balthasar addresses his master as you." See Notes, I.3.9.

17. *well:* Balthasar is trying to break the news gently, using the word to mean (for himself) "in peace."

18. *Capels:* in Brooke's *Romeus and Juliet,* Capel and Capulet are used indiscriminately.

21. *presently:* at once.

 took post: started my journey, using post-horses.

23. *office:* duty.

24. *stars:* my fate.

25-26. *Get . . . to-night:* notice the curt decisiveness of these comments.

28. *import:* mean, signify.

Romeo   Tush, thou art deceived.
Leave me and do the thing I bid thee do.   30
Hast thou no letters to me from the friar?

Balthasar No, my good lord.

Romeo   No matter. Get thee gone
And hire those horses. I'll be with thee straight.
[Exit BALTHASAR]
Well, Juliet, I will lie with thee to-night.
Let's see for means. O mischief, thou art swift   35
To enter in the thoughts of desperate men!
I do remember an apothecary,
And hereabouts 'a dwells, which late I noted
In tatt'red weeds, with overwhelming brows,
Culling of simples. Meagre were his looks,   40
Sharp misery had worn him to the bones;
And in his needy shop a tortoise hung,
An alligator stuffed, and other skins
Of ill-shaped fishes; and about his shelves
A beggarly account of empty boxes,   45
Green earthen pots, bladders, and musty seeds,
Remnants of packthread, and old cakes of roses
Were thinly scattered, to make up a show.
Noting this penury, to myself I said,
'An if a man did need a poison now   50
Whose sale is present death in Mantua,
Here lives a caitiff wretch would sell it him.'
O, this same thought did but forerun my need,
And this same needy man must sell it me.
As I remember, this should be the house.   55
Being holiday, the beggar's shop is shut.
What, ho! apothecary!

[Enter APOTHECARY]

Apothecary   Who calls so loud?

Romeo Come hither, man. I see that thou art poor.
Hold, there is forty ducats. Let me have
A dram of poison, such soon-speeding gear   60
As will disperse itself through all the veins
That the life-weary taker may fall dead,
And that the trunk may be discharged of breath
As violently as hasty powder fired

34.	*I will lie with thee to-night:* as a corpse in a tomb.
35.	*means:* means to do it.
37.	*I do remember an apothecary:* Romeo has quickly found his way about Mantua!
38.	*which:* whom.
39.	*weeds:* clothes.
	overwhelming: overhanging.
40.	*of:* the "of" is inserted because "culling" is a verbal noun.
	simples: medicinal herbs.
	Meagre: thin (from the French *maigre*).
42.	*needy:* in need, bare.
43.	*alligator stuffed:* the sign of an apothecary.
44.	*ill-shaped fishes:* fish of evil shape.
45.	*beggarly account:* very small number.
46.	*bladders:* to hold liquids.
47.	*packthread:* stout thread.
	cakes of roses: rose leaves pressed together (for their scent).
51.	*present:* at present.
52.	*caitiff:* wretched (from its original meaning, captive).
53.	*forerun:* anticipate.
60.	*soon-speeding gear:* something to kill a man rapidly.
63.	*trunk:* body.

Doth hurry from the fatal cannon's womb.   65

Apothecary Such mortal drugs I have; but Mantua's law
Is death to any he that utters them.

Romeo Art thou so bare and full of wretchedness
And fearest to die? Famine is in thy cheeks,
Need and oppression starveth in thy eyes,   70
Contempt and beggary hangs upon thy back:
The world is not thy friend, nor the world's law;
The world affords no law to make thee rich;
Then be not poor, but break it and take this.

Apothecary My poverty but not my will consents.   75

Romeo I pay thy poverty and not thy will.

Apothecary Put this in any liquid thing you will
And drink it off, and if you had the strength
Of twenty men, it would dispatch you straight.

Romeo There is thy gold—worse poison to men's souls,   80
Doing more murder in this loathsome world,
Than these poor compounds that thou mayst not sell.
I sell thee poison; thou hast sold me none.
Farewell. Buy food and get thyself in flesh.
Come, cordial and not poison, go with me   85
To Juliet's grave; for there must I use thee.

[Exeunt]

65.   *fatal:* death-dealing.

67.   *he:* person.
      utters: puts on sale.

68.   *bare:* half-starved.

70.   *Need . . . eyes:* It can be seen from your eyes that
      want and oppression are killing you.

71.   *Contempt:* the cause of other men's contempt.

73.   *affords:* provides.

74.   *it:* the law.

83.   *I sell . . . none:* Gold is a worse poison that this drug.
      (It has been proved so in this transaction.)

84.   *in flesh:* better covered with flesh.

85.   *cordial:* drug with powers of revival (from the Latin
      cor, meaning heart).

COMMENTARY

Romeo walks down a street in Mantua as this scene opens. In contrast with the mournful mood of the previous scene, Romeo is in surprisingly good spirits. He says that "all this day an unaccustomed spirit / Lifts me above the ground with cheerful thoughts" (4–5). He expects happy news from Verona, because his dreams have prophesied good news. The previous night, Romeo dreamt that Juliet found him dead. In the dream, Juliet breathed life back into him with her kisses, and he became an emperor. Although the dream foretells Romeo's death, Romeo isn't worried because the dream also prophesies new life with Juliet. How wonderful love is, he thinks, when even dreams of love bring so much joy.

Romeo's dream is a messenger, but one that he misinterprets. Juliet's kisses won't breathe life into him, although he will be reborn into a new world with his lover—the world of death. Romeo will become the emperor of death that Juliet imagined earlier; his kingdom will be in the stars, where he'll "make the face of heaven so fine / That all the world will be in love with night" (III.2.23–24).

Misguided message

Balthasar, Romeo's servant, enters with a report from Verona. He gives Romeo the shocking news that Juliet's "body sleeps" (18). Balthasar tries to console Romeo, reminding him that Juliet is now in heaven where "her immortal part with angels lives" (19). Romeo's vision of Juliet as a "bright angel" has been fulfilled, although not in the way he had hoped.

Balthasar's message is one of a series of misdirected messages in this play. Others include the illiterate servant's list of party guests (which is mistakenly delivered to Romeo and his friends) and the Nurse's garbled message to Juliet regarding Tybalt's death and Romeo's banishment (which makes Juliet initially believe that Romeo is dead).

The most significant misguided message is Friar Laurence's letter to Romeo, which explains his plan for faking Juliet's death. This scene demonstrates that the letter has not yet been delivered, so Romeo believes that Juliet has actually died. The letter's delay will lead directly to the final tragedy of the play. Besides showing the ease with which communication can be interrupted, these examples highlight the work of fate in the play.

In Act IV, Paris and Lord Capulet lamented Juliet's death using the conventional language of mourning. They tried to outdo each other in their grief. In contrast, Romeo's lament in this scene is brief, heartfelt, and raw: "Is it e'en so? Then I defy you, stars!" (24). Throughout the play, the stars play an important role in determining the fates of these "star-crossed lovers." Earlier in the play, Romeo was willing to be "fortune's fool" (III.1.138), but now he vows to defy the stars and take control of his own fate.

Balthasar describes Romeo as "pale and wild" (28). Unlike the "fire-ey'd fury" that motivated him to kill Tybalt, Romeo's anger is "wild" now but also "pale" and calculating. Earlier in the play, following news of his banishment, Romeo was so hysterical that he was unable to take action to preserve his life with Juliet. He was determined to kill himself until Friar Laurence calmed him down. In this scene, however, his hysteria fills him with energy, propelling him to leave impulsively for Verona. Consider whether the play critiques Romeo's impulsiveness. Also consider whether impulsiveness is associated solely with youth, or if some of the older characters in the play are equally rash.

Returning to Juliet

Romeo plans to sleep with Juliet tonight. He recalls recently seeing an apothecary in the Mantua neighbourhood gathering herbs. Romeo's description of the man's shop, hung with "skins," "bladders," and "old cakes of roses," is a repulsive reminder of the fantasies of the tomb that Juliet experienced as she drank the vial of potion (43, 46–47). Matching the character of his shop, the old man appears like a figure of death—the grim reaper in his "tatt'red weeds" (39). Because this man obviously needs money, Romeo believes that he will sell illegal poisons if the price is right.

When Romeo chooses poison as his means of death, his fate appears symmetrical with Juliet's. But her potion created only an imitation of death while Romeo's poison promises the real thing. The Friar's speech earlier in the play about herbal lore becomes relevant: In the rind of a single flower, "Poison hath residence, and medicine power" (II.3.20). For Juliet, the herbal flowers are medicine—they hold the potential to heal her life by enabling her to be with Romeo. For Romeo, the herbs are poison.

Romeo wants a substance that will steal his life as quickly and violently as "hasty powder fired / Doth hurry from the fatal cannon's womb" (64–65). The cannon's fire comes, paradoxically, from a "womb." The implication is that the poison will lead Romeo to new life after he's reborn in heaven with Juliet. In searching for a hasty, fiery poison, Romeo echoes the Friar's warning against violent loves, which die "like fire and powder" (II.6.10) in their triumph.

Poisonous greed

The apothecary has quick-acting poisons, but he doesn't want to sell them because they are outlawed in Mantua. Romeo comments on the man's appearance, wondering whether such a man could really be afraid of punishment: Famine, need, and oppression are written on his face. The apothecary owes the world nothing, because the world has given him nothing; no law will make him rich, but breaking the law could. Romeo promises to pay the man 40 ducats (a small fortune) for the poison. Finally, the apothecary agrees to sell, warning Romeo that even if he had "the strength / Of twenty men," he could not survive the dose (78–79).

When Romeo pays the apothecary, he comments that money is actually the "worse poison to men's souls / Doing more murder in this loathsome world / Than these poor compounds that thou mayst not sell" (80–82). Romeo believes that his money is poison but the apothecary's herbs aren't. Have you noticed other critiques of money or greed in this play?

For Romeo, poison is transformed into a "cordial" that brings him more quickly to Juliet (85). Word meaning reverses itself here as death becomes a womb, leading Romeo to new life and his heaven with Juliet. The dramatic irony is intense because we know that even as Romeo plans his death, his Juliet is still alive.

Act V, Scene 2

Friar John, whom Friar Laurence sent to inform Romeo that Juliet is not really dead, returns and says he was quarantined because of suspicion of the plague and unable to deliver the news to Romeo. Friar Laurence rushes to the Capulet burial vault because Juliet will soon awaken.

ACT V, SCENE 2
Verona. Friar Laurence's cell.

[Enter FRIAR JOHN to FRIAR LAURENCE]

John Holy Franciscan friar, brother, ho!

[Enter FRIAR LAURENCE]

Laurence This same should be the voice of Friar John.
   Welcome from Mantua. What says Romeo?
   Or, if his mind be writ, give me his letter.

John Going to find a barefoot brother out,   5
   One of our order, to associate me
   Here in this city visiting the sick,
   And finding him, the searchers of the town,
   Suspecting that we both were in a house
   Where the infectious pestilence did reign,   10
   Sealed up the doors, and would not let us forth,
   So that my speed to Mantua there was stayed.

Laurence Who bare my letter, then, to Romeo?

John I could not send it—here it is again—
   Nor get a messenger to bring it thee,   15
   So fearful were they of infection.

Laurence Unhappy fortune! By my brotherhood,
   The letter was not nice, but full of charge,
   Of dear import; and the neglecting it
   May do much danger. Friar John, go hence,   20
   Get me an iron crow and bring it straight
   Unto my cell.

John   Brother, I'll go and bring it thee. *[Exit]*

NOTES

5.   *barefoot brother:* The Franciscans were enjoined to walk barefoot, and friars usually travelled in pairs.

6.   *associate:* accompany.

11. *Sealed up:* put the official seal on, indicating that no one was allowed to enter or leave the house. This was the sixteenth-century method of isolating people with the plague.

12. *stayed:* delayed.

16. *they:* the messengers.

18. *nice:* trivial (full of unimportant details).

     charge: importance, weight.

19. *dear:* great.

21. *crow:* crowbar.

Laurence Now must I to the monument alone.
  Within this three hours will fair Juliet wake.
  She will beshrew me much that Romeo   25
  Hath had no notice of these accidents;
  But I will write again to Mantua,
  And keep her at my cell till Romeo come—
  Poor living corse, closed in a dead man's tomb!

[Exit]

25. *beshrew:* blame.

26. *accidents:* events.

COMMENTARY

Back in Verona, Friar Laurence meets his messenger, Friar John, whom he dispatched to Romeo with the news of Juliet's faked death. Friar John reveals that he was delayed in getting to Mantua because he was suspected of having the plague. Friar John was quarantined, and no messenger would take the letter from him because of fear of the disease. As a result, Romeo never received Friar Laurence's letter.

This situation is the final, and most deadly, example of a message going awry in the play. The Friar's exclamation, "Unhappy fortune!" says it all: Fate is doing all she can to keep Romeo and Juliet from happiness (17). Although Romeo tries to avoid becoming "fortune's fool," he can't escape her powers, as the series of unhappy coincidences that have plagued the lovers exemplify. Friar Laurence immediately realizes the immense danger that may result from the mishandling of this message, so he sends Friar John to find an iron crowbar to help Juliet out of the vault.

Juliet will wake in three hours, and the Friar needs to be at the family vault to help her when she does. The Friar knows that Juliet will be upset that Romeo isn't there to greet her, but he trusts she will be happy because Romeo knows nothing of the strange coincidences that have disrupted the Friar's plans. Friar Laurence decides to change his scheme: He'll recover Juliet from the vault, write a new letter to Romeo, and keep Juliet in his cell until Romeo arrives to take her to Mantua. He feels sorry for Juliet—this poor "living corse, closed in a dead man's tomb" (30). He fears that she is about to confront her worst nightmare, waking alone next to the shroud of her dead cousin. Juliet's doubts about the Friar's plan are becoming reality. Fate, not the Friar, controls her destiny.

Act V, Scene 3

This final scene of the play takes places at the Capulets' tomb. Paris is there to mourn Juliet, and Romeo arrives, behaving wildly. The two fight, and Paris is killed. Overcome by Juliet's beauty, Romeo drinks poison and dies just moments before Friar Laurence arrives to free Juliet. Juliet awakens and, seeing her lover dead, kills herself with his dagger. The Prince, the Montagues, and the Capulets arrive, and the families agree to end their fighting.

ACT V, SCENE 3
The same. A churchyard; in it a monument belonging to the Capulets.

[Enter PARIS and his Page with flowers and sweet water]

Paris Give me thy torch, boy. Hence, and stand aloof.
Yet put it out, for I would not be seen.
Under yond yew trees lay thee all along,
Holding thy ear close to the hollow ground.
So shall no foot upon the churchyard tread   5
(Being loose, unfirm, with digging up of graves)
But thou shalt hear it. Whistle then to me,
As signal that thou hearest something approach.
Give me those flowers. Do as I bid thee, go.

Page *[aside]* I am almost afraid to stand alone   10
Here in the churchyard; yet I will adventure. *[Retires]*

Paris Sweet flower, with flowers thy bridal bed I strew
(O woe! thy canopy is dust and stones)
Which with sweet water nightly I will dew;
Or, wanting that, with tears distilled by moans.   15
The obsequies that I for thee will keep
Nightly shall be to strew thy grave and weep.
[Whistle Page]
The boy gives warning something doth approach.
What cursed foot wanders this way to-night
To cross my obsequies and true love's rite?   20
What, with a torch? Muffle me, night, awhile. *[Retires]*

[Enter ROMEO and BALTHASAR with a torch, a mattock, and a crow of iron]

Romeo Give me that mattock and the wrenching iron.
Hold, take this letter. Early in the morning
See thou deliver it to my lord and father.

NOTES

1. *aloof:* apart.
2. *Yet:* further—an order amending his first.
3. *all along:* flat.

10. *stand:* be, remain.

12. *Sweet flower:* refers to Juliet.

14. *sweet:* perfumed.

16. *obsequies:* rites of burial.
    keep: observe.

20. *cross:* interfere with.

22. *mattock:* like a pickaxe, only with an arched blade at one side.

Give me the light. Upon thy life I charge thee,   25
Whate'er thou hearest or seest, stand all aloof
And do not interrupt me in my course.
Why I descend into this bed of death
Is partly to behold my lady's face,
But chiefly to take thence from her dead finger   30
A precious ring—a ring that I must use
In dear employment. Therefore hence, be gone.
But if thou, jealous, dost return to pry
In what I farther shall intend to do,
By heaven, I will tear thee joint by joint   35
And strew this hungry churchyard with thy limbs.
The time and my intents are savage-wild,
More fierce and more inexorable far
Than empty tigers or the roaring sea.

Balthasar I will be gone, sir, and not trouble you.   40

Romeo So shalt thou show me friendship. Take thou that.
Live, and be prosperous; and farewell, good fellow.

Balthasar *[aside]* For all this same, I'll hide me hereabout.
His looks I fear, and his intents I doubt. *[Retires]*

Romeo Thou detestable maw, thou womb of death,   45
Gorged with the dearest morsel of the earth,
Thus I enforce thy rotten jaws to open,
And in despite I'll cram thee with more food.

[ROMEO opens the tomb]

Paris This is that banished haughty Montague
That murd'red my love's cousin—with which grief   50
It is supposed the fair creature died—
And here is come to do some villainous shame
To the dead bodies. I will apprehend him.
Stop thy unhallowed toil, vile Montague!
Can vengeance be pursued further than death?   55
Condemned villain, I do apprehend thee.
Obey, and go with me; for thou must die.

Romeo I must indeed; and therefore came I hither.
Good gentle youth, tempt not a desp'rate man.
Fly hence and leave me. Think upon these gone;   60
Let them affright thee. I beseech thee, youth,
Put not another sin upon my head

28. *Why:* the reason why.

32. *dear:* important.

33. *jealous:* suspicious.

37. *The time:* Romeo probably means the time after Juliet's death, but perhaps simply the dead of night.

39. *empty:* and therefore savage.

41. *that:* a money present.

43. *For all this same:* notwithstanding all this.

44. *His looks I fear:* Balthasar fears what Romeo may do to himself.

48. *in despite:* against your wish.

55. *Can vengeance . . . death?* Paris thinks that Romeo has come to desecrate the Capulet tomb, in particular the body of Tybalt.

60. *these gone:* the surrounding dead.

61. *affright thee:* the implication is, "And prevent your hindering me."

62. *another sin:* killing you.

By urging me to fury. O, be gone!
By heaven, I love thee better than myself,
For I come hither armed against myself.   65
Stay not, be gone. Live, and hereafter say
A madman's mercy bid thee run away.

Paris I do defy thy conjuration
And apprehend thee for a felon here.

Romeo Wilt thou provoke me? Then have at thee, boy!   70
[They fight]

Page O Lord, they fight! I will go call the watch.
[Exit. PARIS falls]

Paris O, I am slain! If thou be merciful,
Open the tomb, lay me with Juliet. *[Dies]*

Romeo In faith, I will. Let me peruse this face.
Mercutio's kinsman, noble County Paris!   75
What said my man when my betossed soul
Did not attend him as we rode? I think
He told me Paris should have married Juliet.
Said he not so? Or did I dream it so?
Or am I mad, hearing him talk of Juliet,   80
To think it was so? O, give me thy hand,
One writ with me in sour misfortune's book!
I'll bury thee in a triumphant grave.
A grave? O, no, a lanthorn, slaught'red youth,
For here lies Juliet, and her beauty makes   85
This vault a feasting presence full of light.
Death, lie thou there, by a dead man interred.
[Lays him in the tomb]
How oft when men are at the point of death
Have they been merry! which their keepers call
A lightning before death. O, how may I   90
Call this a lightning? O my love! my wife!
Death, that hath sucked the honey of thy breath,
Hath had no power yet upon thy beauty.
Thou art not conquered. Beauty's ensign yet
Is crimson in thy lips and in thy cheeks,   95
And death's pale flag is not advanced there.
Tybalt, liest thou there in thy bloody sheet?
O, what more favour can I do to thee
Than with that hand that cut thy youth in twain

---

65. *armed against myself:* with the poison (suicidal).

68. *conjuration:* sworn warnings.

71. *watch:* the Elizabethan police.

74. *peruse:* look closely at.

75. *Mercutio's kinsman:* Both Mercutio and Paris were kinsmen of the Prince.

77. *attend him:* pay attention to what he was saying.

83. *triumphant:* splendid.

84. *lanthorn:* lantern.

86. *presence:* royal apartment.

87. *Death:* Paris's body.

a dead man: Romeo's body.

89. *keepers:* attendants. Romeo is not necessarily thinking of men at the point of death in prison.

90. *lightning:* lightening (of the spirits)

92. *honey:* sweetness.

94. *ensign:* flag standard.

97. *sheet:* winding sheet.

To sunder his that was thine enemy?   100
Forgive me, cousin! Ah, dear Juliet,
Why art thou yet so fair? Shall I believe
That unsubstantial Death is amorous,
And that the lean abhorred monster keeps
Thee here in dark to be his paramour?   105
For fear of that I still will stay with thee
And never from this pallet of dim night
Depart again. Here, here will I remain
With worms that are thy chambermaids. O, here
Will I set up my everlasting rest   110
And shake the yoke of inauspicious stars
From this world-wearied flesh. Eyes, look your last!
Arms, take your last embrace! and lips, O you
The doors of breath, seal with a righteous kiss
A dateless bargain to engrossing death!   115
Come, bitter conduct; come, unsavoury guide!
Thou desperate pilot, now at once run on
The dashing rocks thy seasick weary bark!
Here's to my love! *[Drinks]* O true apothecary!
Thy drugs are quick. Thus with a kiss I die. *[Falls]*   120

[Enter FRIAR LAURENCE, with lanthorn, crow, and spade]

Friar Saint Francis be my speed! How oft to-night
Have my old feet stumbled at graves! Who's there?

Balthasar Here's one, a friend, and one that knows you well.

Friar Bliss be upon you! Tell me, good my friend,
What torch is yond that vainly lends his light   125
To grubs and eyeless skulls? As I discern,
It burneth in the Capels' monument.

Balthasar It doth so, holy sir; and there's my master,
One that you love.

Friar   Who is it?

Balthasar   Romeo.

Friar How long hath he been there?

Balthasar   Full half an hour.   130

Friar Go with me to the vault.

Balthasar   I dare not, sir.

101. *cousin:* Tybalt would be his cousin (by marriage to Juliet).

103. *unsubstantial:* without a material body.

111. *shake the yoke:* The metaphor is one of a beast of burden coming home at the end of the day and shaking off his yoke.

115. *dateless:* everlasting.

  engrossing: seizing everything.

116. *conduct:* conductor.

119. *true apothecary:* Romeo can feel the poison overcoming him at once; he acknowledges that the apothecary has not misled him.

122. *stumbled:* a sign of ill-omen.

My master knows not but I am gone hence,
And fearfully did menace me with death
If I did stay to look on his intents.

Friar Stay then; I'll go alone. Fear comes upon me.   135
O, much I fear some ill unthrifty thing.

Balthasar As I did sleep under this yew tree here,
I dreamt my master and another fought,
And that my master slew him.

Friar   Romeo!
Alack, alack, what blood is this which stains   140
The stony entrance of this sepulchre?
What mean these masterless and gory swords
To lie discolored by this place of peace?
[Enters the tomb]
Romeo! O, pale! Who else? What, Paris too?
And steeped in blood? Ah, what an unkind hour   145
Is guilty of this lamentable chance!
The lady stirs. *[JULIET rises]*

Juliet O comfortable friar! Where is my lord?
I do remember well where I should be,
And there I am. Where is my Romeo?   150

Friar I hear some noise. Lady, come from that nest
Of death, contagion, and unnatural sleep.
A greater power than we can contradict
Hath thwarted our intents. Come, come away.
Thy husband in thy bosom there lies dead;   155
And Paris too. Come, I'll dispose of thee
Among a sisterhood of holy nuns.
Stay not to question, for the watch is coming.
Come, go, good Juliet. I dare no longer stay.

Juliet Go, get thee hence, for I will not away.   160
[Exit FRIAR]
What's here? A cup, closed in my true love's hand?
Poison, I see, hath been his timeless end.
O churl! drunk all, and left no friendly drop
To help me after? I will kiss thy lips.
Haply some poison yet doth hang on them   165
To make me die with a restorative. *[Kisses him]*
Thy lips are warm!

136. *unthrifty:* unlucky.

138. *I dreamt:* Does Balthasar really believe it to be a dream or does he put it like this to avoid admitting that he had defied his master's orders?

142. *masterless:* abandoned.

143. *To lie:* by lying.

discoloured: by blood.

145. *unkind:* unnatural.

148. *comfortable:* giving comfort.

160. *away:* come away.

162. *timeless:* untimely, and eternal.

163. *churl:* This, of course, is said in a kindly way.

Chief Watchman *[within]* Lead, boy. Which way?

Juliet Yea, noise? Then I'll be brief. O happy dagger!
  [Snatches Romeo's dagger]
  This is thy sheath; there rust, and let me die.   170

[She stabs herself and falls. Enter Paris's Page and Watch]

Page This is the place. There, where the torch doth burn.

Chief Watchman The ground is bloody. Search about the
    churchyard.
  Go, some of you; whoe'er you find attach.
  [Exeunt some of the Watch]
  Pitiful sight! Here lies the County slain;
  And Juliet bleeding, warm, and newly dead,   175
  Who here hath lain this two days buried.
  Go, tell the Prince; run to the Capulets;
  Raise up the Montagues; some others search.
  [Exeunt others of the Watch]
  We see the ground whereon these woes do lie,
  But the true ground of all these piteous woes   180
  We cannot without circumstance descry.

[Enter some of the Watch, with Romeo's Man BALTHASAR]

Second Watchman Here's Romeo's man. We found him in
    the churchyard.

Chief Watchman Hold him in safety till the Prince come
    hither.
  [Enter FRIAR LAURENCE and another Watchman]

Third Watchman Here is a friar that trembles, sighs, and
    weeps.
  We took this mattock and this spade from him   185
  As he was coming from this churchyard side.

Chief Watchman A great suspicion. Stay the friar too.

[Enter the PRINCE and Attendants]

Prince What misadventure is so early up,
  That calls our person from our morning rest?

[Enter CAPULET and his WIFE with others]

Capulet What should it be, that is so shrieked abroad?   190

Wife O the people in the street cry 'Romeo,'

---

173. *attach:* arrest, seize.

180. *ground of:* reason for.

181. *circumstance:* surrounding facts.

187. *Stay:* keep in custody.

188. *up:* going on.

Some 'Juliet,' and some 'Paris'; and all run,
With open outcry, toward our monument.

Prince What fear is this which startles in your ears?

Chief Watchman Sovereign, here lies the County Paris slain;195
And Romeo dead; and Juliet, dead before,
Warm and new killed.

Prince Search, seek, and know how this foul murder comes.

Chief Watchman Here is a friar, and slaughtered Romeo's
man,
With instruments upon them fit to open   200
These dead men's tombs.

Capulet O heavens! O wife, look how our daughter bleeds!
This dagger hath mista'en, for, lo, his house
Is empty on the back of Montague,
And it missheathed in my daughter's bosom!   205

Wife O me! this sight of death is as a bell
That warns my old age to a sepulchre.

[Enter MONTAGUE and others]

Prince Come Montague; for thou art early up
To see thy son and heir more early down.

Montague Alas, my liege, my wife is dead to-night!   210
Grief of my son's exile hath stopped her breath.
What further woe conspires against mine age?

Prince Look, and thou shalt see.

Montague O thou untaught! What manners is in this,
To press before thy father to a grave?   215

Prince Seal up the mouth of outrage for a while,
Till we can clear these ambiguities
And know their spring, their head, their true descent;
And then will I be general of your woes
And lead you even to death. Meantime forbear,   220
And let mischance be slave to patience.
Bring forth the parties of suspicion.

Friar I am the greatest, able to do least,
Yet most suspected, as the time and place

193. *With open outcry:* a metaphor from hunting, when the dogs are "in full cry" after the game.

194. *startles in:* alarms, shocks.

203. *mista'en:* gone to the wrong place.

his house: its sheath (personified, to augment the heinousness of the deed of which it was the instrument).

204. *Montague:* Romeo.

207. *warns:* summons.

209. *down:* dead.

214. *O thou untaught!:* unmannerly, ignorant person!

215. *To press . . . grave?:* as if he were pushing through a doorway in front of his father.

216. *outrage:* passion.

218. *spring . . . head . . . descent:* metaphors from a stream flowing down from its source, standing for the beginning and the sequence of "these ambiguities."

219-220. *general . . . death:* at the head of your woes (to get vengeance or at least inflict punishment) even if it leads to the death of those responsible.

221. *mischance be slave to patience:* disaster be ruled by patience.

222. *parties of suspicion:* suspects.

223. *the greatest:* suspected most.

Doth make against me, of this direful murder;   225
And here I stand, both to impeach and purge
Myself condemned and myself excused.

Prince Then say at once what thou dost know in this.

Friar I will be brief, for my short date of breath
Is not so long as is a tedious tale.   230
Romeo, there dead, was husband to that Juliet;
And she, there dead, that Romeo's faithful wife.
I married them; and their stol'n marriage day
Was Tybalt's doomsday, whose untimely death
Banished the new-made bridegroom from this city;   235
For whom, and not for Tybalt, Juliet pined.
You, to remove that siege of grief from her,
Betrothed and would have married her perforce
To County Paris. Then comes she to me
And with wild looks bid me devise some mean   240
To rid her from this second marriage,
Or in my cell there would she kill herself.
Then gave I her (so tutored by my art)
A sleeping potion; which so took effect
As I intended, for it wrought on her   245
The form of death. Meantime I writ to Romeo
That he should hither come as this dire night
To help to take her from her borrowed grave,
Being the time the potion's force should cease.
But he which bore my letter, Friar John,   250
Was stayed by accident, and yesternight
Returned my letter back. Then all alone
At the prefixed hour of her waking
Came I to take her from her kindred's vault;
Meaning to keep her closely at my cell   255
Till I conveniently could send to Romeo.
But when I came, some minute ere the time
Of her awakening, here untimely lay
The noble Paris and true Romeo dead.
She wakes; and I entreated her come forth   260
And bear this work of heaven with patience;
But then a noise did scare me from the tomb,
And she, too desperate, would not go with me,
But, as it seems, did violence on herself.
All this I know, and to the marriage   265

225.   *Doth make:* do inform, witness.

226-227.   *both . . . excused:* The friar acknowledges that he can be accused of being the cause of these deaths (his condemnation), but not that it was his intention (that is his excuse).

229.   *date of breath:* time I have to live.

233.   *stol'n:* secret.

237.   *siege:* cause (or, which besieged her).

246.   *form:* appearance

247.   *as:* on.

255.   *closely:* secretly.

260.   *She wakes:* notice this dramatic transition to the present tense, making the effect more crisp and forceful.

261.   *this work of heaven:* Romeo's death.

Her nurse is privy; and if aught in this
Miscarried by my fault, let my old life
Be sacrificed, some hour before his time,
Unto the rigour of severest law.

Prince We still have known thee for a holy man.   270
Where's Romeo's man? What can he say in this?

Balthasar I brought my master news of Juliet's death;
And then in post he came from Mantua
To this same place, to this same monument.
This letter he early bid me give his father,   275
And threat'ned me with death, going in the vault,
If I departed not and left him there.

Prince Give me the letter. I will look on it.
Where is the County's page that raised the watch?
Sirrah, what made your master in this place?   280

Page He came with flowers to strew his lady's grave;
And bid me stand aloof, and so I did.
Anon comes one with light to ope the tomb;
And by and by my master drew on him;
And then I ran away to call the watch.   285

Prince This letter doth make good the friar's words,
Their course of love, the tidings of her death;
And here he writes that he did buy a poison
Of a poor pothecary, and therewithal
Came to this vault to die, and lie with Juliet.   290
Where be these enemies? Capulet, Montague,
See what a scourge is laid upon your hate,
That heaven finds means to kill your joys with love.
And I, for winking at your discords too,
Have lost a brace of kinsmen. All are punished.   295

Capulet O brother Montague, give me thy hand
This is my daughter's jointure, for no more
Can I demand.

Montague   But I can give thee more;
For I will raise her statue in pure gold,
That whiles Verona by that name is known,   300
There shall no figure at such rate be set
As that of true and faithful Juliet.

268. *his:* its.

270. *still:* always.

273. *in post:* post haste.

275. *early:* i.e., in the morning,
276. *going:* as he was going.

279. *raised:* sent for, called, summoned.
280. *made:* was doing.

284. *by and by:* at once.

293. *your joys:* your children.
294. *winking at:* closing my eyes to.
295. *a brace of kinsmen:* Mercutio and Paris.

297. *jointure:* that which the bride-groom or his parents settle on the bride.

301. *at such rate be set:* be valued this high.

Capulet As rich shall Romeo's by his lady lie—
Poor sacrifices of our enmity!

Prince A glooming peace this morning with it brings   305
The sun for sorrow will not show his head.
Go hence, to have more talk of these sad things;
Some shall be pardoned, and some punished;
For never was a story of more woe
Than this of Juliet and her Romeo. *[Exeunt]*   310

304.   *sacrifices of our enmity:* offerings of our hatred (which has now ceased).

305.   *glooming:* melancholy.

COMMENTARY

As the final scene of the play opens, Paris and his Page stand in the churchyard at night outside the Capulets' burial monument. Paris posts his Page outside the vault to listen for anyone who may come along and instructs him to whistle if he hears anything. Paris strews Juliet's grave with flowers and plans to cover it each night with perfumed water—his "true love's rite" (20). The Page whistles, and Paris hides. The scene ironically parallels Romeo and Juliet's balcony scene (Act II, Scene 2). In that scene, Romeo, hidden in the darkness, overhears Juliet's feelings for him; here, Paris, also covered by night, listens to Romeo's parting words to her.

Into the "bed of death"

Romeo and Balthasar enter the churchyard. The coincidence is astonishing: Romeo has accidentally learned of Juliet's death and arrives at the tomb exactly when Paris delivers the flowers. Romeo walks to the door of the tomb, rips it open with a mattock (a tool much like an ax or pick), and gives Balthasar a letter to deliver to his father. Romeo threatens to kill Balthasar if he interferes with his plans. Romeo instructs Balthasar that no matter what he sees or hears, he should remain hidden. Balthasar promises to leave but, frightened by Romeo's wild looks, he hides in the trees near the tomb.

Romeo descends into the "bed of death" to see Juliet's face one last time and to take a ring from her finger (28). Romeo's plans are "savage-wild" and "[m]ore fierce" than "empty tigers or the roaring sea" (37–39). In fact, if anyone interferes with his plans, Romeo vows to shred him "joint by joint" and to scatter his limbs in the "hungry churchyard" (35–36). Earth and Romeo are hungry for death on this night.

Romeo's language as he opens the tomb combines a number of images that have recurred throughout the play: The Capulets' vault has become the "womb of death, / Gorged with the dearest morsel of the earth" (45–46). Romeo will force its "rotten jaws" open and "cram" it with more food (47–48). As in Act V, Scene 1, death is a "womb" that will eventually result in new growth. Romeo's language also reminds us of Friar Laurence's claim in Act II, Scene 3 that "[t]he earth that's nature's mother is her tomb: / What is her burying grave, that is her womb" (5–6). For Romeo, the Capulet's tomb has become a womb, which will gorge on him and lead him to new life with Juliet. By "cram[ming]" death with more food, Romeo paradoxically assures the most spectacular rebirth.

Fate claims Paris

Paris sees Romeo enter the tomb and reveals that he believes Romeo is responsible for Juliet's death. (Juliet's family believes that she died from grief as a result of Tybalt's death.) Paris is angry, because he thinks that Romeo came to the tomb to desecrate the bodies of the dead. Paris decides to apprehend Romeo, calling him a "[c]ondemned villain" (56). When Paris tells Romeo that he must die, Romeo agrees. Romeo calls Paris a "youth" and tells him to fear the dead and leave the tomb—"be gone. Live" (61, 66). But Paris refuses, and the two men fight.

By calling Paris a "youth," Romeo draws attention to how much he has changed and matured in the course of the play. In many ways, Paris is Romeo's double. Shakespeare has developed Paris into a notable rival for Romeo: Paris's love is publicly acceptable and sanctioned by Juliet's parents, while Romeo's love is private and romantic and, therefore, preferred by Juliet. Romeo's love is more impassioned than his rival's. Paris is a more proper suitor than Romeo, perhaps in part because his speeches echo those given by Romeo earlier in the play. Romeo's passion for Juliet has overwhelmed the intellectual conventions of love he had once perfected.

As Romeo was entranced by Rosaline (a woman who could never love him), Paris is pledged to Juliet (who is cold to his love). Paris's stilted and conventional language imitates Romeo's praises of Rosaline at the beginning of the play. Creating a contrast between Paris's formal rhymed verses and Romeo's impassioned blank verse, this scene highlights Romeo's growth and development. The stereotypical adolescent has disappeared, and the passionate man has emerged.

Paris's Page sees the fight and runs for the watchmen. Paris is slain and asks Romeo to lay his body next to Juliet's. Romeo agrees, remembering that Paris was to have married Juliet—Romeo knows that both of their names are written in "sour misfortune's book" (82). Fate reaches out to claim Paris because he has come too close to Romeo and Juliet.

The feast of death

Romeo's long soliloquy in this scene repeats many of the motifs that Shakespeare uses throughout the play. For example, consider the emphasis on images of light contrasting with darkness: The dark tomb is brilliantly lit by Juliet's presence, as "her beauty makes / This vault a feasting presence full of light" (85–86). The image of the vault lit for a feast recalls Romeo's words as he entered the tomb. This is the feast of death, who will gorge upon the corpses of three tender youths: Romeo, Juliet, and Paris. The imagery also has a carnivalesque feel: This convergence in the tomb is a carnival feast, a ritual gorging, that will allow the society of Verona to purge itself. Following the deaths of Romeo and Juliet, a more peaceful Verona will be born.

Shakespeare also uses the image of lightning throughout the play. Remember, for example, Juliet's fear that their love will be "[t]oo like the lightning, which

doth cease to be / Ere one can say 'It lightens'" (II.2.119–120). As she predicted, their love blazed quickly across the sky, beginning and ending in a mere few days. In this scene, Romeo likens the merriness he feels before death to a "lightning before death," and he fully understands this phrase for the first time in the play (90). The sight of Juliet's dead body in the tomb shocks him like lightning, yet her beauty also fills the tomb with light and enlightens his heavy heart. Romeo is amazed by the "crimson" in Juliet's lips and cheeks, wondering why she is "yet so fair" (95, 102).

Although Romeo interprets Juliet's lingering beauty as her final bloom before death, the colour in her lips and cheeks is actually a sign that the potion is wearing off and she'll soon wake from her herb-induced trance. If he weren't so hasty and impetuous, Romeo would see her come alive once again. Romeo imagines that death keeps her beautiful so she can be his "paramour" in the dark (105). To protect her from death's fearsome affections, Romeo wants to die with her.

Critics often note the sexual imagery of this scene. In stating that he'll lie and die with Juliet that night, Romeo refers to their literal reunion but also to a figurative sexual reunion (V.1.34). In Renaissance slang, a man dies within a woman during sex. When entering Juliet's tomb, Romeo said that he entered the "womb of death" (45). Romeo uses a round cup, which is circular like a woman, to induce his death. On the other hand, as we see shortly, Juliet will plunge a dagger into her heart—using a more phallic tool to achieve her end. Therefore, their deaths symbolically create a sexual, as well as spiritual, reunion. Through death, they'll finally escape the effect of the "inauspicious stars"—the bad fortune—that has taunted them (111).

Romeo's final words echo the sea imagery that Lord Capulet uses to describe Juliet in Act III, Scene 5: Death is the "desperate pilot" that now dashes him on the rocks in his "seasick weary bark" (117–118). In a final play on words, Romeo states that the drugs are "quick" (120). He means both that the poison works quickly and that it is alive. With a final kiss for Juliet, Romeo dies. By gathering and repeating the imagery that Shakespeare has written throughout the play, Romeo's final soliloquy weaves together an intense, emotional ending to the play.

Moments too late

Immediately after Romeo dies, Friar Laurence arrives in the vault, equipped with his spade and a crowbar. The coincidence is again amazing: Had the Friar arrived five minutes earlier, he could have saved Romeo's life. Fate seems to revel in these near misses. The Friar meets Balthasar outside the tomb, and Balthasar explains that Romeo has been down in the vault "[f]ull half an hour," but he didn't dare investigate because he was afraid of Romeo's wrath (132). While sleeping under a yew tree, Balthasar dreamt that Romeo fought

Romeo and Juliet, by Henry Fuseli, 19th century. David David Gallery, Philadelphia/SuperStock

with someone and "slew him" (139). His dream, of course, is prophetic, like all the dreams in this play.

The Friar enters the tomb, sees blood, and is frightened by "masterless" weapons in this "place of peace" (142–143). Both Romeo and Paris are dead, and he wonders what "unkind hour / Is guilty of this lamentable chance" (145–146). The "unkind hour" and "lamentable chance" have triumphed once more. No individual action or trait could have saved Romeo and Paris from the Wheel of Fortune.

As the Friar contemplates this unlucky event, Juliet wakes wondering where Romeo has gone. The Friar describes the tomb as a "nest / Of death, contagion, and unnatural sleep" (151–152). And, again, the Friar says that a "greater power than [they] can contradict" has thwarted their plans—not the hand of God, but the hand of fortune (153). He explains to Juliet that both Romeo and Paris are dead, and he vows to take Juliet to a nunnery. The Friar wants to escape from the vault before the watchmen arrive.

Juliet refuses to leave, so the Friar goes without her. Leaving is an act of extreme cowardice on the Friar's part. Because he recognizes his role in the tragedy, he leaves Juliet alone in the tomb. Her fears of the Friar's treachery prove to be valid. Like all the other adults in this play, the Friar fails her when she needs him most.

A final kiss

Juliet kisses Romeo's lips in hopes of finding some leftover drop of poison; their first kiss at the masquerade, likened to a prayer, has been transformed into a kiss of death. Not finding sufficient poison on his still warm lips, Juliet stabs herself. In this final moment, Juliet notices even the rust on the sword's blade. Her proximity to death makes her acutely aware of the world around her and, in particular, of the tools of death. In noting that her body is Romeo's "sheath," Juliet uses sexually suggestive language to show that she hopes to die with her lover in more ways than one (170). By plunging Romeo's dagger into her warm flesh, Juliet achieves both sexual and spiritual reunion with her lover.

The watchmen enter the tomb and find the three dead bodies, but they cannot understand the story behind the grisly scene. They wonder why Juliet, who has been buried for two days, appears newly dead.

A Footsbarn Travelling Theatre production, 1993.
Clive Barda/PAL

They question how Romeo and Paris managed to enter the tomb. Other watchmen catch the Friar as he tries to escape from the churchyard with his mattock and spade, and they hold him for questioning.

The Capulets enter, and Lord Capulet notices that Romeo's dagger is "missheathed in my daughter's bosom" (205). His words remind the audience of the sexual implications of the scene; the imagery surrounding Romeo and Juliet's death inextricably links sex and death. The sight of so much death leads Lady Capulet to think of dying herself. Lord Montague and the Prince arrive with the news that Lady Montague died last night over grief at her son's banishment.

Before anyone reenters the tomb, the Prince wants to discover the "head" and "true descent" of the situation, its body and genealogy (218). Notice how the imagery throughout this scene focuses heavily on the body; we've seen "wombs" and "rotten jaws," and we now see that the story of Romeo and Juliet's death also has a body for the Prince.

Re-membering the state of Verona

Symbolically, the body of the community in Verona has become dismembered, fragmented by the feud between the Montagues and Capulets. As the "head" of the state's body, the Prince is responsible for remembering the past: both remembering the community's stories and re-membering or sewing together its dismembered parts.

The Prince's passage structurally parallels his two prior entrances in the play, following the opening street brawl and the fight that resulted in Mercutio and Tybalt's deaths. All three entrances are public communal scenes that contrast with Romeo and Juliet's intense private world. In all of his entrances, the Prince offers judgment on the violence. As explained in the commentary for Act I, Scene 1, the Prince's third entrance into the play is ritually symbolic. On this third occasion, the Prince's judgment will lead to peace and balance between the rival Capulets and Montagues; it will create wholeness in the communal body of Verona.

The Friar provides the first explanation of what happened to Romeo, Juliet, and Paris. Realizing that all situations, as well as all people, have both good and bad sides, the Friar claims that he is both "condemned" and "excused"—both innocent and guilty (227). Although he recognizes his role in the tragedy, he also believes that fate should take some responsibility, because misfortune led to the play's fatal coincidences.

The Friar claims that his explanation will be brief, but he then launches into the longest speech in the play. After a detailed summary of the story (one that adds nothing new to the audience's understanding of the play), the Friar urges that "if aught in this / Miscarried by my fault, let my old life / Be sacrificed, some hour before his time / Unto the rigour of severest law" (266–269).

Always lenient, the Prince pardons the Friar because he is a holy man. The Prince then reads through Romeo's letter to his father and discovers that it supports the Friar's words. Finally, the Prince warns the Capulets and Montagues that "a scourge is laid upon your hate, / That heaven finds means to kill your joys with love" (292–293).

However, no one escapes blame in this play, and the Prince also recognizes his role in the tragedy. If he had disciplined the Montagues and Capulets more completely after earlier incidents, the Prince wouldn't have "lost a brace of kinsmen" (Mercutio and Paris) and Romeo and Juliet may have been saved (295). Everyone is guilty, and everyone has been punished.

A show of reconciliation

Although the love of Romeo and Juliet has flashed as briefly as lightning in a dark sky, the effects of their relationship will have a long-lasting impact on Verona. In a show of reconciliation, Capulet asks for Montague's hand so they can link in friendship, in honour of Romeo's "jointure" with Juliet (297). But Montague doesn't stop with his acceptance of Capulet's offer; he vows to create a statue of Juliet in pure gold. Always ready for a competition, Capulet says that he'll also make a statue of Romeo to lie by Juliet's side—the "[p]oor sacrifices" of their parents' enmity (304).

You can easily view this conversation between the Montagues and Capulets with a cynical eye. Have the heads of the rival families really changed, or have they just exchanged their violent competition with a monetary competition? Either way, the lovers' sacrifice will have a deep impact on Verona. Romeo and Juliet have given their lives to restore civil peace and friendship to this embattled society, and their sacrifice will create unity in both the public and private worlds of Verona.

In the final speech of the play, the Prince provides an example of *pathetic fallacy* (giving human traits to nature) when he argues that the sun won't rise on this day because of its sorrow over the deaths of Romeo, Juliet, and Paris. He vows that the law will enact its judgment so that some citizens are pardoned and some punished, at which point the society of Verona will begin anew.

Shakespeare doesn't make the Prince identify his punishments but instead leaves this facet of the play open to your imagination. In Brooke's version of the story—Shakespeare's source for the play—the Nurse is exiled because she concealed the marriage; the Apothecary who sold Romeo the poison is hanged; and the Friar is released, becomes a hermit, and dies soon after. By focusing on the Prince's leniency in this passage, Shakespeare reminds us that the proper function of the law is not violence, but the creation of harmony and justice. Unlike the other men of authority in this community—in particular, Lord Capulet—the Prince is fair and thoughtful, not despotic and careless.

Perhaps Shakespeare didn't assign punishments because part of the play's message is that such judgments would be arbitrary. As the play emphasizes, distinguishing good from bad is often difficult because context plays such a strong role in creating values. Was the Friar corrupt because he attempted to help Romeo and Juliet? Should he have simply reported them to their parents? Was the Nurse immoral in advocating that Juliet marry Paris rather than Romeo? Was it wrong of the Apothecary to sell poison to Romeo? Was fate to blame for Romeo and Juliet's misfortune or were the actions of people? Clear answers for these questions don't exist. All of these actions are morally ambiguous, so it's impossible for the play to punish anyone for a role in the tragedy.

Ending the play, the Prince says, "For never was a story of more woe / Than this of Juliet and her Romeo" (309–310). Obviously, this story of woe has had a strong impact on audiences throughout the centuries. Even today the names Romeo and Juliet are culturally synonymous with the idea of deep but tragic love. Recent film adaptations of the play show that Shakespeare's vision of romantic love continues to appeal to people today. Not a fleeting light, their tragic story continues to flash like never-ending lightning in movie and theatre productions around the world, showing that all lives need a little poetry and love.

Notes

Notes

Notes

REVIEW

Use this Review to gauge what you've learned and to build confidence in your understanding of the original text. After you work through the review questions, the problem-solving exercises, and the suggested activities, you're well on your way to understanding and appreciating the works of William Shakespeare.

IDENTIFY THE QUOTATION

Answer these questions as you identify the quotations listed below:

* Who is speaking? Who (if anyone) is listening?
* What does the quotation reveal about the speaker's character?
* What does the quotation tell you about other characters within the play?
* Where does the quotation occur within the play?
* What does the quotation show you about the play's themes?
* What significant imagery do you see in the quotation, and how do images in this passage relate to images in the rest of the play?

1. The earth that's nature's mother is her tomb.
What is her burying grave, that is her womb;
And from her womb children of divers kind
We sucking on her natural bosom find,
Many for many virtues excellent,
None but for some, and yet all different.

2. 'Tis but thy name that is my enemy.
Thou art thyself, though not a Montague.
What's Montague? It is nor hand, nor foot,
Nor arm, nor face, nor any other part
Belonging to a man. O, be some other name!
What's in a name? That which we call a rose
By any other word would smell as sweet.

3. Sweet flower, with flowers thy bridal bed I strew.
(O woe! thy canopy is dust and stones)
Which with sweet water nightly I will dew;
Or, wanting that, with tears distilled by moans.
The obsequies that I for thee will keep
Nightly shall be to strew thy grave and weep.

4. Death, that hath sucked the honey of thy breath,
Hath had no power yet upon thy beauty.
Thou art not conquered. Beauty's ensign yet
Is crimson in thy lips and in thy cheeks,
And death's pale flag is not advanced there. . . .
Shall I believe
That unsubstantial Death is amorous,
And that the lean abhorred monster keeps
Thee here in dark to be his paramour?

5. Why, is not this better now than groaning for love? Now art thou sociable, now art thou Romeo;
Now art thou what thou art, by art as well as by nature.
For this drivelling love is like a great natural that runs
Lolling up and down to hide his bauble in a hole.

6. Where be these enemies? Capulet, Montague,
See what a scourge is laid upon your hate,
That heaven finds means to kill your joys with love;
And I, for winking at your discords too,
Have lost a brace of kinsmen. All are punished.

7. O heavy lightness, serious vanity,
Misshapen chaos of well-seeming forms,
Feather of lead, bright smoke, cold fire, sick health,
Still-waking sleep, that is not what it is!
This love feel I, that feel no love in this.

8. Beguiled, divorced, wronged, spited, slain!
Most detestable Death, by thee beguiled,
By cruel, cruel thee quite overthrown.
O love! O life! not life, but love in death!

9. O serpent heart, hid with a flow'ring face!
Did ever dragon keep so fair a cave?
Beautiful tyrant! fiend angelical!
Dove-feathered raven! wolvish-ravening lamb!
Despised substance of divinest show!
Just opposite to what thou justly seem'st—
A damned saint, an honourable villain!

10. This night you shall behold him at our feast.
Read o'er the volume of young Paris' face,
And find delight writ there with beauty's pen,
Examine every married lineament,
And see how one another lends content;
And what obscured in this fair volume lies
Find written in the margent of his eyes.
This precious book of love, this unbound lover,
To beautify him only lacks a cover.

11. No, 'tis not so deep as a well, nor so wide as a church door; but 'tis enough, 'twill serve. Ask for me to-morrow, and you shall find me a grave man. I am peppered, I warrant, for this world. A plague o' both your houses!

12. Hang thee, young baggage! disobedient wretch! I tell thee what—get thee to church a Thursday Or never after look me in the face.

TRUE / FALSE

1. T F When the play begins, Romeo is in love with Rosamund.

2. T F Rome is the setting of this play.

3. T F Tybalt kills Mercutio.

4. T F Juliet's Nurse tells her about Tybalt's death.

5. T F Friar Laurence banishes Romeo to Mantua.

6. T F When the play begins, Juliet is in love with Paris.

7. T F Benvolio encourages Mercutio to fight with Tybalt.

8. T F Friar John marries Romeo and Juliet.

9. T F Paris commits suicide when he realizes that Juliet is dead.

10. T F The Prince banishes Friar Laurence to Mantua at the end of the play.

11. T F Tybalt is Juliet's cousin.

12. T F Juliet's Nurse thinks that she should marry Paris.

13. T F Mercutio sympathizes with Romeo's love for Juliet.

14. T F Juliet's Nurse makes a potion for Juliet that imitates death.

15. T F Lady Capulet opposes Juliet's marriage to Paris.

MULTIPLE CHOICE

1. When the play begins, Juliet is how old?

a. 21

b. 18

c. 16

d. 13

2. Which characters are related to Prince Escalus?

a. Mercutio

b. Benvolio

c. Paris

d. More than one of the above.

3. What caused the feud between the Capulets and Montagues?

a. Lord Capulet killed Lord Montague's nephew.

b. The Capulets stole land from the Montagues.

c. Lady Montague insulted Juliet.

d. None of the above.

4. Why does the Friar agree to marry Romeo and Juliet?

a. He hopes that the marriage will help end the feud between the Montagues and Capulets.

b. He believes that Romeo and Juliet are deeply in love.

c. He's afraid of offending Romeo's father.

d. None of the above.

5. Why does Friar Laurence's message not reach Romeo in Mantua?

a. Romeo has moved to a new house, and Friar Laurence doesn't have the correct address.

b. A civil war in Italy has blocked all roads to Mantua.

c. Friar John can't get to Mantua because of an outbreak of the plague.

d. None of the above.

6. Mercutio doesn't like Tybalt because:

a. Tybalt is in love with Mercutio's sister.

b. Tybalt is too fashionable for Mercutio.

c. Tybalt's style of fencing is too formulaic.

d. More than one of the above.

7. According to the Prince's opening speech, brawls between the Montagues and Capulets have disturbed the streets of Verona how often:

a. Three times

b. Five times

c. Two times

d. Ten times

8. What is the name of the Nurse's servant?

a. Samuel

b. Abram

c. Peter

d. Balthasar

9. What is Mercutio's nickname for Tybalt?

a. Tricky Ty

b. Brawling Boy

c. Prince of Cats

d. King of Compliments

10. Which of the following characters did Romeo kill?

a. Paris

b. Tybalt

c. Mercutio

d. More than one of the above.

11. How much time elapses in the play?

    a. Five days

    b. One week

    c. Three weeks

    d. Six months

12. Whose body is in the tomb with Juliet when she is under the spell of the potion?

    a. Mercutio's

    b. Lord Capulet's

    c. Benvolio's

    d. Tybalt's

13. What time of day seems to best suit Romeo and Juliet?

    a. Dawn

    b. Late afternoon

    c. Night

    d. Noon

14. Mercutio explains the reason why people dream by describing the actions of which mythical character?

    a. Diane

    b. Cupid

    c. Queen Mab

    d. Venus

15. The musicians appear in the play because they are hired for what occasion?

    a. Romeo and Juliet's wedding

    b. Paris and Juliet's wedding

    c. The masquerade

    d. Juliet's funeral

FILL IN THE BLANKS

1. Romeo: But soft! What light through yonder window breaks?

It is the East, and Juliet is the _____!

2. Chorus: Two households, both alike in dignity,

In fair _____, where we lay our scene

From ancient grudge break to new mutiny,

Where civil blood makes civil hands unclean.

3. Mercutio: O, then I see Queen _____ hath been with you.

She is the fairies' midwife . . . .

4. Romeo: My lips, two blushing _____, ready stand

To smooth that rough touch with a tender kiss.

5. Juliet: My only love, sprung from my only _____!

Too early seen unknown, and known too late!

6. Friar: _____ itself turns vice, being mis-applied,

And vice sometime's by action dignified.

7. Friar: Young men's love then lies

Not truly in their hearts, but in their _____.

8. Juliet: Give me my Romeo; and when he shall die,

Take him and cut him out in little _____,

And he will make the face of heaven so fine

That all the world will be in love with night.

9. Juliet: 'Romeo is _____'—to speak that word

Is father, mother, Tybalt, Romeo, Juliet,

All slain, all dead.

10. Montague: But I can give thee more;

For I will raise her _____ in pure gold,

That whiles Verona by that name is known,

There shall no figure at such rate be set

As that of true and faithful Juliet.

DISCUSSION

Use the following sets of questions to generate class/group discussion:

1. Love is one of the primary themes in the play. Consider the following questions about love. What different types of love does Shakespeare represent in the play? Which characters are associated with which types of love? How does Mercutio's notion of love compare with the Nurse's? How does it compare with Romeo's or Juliet's? What differences can you find between Paris and Romeo in their descriptions of love? What kind of love is best?

2. Compare and contrast the women of the play. What do you think Shakespeare is saying through his representations of these specific types of women? For example, what differences do you see between Juliet and Rosaline? How does Juliet differ from her mother and her nurse? What negative views of women can you find in the play? What positive views can you find?

3. In *Romeo and Juliet*, as in most of his plays, Shakespeare presents his main themes in various shapes and forms. (The Friar isn't the only character trying to distinguish between good and evil, for example.) Make a list of what you perceive to be the play's major themes (friendship, violence, marriage, and so on), and then see how many different ways you can identify that Shakespeare treats those themes in the play. For example, how do Benvolio, the Prince, and Mercutio differ in their positions on violence? How do Lord Capulet, Lady Capulet, the Nurse, and Juliet differ in their views of marriage?

4. Trace the image of blind Cupid in the play. Where does the image appear in the text? Which characters refer to him? What purpose does he seem to serve?

5. Using the text of *Romeo and Juliet*, find examples of definitions of masculinity. What are some of the traditional stereotypes associated with men in modern society? How do they compare with Shakespeare's views of men? Does Shakespeare seem to like the men in the play? Given the power, how might he change the stereotypes of men?

6. Many critics believe that Mercutio's death is unnecessary. Do you agree? What functions might his death serve in the play?

7. Look at some of the other supporting characters in the play—the Nurse, Benvolio, Lord and Lady Capulet, the Prince, and Friar Laurence, for instance. Referring to the text of the play, characterize the supporting characters and determine what they contribute to the play's unfolding action. What purpose do they serve? How would the play differ if any one of them were missing?

8. Fate plays an important role in the play. What examples can you find of fate working against Romeo and Juliet? In your opinion, how much do the personal characteristics of the two main characters contribute to their tragedy? Do factors other than fate seem to be at work? How much does Friar Laurence contribute to Romeo and Juliet's tragedy?

9. Marriage is a central theme in *Romeo and Juliet*. Compare and contrast the views characters in the play express by finding passages that discuss marriage and, in a larger sense, men's perceptions of women and women's perceptions of men. What does Shakespeare seem to think about marriage?

IDENTIFYING PLAY ELEMENTS

Find examples of the following in the text of *Romeo and Juliet*:

* **Verbal Irony:** A statement in which there is a large difference between the literal meaning and the implied meaning.

* **Dramatic Irony:** A plot device in which a character has an experience that is unexpected to him or her, but that the audience had anticipated because our knowledge of the situation is more complete than the character's.

* **Cosmic irony:** The suggestion that a god or fate controls and meddles with human lives.

* **Soliloquy:** A monologue in which a character in a play is alone and speaking to him or herself.

* **Foreshadowing:** The introduction early in the play of verbal and dramatic hints of what will happen later.

* **Ambiguity:** The use of a word or expression to mean more than one idea.

* **Analogy:** A comparison based on resemblances between things that are otherwise unlike.

* **Apostrophe:** An address to someone who is absent and cannot hear the speaker or to something nonhuman that cannot understand. An apostrophe allows the speaker to think aloud.

* **Symbol:** A person, place, or thing in a literary work that figuratively represents something else. Often the idea represented is abstract, while the symbol itself is concrete.

* **Oxymoron:** A figure of speech that combines two apparently contradictory words (e.g., "wise fool").

ACTIVITIES

The following activities generally work best with small groups, and you can modify them to fit individual needs. Use them as springboards for further discussion and activities.

1. As a precursor to studying the text, ask your students to research not only Shakespeare's life, but his culture as well. Have students explore the politics, religion, theatre, and daily life of Early Modern England. (You can use the Introduction to Early Modern England at the front of this text as a starting point.) Have your students respond to a specific set of questions. For example, what was a normal day for a teenager? What could one expect from his or her life in that time period? What types of jobs might be available? What types of foods would be on the table for an evening meal? What would someone wear?

2. Randomly assign students one of the play's characters. (For students who are just beginning to study Shakespeare, use only the main characters. More advanced students can tackle the minor characters.) Ask each student to write a letter of introduction (from one paragraph to several pages in length) from the perspective of that character. Consider asking the students to address specific topics in the letter, such as the character's station in life (social class), his or her relationships with other characters in the play, and his or her views on love and marriage.

3. As a follow-up to the previous activity, have each student's character write a question that he or she has for each of the other characters. For example, have Juliet write a question that she is likely to ask each of the other characters. (She might ask her father, for instance, why he wants her to marry Paris.) In a discussion group, have students ask their questions and allow the appropriate character to respond. Ask other students to consider whether that character has responded appropriately based on his or her behaviour in the play.

4. If your school has access to electronic discussion boards or an asynchronous discussion forum such as *TopClass* or *Web Crossing*, have students post questions and responses as they read through the text. Consider asking students to post a minimum number of questions (two, perhaps) and a minimum number of thoughtful replies (four, for example). Also, consider imposing qualifiers on the types of replies. For example, a brief response such as, "I couldn't agree more" might not count as a reply, but a response that says, "I couldn't agree more" and then substantiates why the student thinks so would be acceptable.

5. Select a few short scenes (or edit the longer ones) and assign a group of students to each scene. Have the students make a *prompt book* for their scene. The prompt book will use a three-column format. Have students copy and place the text of the play in the middle column. In the left column, ask them to write a literal translation of the action occurring on that page. In the right column, students should write the stage directions they would consider appropriate for acting the play.

6. Have student groups perform short scenes for the class (perhaps as a follow-up to the previous activity). In order to increase student participation, have each student audience member serve as a reviewer. Make small slips of paper with two or three open-ended questions for audience members to respond to after each group's performance.

7. Ask students to keep a dialectical reading journal as they work through *Romeo and Juliet*. Students can either purchase dialectical notebook paper or make some by dividing regular notebook paper into two columns (the left about 3½ inches and the right about 5 inches). In the right column, have students keep track of the plot of the play. Ask them to put in headings indicating act, scene, and line number references so they can quickly locate passages for class discussion. In the smaller column on the left, have students write their personal responses to what they've just read. For example, students may offer commentary or questions regarding the action in a particular scene. Working dialectically helps students engage the text and read actively rather than passively.

8. Using an Internet search engine such as *Google*, have students do a search for websites related to *Romeo and Juliet*. Ask students to assemble a list of sites, critically annotating each one with a few sentences (not just summarizing its content, but really considering the credibility of each site). All students can then pool their findings to create a master list of Web sources. Developing a system for classifying their findings is also a good way to advance the students' analytical skills.

9. Have students make websites for *Romeo and Juliet*. Small groups can each work on an act, or each group can make a site for the entire play. In lieu of summarizing action, students can discuss film adaptations; research critical approaches to the text and present their findings; make a concordance to the play; discuss visual representations of the text (for example, scan in drawings and engravings that have accompanied various printed versions of the text, analyzing which themes and ideas the artworks provide); start a discussion board; and so on.

10. Show scenes from selected film adaptations of *Romeo and Juliet* (such as *William Shakespeare's Romeo + Juliet* or *Shakespeare in Love*). Have students look for specific things, such as how the film depicts Romeo and Juliet's relationship; outright deviations from the text; how music, settings, and costumes contribute to their understanding of the play; the characterizations of Mercutio and the Friar; and so on. You can then ask students to discuss their findings.

ANSWERS

Identify the Quotation

1. This passage is spoken by Friar Laurence in Act II, Scene 3. He is alone in his garden, reflecting on the dual nature of plants, human beings, and all of creation.

2. Juliet speaks these words in Act II, Scene 2 from her balcony. She believes she is alone, but Romeo is actually in the orchard below listening to her. In this passage, she notes how arbitrary and insignificant names are, casting new light on the feud between her family and the Montagues.

3. Paris says these words in Act V, Scene 3—the final scene of the play. He is in the churchyard where Juliet is buried, mourning her loss. Notice the formal language and imagery he uses to express his grief.

4. Romeo speaks these words to Juliet's "corpse" in Act V, Scene 3. He wonders how she looks so beautiful, not realizing that she is on the verge of awaking from her potion-induced sleep.

5. Mercutio, in Act II, Scene 4, is happy to see the sociable side of Romeo emerge again. Mercutio does not understand Romeo's lovesick melancholy and dislikes the way it has altered his friend's personality.

6. Prince Escalus chides the Capulets and Montagues in Act V, Scene 3, for the deadly results of their senseless feud. Not only have Romeo and Juliet perished because of it, but the Prince has lost two family members.

7. In Act I, Scene 1, Romeo uses formalized Petrarchan language to describe his supposed love for Rosaline. His emphasis on form rather than feeling changes when he meets Juliet and begins to experience real passion.

8. Paris speaks this passage in Act IV, Scene 5, when he is in Juliet's chamber mourning what appears to be her death. He and Lord Capulet seem to use language to outdo each other in their grief, piling adjective upon adjective to describe their feelings.

9. Juliet says these words in Act III, Scene 2, when she learns from the Nurse that Romeo has killed her cousin, Tybalt. She uses the device of oxymoron to describe the seeming oppositions in Romeo's character. Her speech reminds us of the Friar's musings in his garden about the duality of all things and all people.

10. Lady Capulet speaks to Juliet in Act I, Scene 3 about Paris's charms, using heavy book and reading imagery to communicate her message.

11. Mercutio says these words as he is dying in Act III, Scene 1. Even on the verge of death, he puns on the word "grave." He also refuses to accept responsibility for his own actions, blaming the "houses" of Capulet and Montague for his demise.

12. Lord Capulet chastises Juliet in Act III, Scene 5 for disobeying his wishes by refusing to marry Paris. Showing his hot temper and questionable concern for his daughter's happiness, he demands her obedience and threatens to abandon her if she won't give it.

True / False

1. False 2. False 3. True 4. True 5. False 6. False
7. False 8. False 9. False 10. False 11. True
12. True 13. False 14. False 15. False

Fill in the Blank

1. sun 2. Verona 3. Mab 4. pilgrims 5. hate
6. Virtue 7. eyes 8. stars 9. banished 10. statue

Multiple Choice

1. d 2. d. 3. d. 4. a. 5. c. 6. d. 7. a. 8. c. 9. c.
10. d. 11. a. 12. d. 13. c. 14. c. 15. b.

Romeo and Juliet
RESOURCE CENTRE

The learning doesn't need to stop here. The Resource Centre shows you the best of the best: great links to information in print, on film, and online.

FILMS

Romeo and Juliet. Directed by Franco Zeffirelli. Performed by Olivia Hussey and Leonard Whiting. 1968.

Starring Olivia Hussey and Leonard Whiting (who were 15 and 17 when this film was made), this production was one of the first to use teenage performers in the lead roles. The preserved medieval towns of Tuscany, Italy and the Borghese Palace, where the balcony scene is set, provide accurate glimpses of Renaissance culture. Zeffirelli shortened the original script, but the screenplay maintains the most essential scenes.

Shakespeare in Love. Directed by John Madden. Performed by Gwenyth Paltrow and Joseph Fiennes. 1998.

This Oscar award-winning film offers exciting speculation about a love affair that inspired Shakespeare to write *Romeo and Juliet.* Alternately comic and romantic, the film depicts young Will Shakespeare's battle with writer's block as he works on his most recent comedy, *Romeo and Ethel, the Pirate's Daughter.* Beautiful Viola de Lessels, disguised as a man, auditions for the play. Will falls deeply in love after discovering her true identity, and the pirate comedy is transformed into *Romeo and Juliet.* The film includes entertaining parallels with *Romeo and Juliet* and offers a convincing performance of the play, which captures the atmosphere of the sixteenth-century theatre.

West Side Story. Directed by Robert Wise and Jeremy Robbins. Performed by Natalie Wood and Richard Beymer. 1961.

An adaptation of *Romeo and Juliet* set in New York in the 1950s, this film tells the story of two teens, one white and the other Puerto Rican, who fall in love despite cultural tensions. Considered one of the best musicals ever made, the film features the music of Leonard Bernstein and the lyrics of Stephen Sondheim. The film is especially noted for the exuberance of the dancing by the rival male gangs, the Sharks and the Jets.

William Shakespeare's Romeo + Juliet. Directed by Baz Luhrmann. Performed by Clare Danes and Leonardo DiCaprio. Twentieth Century Fox, 1996.

Explosive, excessive, and original, this MTV-style version of the play is clever and compelling. While the words are all authentic, Luhrmann updates the tragedy with inventive changes of Shakespeare's scenes and characters. Mercutio becomes a flamboyant cross-dresser, for example, and the opening Montague-Capulet fight scene is transformed into a shootout at a self-service gas station.

INTERNET

"A Freshy's Guide to *Romeo and Juliet*."

www.angelfire.com/hi/romeoetjuliet

Designed as a guide for first-time readers of the play, this website has a variety of useful sections: vocabulary, homework problems, poems, essays, and a comparison of the 1968 and 1996 film versions of the play. The site also includes links to other *Romeo and Juliet* pages, providing access to play-related illustrations, a study guide, quizzes, and more.

"Mr. William Shakespeare and the Internet."

http://daphne.palomar.edu/shakespeare/

According to the creators of this site, its primary aim is to provide a complete annotated guide to all of the Shakespeare resources available on the Internet. In addition, it presents Shakespeare information unavailable elsewhere on the Web. Some of its unique features include a Shakespeare Timeline that highlights the main events of Shakespeare's life and work (includes a Shakespeare Biography Quiz), prefatory materials from the First Folio, and so on. It also provides links related to teaching Shakespeare and lists of other Shakespeare resources available on the Web.

BOOKS AND ARTICLES

Bristol, Michael D. "Funeral Bak'd-Meats: Carnival and the Carnivalesque in *Hamlet*: Complete, Authoritative Text with Biographical and Historical Contexts, Critical History, and Essays from Five Contemporary Critical Perspectives." *Case Studies in Contemporary Criticism.* Ed. Susanne L. Wofford. New York: Bedford Books, 1994.

This article contains information on the literary styling that Mikhail Bakhtin called carnivalesque, discussed in the commentary to Act II, Scene 4 of this text.

Doyle, John and Ray Lischner. *Shakespeare For Dummies.* Foster City: IDG Books Worldwide, Inc., 1999.

This guide to Shakespeare's plays and poetry provides summaries and scorecards for keeping track of who's who in a given play, as well as painless introductions to language, imagery, and other often intimidating subjects.

Gibbons, Brian, ed. *The Arden Shakespeare: Romeo and Juliet.* Walton-on-Thames Surrey: Methuen, 1980.

The Arden edition of the play contains detailed notes and background information. For readers who are interested in taking a scholarly approach to the text, this edition gives an exhaustive introduction of the critical and historical background to the play. It also explains the academic and editorial controversies surrounding the text.

Halio, Jay L., ed. *Shakespeare's Romeo and Juliet: Texts, Contexts, and Interpretation.* Newark: U of Delaware P, 1995.

The essays in this collection provide a fairly traditional glimpse of the play, offering in-depth information about the text and Shakespeare's sources. Articles assess topics such as the differences between various versions of the play; the function of the play's use of subversive wordplay; Shakespeare's mythic and symbolic use of sleep-related imagery; the play's subversion of original source material, such as Thomas Nashe's *The Terrors of the Night*; and the functions of the play's depiction of duelling.

Holmer, Joan Ozark. "'O, what learning is!': Some Pedagogical Practices for Romeo and Juliet." *Shakespeare Quarterly* 41.2 (1990): 187–194.

This article provides an overview of an educational workshop on *Romeo and Juliet* at the 1989 annual meeting of the Shakespeare Association of

America. The article explores strategies for engaging students with the play, discusses the most intriguing problems participants' encountered while teaching the play, and evaluates the art of teaching Shakespeare using *Romeo and Juliet* as a touchstone. Is there still a place in the new performance-oriented pedagogy for such old-fashioned methods as lecture and discussion? These authors say yes.

Wells, Stanley, ed. *Shakespeare Survey: An Annual Survey of Shakespeare Studies and Production—Romeo and Juliet and its Afterlife*. Vol. 49. Cambridge: Cambridge UP, 1996.

This edition of *Shakespeare Survey* offers a variety of approaches to the play. In addition to traditional analyses of the play's history, the *Survey* also provides insightful and contemporary theoretical approaches. Topics range from an exploration of the play's ideology to an analysis of the film representations of the play to a discussion of nineteenth-century depictions of Juliet.

Romeo and Juliet

READING GROUP DISCUSSION GUIDE

Use the following questions and topics to enhance your reading group discussions. The discussion can help get you thinking—and hopefully talking—about Shakespeare in a whole new way!

DISCUSSION QUESTIONS

1. Some scholars have called Shakespeare's *Romeo and Juliet* "a play that starts out as comedy, then goes terribly wrong, and finally becomes a tragedy." Do you agree with this statement? What comic elements do you see in the play? How does the first half of the play feel like a comedy? When does the play become a tragedy?

2. Given that so many stories of ill-fated lovers exist, what makes Shakespeare's *Romeo and Juliet* arguably the greatest ill-fated love story ever told? In what ways are Romeo and Juliet the archetypal ill-fated lovers for all other love stories?

3. Throughout *Romeo and Juliet*, you can view many of the characters' actions as based on choice (or *free will*) or based on fate (or *destiny*). Which of Romeo's actions seem to come from free will? Which seem to come from destiny? What about the actions of Juliet? Friar Laurence? Juliet's Nurse? What relationship between free will and destiny does Shakespeare suggest?

4. By having a Prologue at the start of Act I, Shakespeare essentially gives away the entire plot of *Romeo and Juliet*. Why do you think Shakespeare included the Prologue to Act I? What does it take away from the action of the play? What does it add to your appreciation of the play?

5. Directors of stage and film productions of *Romeo and Juliet* often have a difficult time casting the lead roles of Romeo and Juliet. The characters in the play are young teenagers, but the play's language and emotion require talented and accomplished (and often older) actors to play the roles. If you were directing a new production of *Romeo and Juliet,* what casting choices would you make? What are the pros and cons of casting teenagers in the roles? Of casting older actors?

6. *Romeo and Juliet* has served as inspiration for several musical creations—notably, Tchaikovsky's score of *Romeo and Juliet* and Leonard Bernstein and Stephen Sondheim's score for the musical *West Side Story.* Why do you think composers are drawn to Romeo and Juliet? What scenes feel like they could have musical underscoring? What speeches and dialogues seem like they could be converted easily into song?

7. *Romeo and Juliet* features numerous supporting characters. Why did Shakespeare include the characters of Benvolio? Mercutio? Friar John? Peter? Lady Capulet? Tybalt? What do these characters add to the play? How would the play be different if you took away each of these characters?

8. Female characters in *Romeo and Juliet* sometimes seem to have a secondary importance in the play. Where in the play do you feel like decisions are made *for* women? Where do you feel that things happen *to* them? Where do women make decisions and take some control of the action of play? What are the consequences of these actions? What might Shakespeare being saying about the roles of women in society?

9. In some rewritten productions of *Romeo and Juliet* during the Victorian era, the characters of Romeo and Juliet were still alive at the end of the play. In Leonard Bernstein, Stephen Sondheim, and Arthur Laurents' *West Side Story,* the character of Maria (*West Side Story's* Juliet) is alive at the end of the musical. Is it necessary for Romeo and Juliet to die at the end of the play for the story to be truly tragic? How does having one or both of the lovers alive at the end of the play change the play's meaning and effectiveness?

10. Film and stage productions of Romeo and Juliet have been set in literally hundreds of different locations and historical time periods. Select a location or historical time period (Victorian England, 1920s Chicago, a present-day mall, a futuristic space colony, and so on) and suggest how you would stage the following:

* The Capulets' party
* Romeo and Juliet's first meeting
* The balcony scene
* The fight between Romeo, Tybalt, and Mercutio
* Romeo and Juliet's wedding
* The final death scene

Notes

Notes

Notes

Notes